RERUNS:
FIFTY MEMORABLE FILMS

RERUNS:
FIFTY MEMORABLE FILMS

by
Bosley Crowther

author of Vintage Films

G. P. PUTNAM'S SONS • NEW YORK

Copyright © 1978 by Bosley Crowther
All rights reserved. This book or parts thereof may
not be reproduced in any form without permission.
Published simultaneously in Canada by
Longman Canada Limited, Toronto.

Designed by Rick Celano

SBN: 399-12112-9 (hard cover) 399–12230–3 (soft cover)

Library of Congress Cataloging in Publication Data

Crowther, Bosley.
  Reruns: fifty memorable films.

  Continues the author's Vintage films.
  1. Moving-picture plays—History and criticism.
I. Title.
PN1995.C757   791.43′7   78-6271

PRINTED IN THE UNITED STATES OF AMERICA

For Florence

Contents

FOREWORD

We are facing a showdown situation in the art and culture of the screen that may end in the virtual extinction of the kinds of movies remembered in this book. Many sober soothsayers in the entertainment and financial industries are coming right out and admitting they are fearful for the future of theatrical films—meaning, of course, the kinds of movies that are made for primary showing in theaters, as against the ever increasing number made solely for showing on TV. Long since, the popular attraction of free television shows in the home has cut deep into attendance at movie theaters and resulted in the closing of hundreds of those old emporia. The round-the-clock competition of endless TV family comedies, violent crime melodramas, idiot game and variety shows, sportscasts, spinoffs from popular movies, and badly butchered old theatrical films has pulled the mass audience away from theaters, where its options were at least more circumscribed, and has turned it back into its dwelling places, where it is being methodically homogenized. Not just the *mass* audience, either; it is leveling the minds of *everyone.*

This is not news. It is a process that has been going on for years and against which assorted critics have been howling in agonized alarm. I wrote my first jeremiads on it a good quarter-century ago, when I was the motion picture critic for *The New York Times* and was dismayed by the evident defection of moviegoers to what we then called "the box." To be sure, what the mass was being lured *from* was not so much better, by and large, than the junk it was being lured *to.* (It may have been worse, indeed, since some of the early TV dramas were comparatively original and good.) No one could ever make a strong claim that the run of theatrical films was above severe criticism or that it teemed with intelligence and taste. But, at least, within the area of theaters and in the output of the top talented individuals it en-

couraged, one did find an occasional treasure of cinematic substance and artistry. One could find a film that moved the spirit with noble drama, humor, poetry, grace—that tingled the taste buds of the intellect as does the bouquet of a vintage wine.

But now, even that satisfaction is being threatened by the steady decline in the numbers of films being made for theaters, and this reflects the equally ominous increase in the costs of making them. All sorts of complicated factors are involved in the financing and production of theatrical films, including the recent loss of tax shelters which gravely curtailed the flow of risk funds. The consequence is a vicious cycle of more and more money being spent on fewer and fewer films. And the fewer films made means fewer chances for exceptional ones of intelligence and taste and the greater inducement for producers to place their wagers on the sorts presumed to have large mass appeal. The ins and outs of film economics are too tangled to be gone into here and too full of contradictions and anomalies that defy the understanding of reasonable minds. For instance, while revenues from movies are greater than they've ever been, largely because of the inflated prices and success of such huge hits as *Star Wars, Close Encounters of the Third Kind,* and *Jaws,* those proceeds are deceptive because only one movie out of ten makes a profit for the producer-distributor and those profits have to cover the costs of the rest. As a consequence, the theatrical film business is constantly teetering on the brink, depending upon those occasional blockbusters to keep it from falling into the pit. Is there any wonder soberer soothsayers are perceiving the possibilities of its doom?

In the face of this dire situation, it would seem that two things should be done consciously by movie-lovers if they hope to save the objects of their love. First, they *must* patronize those new films which have recognized quality and class with a fervor and determination even greater than they have shown in the past. And I do not mean simply the "cult" films, the sort that are most vigorously endorsed by those cinema critics and addicts who form small, violent coteries. Exclusive encouragement for such movies only leads the ardent factions into small metropolitan "art" theaters where broader, more catholic tastes and interests tend to flounder and expire. Nor do I mean the sort of movies that appeal by their sensational tricks, no matter how skillful and dazzling, to the actual and perennial juveniles. I mean films that convey sensibility and adult intelligence, in ways that advance the aesthetics and traditions of the great films of the past.

Fortunately, it does appear that audiences are finding and attending such films in large numbers—at least, in the large cities—and this is doing a bit to stem the down-pull of the vicious cycle. But where effort is needed is in the smaller cities all across the nation, in most of which suitable theaters do not even exist for showing the kinds of exceptional movies, often foreign-made, that adult patrons want. In these areas, the culture-minded people must join with enterprising theater men to set up the kinds of operations that will serve their communities with adult films.

The other big thing that movie-lovers can do quite beyond and apart from the primary need of patronizing the good films as they come along (and, oh, how often that exhortation was the theme of my journalistic screeds!) is to form ever closer attachments to the abundant stores of classic films that exist and cry out for rescue from the clutches of voracious commercial TV. I am speaking of the excellent collections of old films that have been made by such valuable archival bodies as the Museum of Modern Art in New York, the Eastman House in Rochester, and the American Film Institute in Washington and Los Angeles, and also the film-rental enterprises that circulate vast numbers of old films that have been turned over to them for subsequent distribution by their original distributors.

This entails more than paying lip-service to the classics of the screen the way we perfunctorily pay lip-service to the classics of literature without seeing to it that our children even stick their noses into them. And it entails more than simply giving money to the support of those film archives which must, by the nature of our system, seek support from the rich and the socially elite. We have to make positive efforts to see that more of the fine old films are shown not only in schools and colleges and film societies of the sort that have been in existence in cultural centers across the country for many years, but shown also in combination theaters where revival showings of memorable movies of the past may alternate with the showing of new adult films as mentioned above. There are already operating such first-rate revival theaters as the Carnegie Hall Cinema, the Bleeker Street Cinema, the New York Theater, the Thalia, and the Regency in New York City and others in Boston, Chicago, Washington, Los Angeles, and San Francisco. We need more—and they need to be patronized and cherished as much as are our opera companies, symphony orchestras, and art museums.

It is because I feel so strongly about this matter that I have added this book to the two I have already written and had published—*The Great Films* and *Vintage Films.* In them, my intention has been to single out and reexamine such films as I feel have enduring value as entertainment and in what they have to say about society and tastes as they were in the times these films were made. I have chosen films that were significant for reasons not always recognized at the time of their release—because they were breakthrough pictures, either in subject matter or techniques, that opened new social vistas and devices for cinema craftsmanship; because they were meaningful and vital as psychological and philosophical weather vanes, and because (in a few conspicuous cases) they simply entertained so charmingly. Some of my selections may seem obvious to cinema scholars, who probably know them by heart and whose interests understandably run to more advanced and esoteric things. (One young man, reviewing my last book, *Vintage Films,* chided me for celebrating "all those tedious films that once passed for great—*The Ox-Bow Incident, Great Expectations, Ben Hur*—and which are now finding their well-deserved obscurity.") Obviously it is not for such pedants that I have written my books, but rather for those general readers whose acquaintance with movies is such that they may welcome reminders and reintroduction as to the great ones, why they were—and *are*!

To this end, I have gone into some details as to the contents of most of these films, recalling their plots and implications so the reader may envision them again or grasp the scope of those that he or she may not have seen. Movies are, of course, a visual medium and *seeing* them is the only way to get a complete comprehension of what they have to communicate. But I have always found that comprehension and appreciation can be assisted by the comments and clarifications of others who are qualified to analyze and criticize. That is what I have endeavored to provide the readers of this book. As further aids to revisualization, I have included as many scene photographs as diligent research could turn up and my generous publisher could reasonably allow.

I am also hopeful that this volume will prove of value to those who want a general overview and summation of the history of films since sound. I have purposely framed my contemplations with historical fingerposts, anecdotes, and all such matters as may set these films in time and give perspectives that will aid the reader in seeing how films have changed in the past half-century. Thus I have blocked out my selections in very general groups to give an idea of the major transitions in the characteristics of films. My first group is labeled The Venerables and here are samples of the early sound films which still have significances and values that render them viable today. Following is a group of films I categorize as representative of The Grand Tradition—the years of the 1940s and the 1950s when the output, especially of Hollywood, was generally glossy and romantic and brought in a lot of gold. Next is a group that constituted what we called The New Cinema, films of the late 1950s and the 1960s that brought large departures from the subject matter, cinema styles and viewpoints of films that had gone before. These films were largely from Europe— from France, Britain, Sweden, and Italy, as well as from Czechoslovakia—and embraced the spirit and attitudes of the "new wave." And finally I have lumped in one group, which I call Here and Now Cinema, those films that have reflected the disorders, cynicisms, and escapist longings that have been so prevalent in recent years. I have not tried to line them up in strict chronological order,

but it is remarkable how little shifting was necessary to have them fall into place.

It should be obvious that my selections are arbitrary, nobody else's but my own, based upon what has been an extensive familiarity with films (when people ask me how many I've seen in my lifetime, I can honestly answer six thousand, at least) and twenty-seven years as film critic for *The New York Times.* Exception may be taken to my choices, and I welcome well-reasoned challenges. But please don't berate me for neglecting films that I have already covered in my previous books. When occasion has come up to mention one of those in this volume I have clearly noted the inclusion with one or two asterisks—one (*) for those I have covered in *The Great Films* and two (**) for those in *Vintage Films.* I have also given full lists of the contents of both previous books in the appendix of this volume.

Lest it may seem that I have come down too hard and heedlessly on TV, let me slip in this explanation before I finish with the subject. Certainly television does provide some commendable fare: interesting and valuable news events coverage, occasionally good dramatic shows (when they are done without commercial interruptions!), a well-presented old film now and then (again when shown without commercials, as the Public Broadcast Service does), and, of course, some very fine and truly priceless musical offerings. But it is the endless and overpowering *trivia* it throws off that is so deadening and damaging, not only because it *is* trivia but because it is so shoddily and senselessly done. This is the stuff that contributes to the softening of the mass audience brain and arrests the development and expansion of any possible sophistication and taste. It reduces all thinking to a sameness, contracts the attention span, and destroys the ability of the viewer even to follow a simple story line. That is what TV does to the viewer. What it does to old films is on a par. It diminishes them to dwarf size, distorts or drains the color out of them, and fragments the story continuity with so many commercials that often it doesn't make sense. For all the seeming service TV does to keep old films alive, it turns right around and kills them to feed its own commercial appetite.

So what is to be the future of theatrical films? Will they live for a few more generations in a limited number of smaller theaters, or will they go the way of the transatlantic liners, the luxury trains, or perhaps Radio City Music Hall? Will their souls be transmigrated through space-age transmission techniques onto large, commercial-free wall panels in dwelling places and culture centers all over the world, or will they be packaged for delivery in the home on electronic tapes?

I am sure I don't know the answer any more than the soothsayers do—nor any more than I have the slightest notion of what the future of civilization will be.

While waiting for the answer, however, there are the treasures of fine old films to be enjoyed, and it is to the encouragement of this pleasure that I am hopefully offering this book.

The Venerables

THE LOVE PARADE

1929

Considering the large importance historically of the musical film in the culture and economy of American movies, it is appropriate that the first sound film to merit contemplation in this book should have been an outstanding example of the genre in its infant stage. Directed by the great Ernst Lubitsch, *The Love Parade*, starring the then fresh Jeanette MacDonald and Maurice Chevalier, was by far the most original and exciting sound film to reach the screen at the time of its unveiling in the fall of 1929; and it still stands as a distinctive model of the advancement of cinema art.

Young people of today who assume that they exclusively constitute what they like to call the "film generation" because they were born and weaned on films and therefore possess a kind of insight and wisdom about them superior to that of previous generations might do well to contemplate this picture, consider what lay behind it and its historic impact on the medium.

Lubitsch, who made his first excursion in sound with *The Love Parade*, was then thirty-six and had been active as a creator of silent films in Germany and Hollywood for fifteen years. When he came to America, he soon proved himself to be a master of witty, suggestive, and somewhat cynical silent comedy with such films as *The Marriage Circle*, *Forbidden Paradise*, and *Lady Windermere's Fan*. So he wasn't precisely a yahoo who didn't perceive and understand the uniqueness and possibilities of the medium when he made *The Love Parade*.

Its precursors, which had sought intensely for a thoroughly happy marriage of musical expression with cinema were, on the whole, stiff and static, including *The Broadway Melody*,** which

Queen Louise (Jeanette MacDonald) of Sylvania does a military drill with her palace guards in the musical number, "My Royal Grenadiers."

The about-to-be Prince Albert (Maurice Chevalier) pays preliminary respect to his haughty but interested queen, Louise.

13

A display of Lubitsch extravagance was the wedding ceremony of Queen Louise and Prince Albert. The bridal veil alone was reported to have cost $10,000.

was solely distinguished as the first original musical film. There were other such shaky productions as Richard Wallace's *Innocents of Paris* (starring none other than the newly imported French music hall favorite Maurice Chevalier); Roy del Ruth's duplication of Broadway stage musical *The Desert Song;* and the Four Marx Brothers photocopy of the stage hit *The Cocoanuts.* There was a spate of vaudeville movies such as MGM's *The Hollywood Revue* and Warner Brothers—First National's *The Gold Diggers of Broadway.* These productions did little more than put on film the familiar routines and devices of the stage musical. The advent of Lubitsch's distinctly cinematic and blithely witty *The Love Parade* marked the first big boost up of the new genre.

Those whose memories of movie musicals begin with such finished and color-drenched achievements in the genre as *Meet Me in St. Louis*** and *Singin' in the Rain,*** may regard this venerable black and white classic as a labored antique just on the strength of its paleozoic story and the unblushingly obvious ways it moved into its musical numbers and used dissolves to accomplish pictorial surprise—through frank camera tricks and passé optical allusions which have long since become clichés. Nevertheless, here is pre-

cisely where those filmic flexibilities began, and to audiences which saw them for the first time they were as thrilling as an introductory kiss.

Admittedly, the story was a chestnut, even at the time the film was made. But that was not unintended; in fact, it was carefully selected as such. Stories of Ruritanian kingdoms and of star-crossed romances among sovereigns and their subjects were familiar in operettas and silent films. So familiar were they—so hackneyed—that Lubitsch deliberately set out to kid one of these old situations with the splendid new device he had at hand. Indeed, his story was adapted by Ernst Vajda and Guy Bolton from a remote Hungarian stage play of the sort that was invitingly loaded with romantic absurdities.

How ridiculous and unrealistic it was to assume that the beautiful virgin queen of the European kingdom of Sylvania should suddenly fall in love with the debonair rake whom the ministers of the country had been compelled to order home from Paris because of his scandalous philandering with the wives of Parisian diplomats. Another great stretch of plausibility was to have the queen choose to make this patently frivolous fellow her prince consort and demand that he keep only unto her! Such far-out fictitious fabrication could only be tolerated in a piece of entertainment that

14

was intended to provide escape. But I am sure that Lubitsch also intended an edge of satire to sharpen this spoof—a slight thrust of adult derision at the pomposities of royalty which had been dethroned, or was largely obsolescent, after the First World War. For the easy conclusion of this fiction which had the prince consort forcing the queen to give him a voice in the government, on the threat of leaving her, was a moderately practical solution that settled the gross absurdities.

But it really wasn't the story that was paramount in *The Love Parade.* It was the wonderful way that Lubitsch made it soar and spin, the airiness and charm that he gave it with wit and an uncommonly crisp pace, and also with the waves of sex vibrations that he was able to agitate. Since Miss MacDonald and M. Chevalier were practically new to films, he had clean slates on which to scribble his cautious but clear erotic hints. Though Miss MacDonald was not exactly what one would call today a Raquel Welch, she was able with her fair skin and fine voice to suggest a warm afflatus of sex. And, of course, M. Chevalier, trim and youthful, was the image of the blithe Parisian buck.

"What would you do if we were meeting for the first time," the queen coyly asked in her first interview with the rascal, "and I were a mere woman?" His reply was a pantomime exhibit of a man paying ardent court to a lady, approaching her boldly, and concluding with a sudden, passionate kiss. "And what would be left for later?" she asked after catching her breath. He, beaming brightly and slyly, answered, "Plenty!" followed by a throaty laugh suggesting voluptuous possibilities. This was quite sufficient to agitate audiences of that day. Thereupon he slid easily and gracefully into the theme song, "The Love Parade," wherein he proudly recounted all the ladies he had loved but would forsake. Such was the way that Lubitsch used music to annotate the plot and convey as much in lyrics as was supplied in the straight dialogue. And since he had excellent music by Victor Schertzinger, a former concert violinist who had an appropriately lush lyric style, he was able to use the dissertative in a conversational way so that audiences either didn't notice or were delighted by the novelties they heard.

The happy couple enter their bridal bower, to pursue their nuptial activities behind closed doors.

This typical 1929 show-girl tableau helped to suggest the tone of Parisian night-life as described in Prince Albert's farewell song, "Paris Stay the Same."

For instance, again, in the opening sequence, when the nonchalant roué was ordered home from Paris and was moderately saddened thereby, Lubitsch had him step onto a handy balcony, a convenient straw hat in hand—the trademark of the elegant boulevardier—and start chortling out into the night air "Paris Stay the Same." This was picked up in turn by a group of ladies on a balcony across the way who lifted champagne glasses in a wistful salute to him, then by his valet downstairs singing a chorus to a cluster of doting maids. The number was cleverly concluded with a switch to his dog in the garden below barking in an imitative rhythm that brought a swarm of canine cuties on the run. That was a visual transition that encapsulated the whole idea. Or when the queen was introduced in her bedchamber awakening from an obviously erotic dream, she simply sat up in bed and started singing "My Dream Lover," with full orchestral accompaniment, which quickly conveyed to her ladies-in-waiting and to the audience her exact feelings.

A contrapuntal arrangement to the romancing of the principals was a comical courtship conducted belowstairs by the valet and a maid, played broadly by the English music hall comedian Lupino Lane and Lillian Roth, a nimble and briefly popular American ingenue. Their sardonic singing and hoofing to "Let's Be Common and Do It Again" was a popularly slanted mockery of the gaudy formalities upstairs.

There were numerous other witty "touches" in this cheerfully artificial film that prompted immediate recognition and therefore appreciative laughs: shots of the queen's dignified ministers undignifiedly listening at the doors and peeping through keyholes to glimpse the progress of the royal romance; or the moment of sudden hesitation in the wedding ceremony when the prince balked at responding directly to the bishop's demand that he vow to love, honor, obey, and remain discreetly subservient to the absolute authority of the queen. The way M. Chevalier milked that moment, rolling the thought in his impudent eyes as Lubitsch scanned the faces of anxious onlookers and cut fast to the face of the astonished queen, signaled at once the frank rebellion that the audience could later expect. This sort of visual innuendo was a mark of the Lubitsch style.

I suppose the unconcealed male chauvinism that is evident in this film may today appear downright antediluvian, though I doubt that many ladies now see this evidence of early-pig behavior as anything but a quaint absurdity—that is, unless they, like their mothers or grandmothers, are susceptible to the early-Pigalle charm and self-esteem of M. Chevalier. But, after all, this fairly frank appropriation of the theme of *The Taming of the Shrew* made no more of a dent on sex equality than do performances of Shakespeare's play. It was just a delightful projector of the potentials of the screen musical, which Lubitsch and others expanded in the years ahead.

The Little Tramp (Charlie Chaplin) makes a heroic effort to prevent the Eccentric Millionaire (Henry Meyers) from committing suicide by drowning.

CITY LIGHTS

1931

Some purists insist that Charlie Chaplin's *City Lights* was a silent film and thus deserves no place in a book about vintage sound movies. Silent? *City Lights* was no more silent than Keats' "Ode to a Nightingale," no more without aural impact than the proverbial music of the spheres! What more piercing and expressive sound intrusion has there ever been in a film than that surprising little beep of the toy whistle the Little Tramp swallowed in the gala party scene and couldn't prevent from squeaking every time he embarrassingly burped! Yes, *City Lights* was Charlie Chaplin's cautious passage into the realm of talking films. An audacious ad writer might have hailed it "Chaplin speaks!"

To be sure, there was no substantial placement of spoken dialogue in the film. When a verbal ex-change was called for, a traditional subtitle was employed. But that, too, was a subtle indication that Chaplin was deliberately bifurcating sound because he saw no psychological necessity at this point for leaping quickly to the banalities of dialogue. And he was absolutely right, when one considers the aesthetic of his style of pantomime. Spoken words in this particular picture would have been anachronistic and dull. Chaplin was still operating in the fanciful realms of make-believe, conjuring up situations and comic mix-ups that were no more literal and plausible than his eclectic Little Tramp costume. Words would have been *unrealistic* in this elusively surrealistic realm.

A good test of what I am saying is to see this great picture with a child. You will probably discover that the youngster is not in the least concerned about the fact that the characters are not communicating—out loud that is. His or her undivided attention will be on visual perceptions,

The Little Tramp lavishes adoration upon his newly discovered idol, the Blind Flower Girl (Virginia Cherrill).

while the ears are unconsciously responding to occasional ideographic sounds: a pistol firing (in the scene where the drunken millionaire threatened to shoot himself); screaming police car sirens when the Little Tramp tried to escape from the millionaire's mansion with a bundle of money to give to the blind girl; and the sound of the toy whistle, of course!

Yes, the child, if too young to read, may ask you, "What'd he say?" when the subtitles flash, but that's a simple curiosity reflex, a request for scraps of random information. I've never known a child to lodge a protest that the actors didn't *speak*. The child's mind is generally quite contented with what he *sees* within the atmosphere of sounds that his imagination is supplying, along with the carefully directed stimulation of Chaplin's eloquent musical score.

City Lights is full of "heard melodies," as well as a constant flow of "unheard" ones. So let's not hear any more about it being a silent film!

As a matter of fact, Mr. Chaplin may very well have purposely arranged the opening scene in his picture to establish an aural style that would embrace satiric comment with music, as well as a full range of emotional stimuli. It was well known, of course, that he was nervous about what effect the introduction of sound would have on his kind of pantomimic playing and thus his audience response. He knew he was at a dangerous crossroads with this his first film après sound.

It opened with a characteristically saucy Chaplin scene in a city park. A crowd of people was gathered for the unveiling of a monument, with a speaker elaborately orating in front of a shrouded bulk of statuary. But instead of the usual clutter of words coming out of his mouth, a saxophone sounded loudly, mocking him with a clear sound-film cliché, and repeated itself, only in higher register, when a woman took over to speak. Thus, when the shroud was ripped off the statue, revealing the Little Tramp peacefully sleeping in the lap of one of the huge stone figures, the convention had been established and the Little Tramp was released from reacting in any way but his familiar pantomime. Suddenly awaking and being startled by the surrounding crowd, he scuttled to climb down from the statue but caught his baggy pants on a sword brandished by one of the figures. As he dangled there, while the band played "The Star-Spangled Banner," his nose kept colliding with the thumb on the outstretched hand of another statue. Making a perfect Chaplin gesture toward the crowd, the Tramp tipped his hat in mock apology, fell loose, and swiftly waddled away.

In the next scene the Little Tramp was strolling along a city street, aimless and alone, peeping in fancy shop windows—especially in one that held a nude statuette—chasing off bothersome newsboys, and having a bit of a contretemps with a rising sidewalk elevator on which ascended a towering man. Suddenly he spied a beautiful flower girl who, thinking him a passing gentleman, offered to sell him a posy which he accidentally knocked from her hand. Then, when he saw her groping for it on the sidewalk, he realized to his chagrin that she was blind. He gave her his last coin, smiled sweetly, and moved away to sit and feast his eyes upon her.

Thus was established the first involvement in this significantly multi-level film—that of the Little Tramp with the flower girl, for whom his sympathy and dedication became intense. He thereafter lovingly served her (even though she once accidentally knocked a flowerpot on his head) and basked in the concept of the image he hoped she had of him in her sightless eyes.

A point that I have never seen examined very closely in the studious commentaries on the film was this interesting juxtaposition of a girl who was blind with a man who was mute—at least, to the extent that his exchanges of conversation with her could not be heard. The depth and extent of his feeling were communicated to the audience through his eyes—those incomparable eyes of Charlie Chaplin which crinkled rhapsodically with joy, grew dark with pain, flashed with excitement, and became absolutely lusterless with grief! There he was, articulating most eloquently to a girl who could not see, while she, forming unrevealed visions of her suitor, stared blankly into space. Thus he had her at a disadvantage, for his eyes were *his* vocal cords while she was without that facility to reach the audience. I do not think this ambiguity was consciously contrived. But it was an acutely ironic and poignant coincidence.

The other major involvement of the picture was played on the level of familiar slapstick farce and had to do with the Little Tramp's relations with the schizoid millionaire, who was boundlessly affectionate and generous toward the tramp when he was drunk and totally unrecognizing when he was sober and depressed. Those erratic tangles and experiences of the two which superlatively conveyed the essential instability and menace of the Little Tramp's world, were some of the most penetrating and amusing in all Chaplin's films. One hilarious scene was their first meeting in which the Little Tramp tried to prevent the despondent fellow from jumping into a river with a rock tied around his neck. In this magnanimous endeavor, the Little Tramp became entangled and was dumped into the river instead. Another was the subsequent visit of the convivial pair to an expensive nightclub, both of them handsomely soused, the Little Tramp dressed in a borrowed tuxedo and working hard to appear suave and nonchalant, but having his usual trouble keeping his footing on the slippery dance floor, mistaking the menu for a sheet of music and starting to sing, then squirting seltzer on a lady who had been set afire by his cigar. There was also the later party

The Eccentric Millionaire and the Little Tramp, decidedly in their cups, cause hilarity and confusion on one of their inflated visits to a night club.

The Little Tramp, puzzled but perfectly submissive, wallows in the lap of luxury in the home of the momentarily expansive Millionaire.

19

The potency of a good-luck charm is offered by a neighborly pugilist to the nervous Little Tramp as he awaits his turn to go into the ring.

where the toy whistle episode occurred, and a couple of those bleak, confusing mornings when the millionaire woke up sober and blindly ordered the Little Tramp thrown out of the house.

There were countless such episodes and "touches" in this extraordinary film, all of them manifestations of Chaplin's sense of the illogical in life and his skill at anatomizing human nature. My favorite was the occasion when the Little Tramp, needing some cash to buy the girl a sight-restoring operation, was lured into a prizefight with a small-time club professional who promised to take it easy with him and split the purse. But, unfortunately, at the last moment, the expected opponent had to flee to avoid the police, and the Little Tramp, suited up but wearing his derby, found himself trapped in the ring with a silent, uncompromising brute. The wild maneuvers of the little fellow to avoid disaster—rubbing his face with a rabbit's foot, a brash attempt to seduce the new opponent with arrant coquetries, and finally his frantic sidestepping and evasive tactics to distract his opponent in the ring—were

grandly ingenious expedients of the hapless humanitarian to survive.

But, of course, the conclusion of the picture was the height of Chaplin's poignancy. The Little Tramp, having snitched the money for the girl's operation from the millionaire (and avoided two robbers and the gendarmes in getting it to her), was later arrested by detectives for robbery and hustled off to jail. Months later, released from prison and wandering the streets again, he passed a prosperous flower shop and there, at the window, who should be but the former blind girl, now radiant and miraculously able to see! We were given to understand that she was watching, watching every day, for the return of the handsome Prince Charming whom she imagined her benefactor to be.

When the Little Tramp caught a glimpse of her he was tranfixed with joy and sudden dread, obviously realizing how painful it would be if she found out who he was. So he started to flee in panic, but she, thinking him merely a passing tramp, came out of the shop, called him back, and insisted upon placing some money and a rose in his hand. Fearfully, he allowed her, but when her hand touched his, she started in recognition, ran one hand inquisitively across his face, looked at him unbelieving, and formed one word: "You?" The Little Tramp hesitantly nodded and, with adoration in his eyes, simply asked, "You can see now?" "Yes, I can see now," she replied. And, with their hands locked, they stood there, looking into each other's eyes while the soft strains of the sentiment-dripping theme song, "La Violetera," played. The last shot was a heartmelting close-up of the Little Tramp's eager, questioning face, with one sensitive, timorous forefinger and the rose barely touching his lips.

In all of motion pictures, that is perhaps the single most eloquent and significant fade-out. For it symbolically posed the crucial question of Chaplin's beloved Little Tramp not to the girl alone but to the audience that had adored him over the years: Do you still love me? Where do I go from here?

The arrogant Prussian, Preysing (Wallace Beery), introduces himself at the switchboard in the opening scene of "Grand Hotel."

GRAND HOTEL

1932

Metro-Goldwyn-Mayer's and Edmund Goulding's production of Vicki Baum's novel and stage play, *Grand Hotel*, ranks, for a number of reasons, as one of the most conspicuous breakthrough movies ever made. It was a prime example of how to make profitable use of the rich and increasingly attractive multi-star facilities of Hollywood, especially those of its largest and most opulent studio, MGM. Into it the studio threw a platoon of top performers, including Greta Garbo, Wallace Beery and John Barrymore. It mingled a motley assortment of interesting characters in a rigidly circumscribed location, wherein to reveal their various character traits and, within a limited time, resolve their problems or be propelled toward their destinies. And it proved that the multiple-story format, which had seen service in novels and plays, could be more swiftly manipulated on the ever more flexible screen without confusing the audience's attention by its shifting story lines.

Here, in this creative venture, the smoothly rolling cameras had the range of the multiple locations within a Berlin grand hotel—the telephone switchboard, which was focused as a sort of nerve center at the start; the elaborate and always busy lobby and reception desk; the upstairs halls and various guest rooms where most of the

Weary and bored, the aging ballet star, Grusinskaya (Greta Garbo), causes alarm among her managers and maid by refusing to make a scheduled appearance.

intimate dramatic action took place. And through the new conceptions of cutting, the flow was smooth, the cuts were sharp, and the whole production was given an uncommon and electrifying pace.

At the outset several key guests arrived at the switchboard and placed phone calls to unseen parties, a clever expository technique. There was Kringelein, played by Lionel Barrymore, who imparted to a distant friend that he, an aging bachelor and a meek accountant, had been told by his doctor that he had only a short while to live and

that he had decided to take all his money and have one last fling in a luxury hotel. There was Preysing, played by Wallace Beery, a big, bruising Prussian business man, later to be revealed as a rogue and lecher, who made an unctuous call to someone he addressed as "Mama" (wife or mother?) to report all was well. Then came the prim secretary of a Russian ballerina to alert one of the managers of the dancer that he had better come quickly to her suite because the distinguished lady was in an alarming state. And lastly there came The Baron, played by John Barrymore, who assured some mysterious confederate that he had arrived and would be doing a certain ''job'' all in good time.

Meanwhile, the torpid house physician, played by the ageless Lewis Stone, observed, in what was probably the prize understatement of all time, ''People come and people go but nothing ever happens in the Grand Hotel.'' For plenty did happen in this picture, most of it gripping, some banal, as the threads of dramatic complications were rapidly pursued. A pretty secretary named Flaemmchen, played by Joan Crawford, arrived to report for work to the businessman Preysing and paused for a brief but promising flirtation with The Baron outside Preysing's suite. The ballerina, Grusinskaya, who was unforgettably played by a beautifully solemn Miss Garbo, arose and wanly informed her managers and her secretary that she would not be able to perform that evening because of exhaustion (merely a symptom of her increasing despair). Old Kringelein angrily protested to the management that he had not been placed in the most expensive suite (which he soon was), and The Baron, an elegant smoothie, postponed Flaemmchen to walk his dog conspicuously through the lobby while biding his time to do his ''job.''

Résumés of the various dramas that occurred in the next thirty-six hours are sufficient. The Baron, attempting at first to steal the pearls of Grusinskaya while she was out of her suite, was found there when she returned and paid her such swift and ardent suit that she willingly fell in love with him and was inspired to go on with her career. Preysing, exposed in a mammoth swindle, tried to persuade little Flaemmchen to flee to England with him. Kringelein, drinking and carousing, got into a gambling game and ironically won for himself a lot of money while The Baron, who could have used it, lost.

The climaxes came in quick succession: The Baron, next attempting to rob the suite of Preysing while the latter and Flaemmchen were preparing to skip, was caught and killed by Preysing, who was thereafter hauled off to jail. Flaemmchen was persuaded by old Kringelein, remarkably revivified, to go to Paris with him. And the beautiful, somber Grusinskaya, guarded from knowing that her beloved Baron had been killed, departed to take the train for Italy, expecting him to join her there.

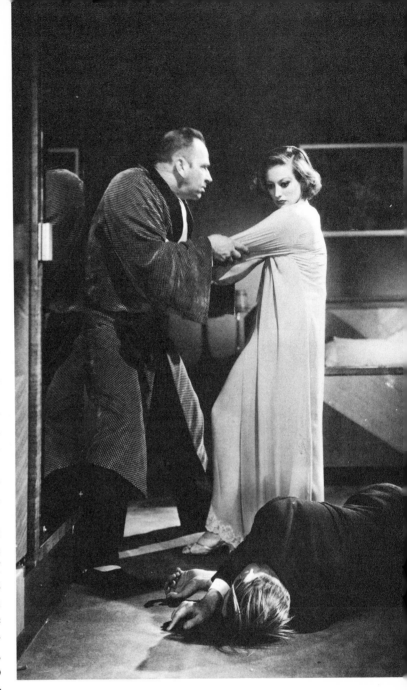

Melodramatics flare as Preysing attempts to divert an aghast Flaemmchen from the body of the Baron, whom he has just shot and killed.

As one can see, the thrust of these small dramas was to point up the ironies of life, the unsuspected and bizarre twists of fortune and fate that may occur without others being aware of them in a grand hotel. To be sure, they were rather obvious, shallow, and contrived, but the characters involved were engrossing and, in general, very well played.

Most conspicuous, of course, was Garbo, whose conveyance of a Russian temperament,

The Baron (John Barrymore), looks on with contempt as Preysing browbeats his temporary secretary, Flaemmchen (Joan Crawford).

Kriengelein (Lionel Barrymore), presumably doomed to an early death, lavishly entertains a sympathetic Flaemmchen and the Baron during his last fling in "Grand Hotel."

the dark moods and suddenly soaring spirits of an international ballet star was tremendously impressive when first seen. She still is today. In one of the most affecting moments, the dancer swept out of the grand hotel, swathed in ankle-length chinchilla, surrounded by her entourage, serenely anticipating the pursuit of her new love affair; unlike the audience, she was unaware that her lover was dead and her happiness doomed. The lovemaking scene was also memorable. The Baron, cued by having heard her despairingly utter the classic supplication "I vant to be al-lone," emerged from behind the draperies and skillfully began to comfort her. That line, now worn by repetition as a Garbo idiom, then conveyed all the woe and desperation of the waning dancer who was giving up hope. It is astonishing to realize that Garbo, at that time, was only twenty-six years old.

Supporting her superbly in this picture was the

glamorous John Barrymore, who got the role because MGM's top lover, John Gilbert, was having contract trouble with Louis B. Mayer. Mr. Barrymore, whose reputation was predominantly made on the stage, certainly gave ground to nobody when it came to playing love scenes. His initial compassion for the dancer, his endearments as he softened her up, and then his passionate embraces and kisses were on a par with Mr. Gilbert's in past films. Here was a classic confrontation, Garbo and Barrymore! Indeed, Director Goulding, could not bear to pass up such a chance. He sneaked in one stylized close-up of their two classic profiles *vis-à-vis*!

Otherwise, Mr. Barrymore was romantic in the custom-built role of a lovable scoundrel with a heart, at least, of gold, and with an air of infinite languor and a hint of inevitable doom on his face. In this film he was better than his brother, Lionel, who played the senescent Kringelein in a style of forced gaiety and self-pity that appears downright hammy now.

Wallace Beery as the porcine Preysing was a veritable George Grosz character, exuding greed and vulgarity with ugly unction and pomposity; and Joan Crawford as the amiable Flaemmchen seemed a nice American girl, given to coquetry and striving, which dropped her somewhere between a debutante and a whore. As a consequence of this role, however, Miss Crawford emerged as a serious dramatic star. Jean Hersholt as Senf, the doorman, and Lewis Stone as the house physician whose medical skill, one hoped, was better than his powers of observation, were up to the little they had to do.

A word should be said for the music that was used to background certain scenes—Strauss's "The Blue Danube," for instance, to set the general mood of the hotel, and "Wien, Wien," the old waltz number, to express the sadness of Grusinskaya. Clichés, beyond any question, judged by the standards of today; but in 1932 they were precisely what this sort of picture required.

Inspired by the great success of it, MGM came through the following year with a similarly constructed multi-star and multi-story drama from the stage play *Dinner at Eight*, in which Mr. Beery and John Barrymore also appeared. Thus began a succession of such pictures which have run into hundreds over the years and have acquired a characterizing identification as a genre—a "Grand Hotel."

A power struggle in the kingdom of Klopstokia is waged between the President (W.C. Fields) and the Secretary of the Treasury (Hugh Herbert).

MILLION DOLLAR LEGS

1932

Not many people remember and some have never even heard of the great 1932 slapstick *Million Dollar Legs*. It seldom shows up on revival programs and I have never spotted it on TV. Yet to my mind it was the most aggressive, the liveliest and zaniest film in that post-silent period when Hollywood was trying to recapture the spirit of the old Keystone comedies with sound. It had it all over the blatherings, for instance, of the initially popular Joe E. Brown (who was seen in a total of fifteen pictures between 1928 and 1932) or the first stage larks of the Marx Brothers, who were pioneering a new kind of verbal slapstick on the screen.

Furthermore, it was not without a certain erratic but sharp satiric thrust, which the three prior

Peeking and peering through the picture was this Mysterious Man (Ben Turpin), spying—but for whom and for what? That was never explained.

A secret meeting of the cabal of ministers conspiring to overthrow the President was chaired by the Secretary of the Treasury. Among those present: the Secretary of War (Teddy Hart), the Secretary of the Navy (Irving Bacon), the Secretary of Agriculture (Billy Gilbert, etc.)

films of the Marx boys conspicuously lacked. The picture—set in a mythical land called Klopstokia, which was administered by a lunatic government and whose "principal exports were goats and nuts"— made great sport of the confusions of dictatorial rule. Its autocrat, called the President, was played by the amazing W. C. Fields, who bore no more resemblance to Mussolini or Hitler than did Groucho Marx in his characterization of a mythical dictator in the 1933 production *Duck Soup*. But the folly of such presidential tyranny as Mr. Fields elaborately exercised was, for the purpose of humor, prophetically bombastic and absurd.

Actually, the satire was originally aimed not so much at dictators as at the pious solemnity of the Olympic Games, which were held in the summer of that year—1932—in Los Angeles. Joseph L. Mankiewicz, newly arrived in Hollywood, had been commissioned by Paramount the year previous to prepare a comedy that would be based

upon the upcoming Olympic folderol. Being a bright and brash young fellow, eager to make his mark, Mr. Mankiewicz wished to bypass the conventional story wherein the hero-athlete had to decide between winning the race or winning the girl. He opted for a script in the realm of make-believe, starting in a Graustarkian country of absolutely no consequence, except for an unsung nucleus of its citizenry who could run remarkable distances at prodigious speeds in order to flee from bill collectors who were always on their heels.

In order to get some notice for the country, and thus replenish its empty treasury, the President was persuaded by a visiting American brush salesman who had fallen in love with the President's daughter to send the pick of those runners to the Olympic Games. Since the President himself was an accomplished weight-lifter and one-arm Indian wrestling champ, it was decided that he would accompany the team. This was the angle that supposedly fulfilled the initial requirement for the film.

An experienced comedy cast was assembled. It included, among others, Jack Oakie, Ben Turpin, Billy Gilbert, Lyda Roberti, Hugh Herbert, Andy Clyde, and above all the uniquely erratic but still not too widely recognized Mr. Fields. This remarkable American comedian, who had begun his career in vaudeville and had been a perennial fixture in the Ziegfeld Follies in the early 1920s before going on to silent films, presented a personality that boiled with incongruity and surprise. Squat and rotund of figure, with a round and bloated face, he came on as a noisy old windbag exhaling a foul pomposity. Highly rhetorical pronouncements would flow from him in a gravelly whiskey voice which, like his affectations of wisdom, were soon apparent as lush absurdities. Along with this studied simulation of a familiar faker and bibulous bore there came a delicious cascade of amazing non sequiturs, such as, for instance, the ceremonial entrance of his President into a meeting of his cabinet, wearing a top hat and swallowtail coat, banging on a bass drum, with a trombone lashed to his face, and beating out, "You're in the Army Now." When he ceased, he abruptly growled to his subordinates, "Any of you mugs been playing on my harmonica? It's busted."

Or, in the course of the cabinet meeting, when it was observed that the country was broke and needed $8 million, and one of the members remarked that $8 million was no problem, "Just a lot of zeros," the President shot back with a stern look at his subordinate, "We've got the zeros. What's bothering me is the eight."

This sort of whacky conversation, flying back and forth like Indian clubs, provided the kind of grotesque humor and peculiarly laughable "hurt" that came in the silent farces from seeing a person suddenly fall through a manhole or get bopped on the head by a brick.

But the "chase" and the sight gag were not abandoned in this new kind of sound comedy. Far from it. These fixtures of the old school were as diligently utilized as before. And it was in his command of the old techniques that Eddie Cline, the director and eminent veteran of silent slapstick comedy, was effective in this film.

The picture opened with Jack Oakie as the brush salesman and his boss, Mr. Baldwin, played by George Barbier, preparing to leave Klopstokia by ship under the persistent surreptitious surveillance of silent, dark-suited Ben Turpin, cast as a grotesquely cross-eyed spy. (Why Mr. Turpin was spying, or for whom, was never explained. He was just a comical addition—and, as it turned out, a farcical anticipation of the Nazi

A female rivalry flares in the dressing room of the Olympic team of Klopstokia between Mata Macree (Lyda Roberti) and the President's daughter (Susan Fleming), as the American brush salesman, Migg Tweeny (Jack Oakie), watches apprehensively.

A shapely distraction catches the eye of Klopstokia's champion distance runner, the Major Domo (Andy Kline), as he works out by racing alongside a moving train.

SS or the Soviet GPU.) Jack spilled his satchel full of brushes and when he bent over to retrieve them a mischievous brat in the background plugged him in the seat of the pants with an arrow. That was a notice of irreverence that everyone in the audience could recognize.

Or, when moving to pick up his brushes, Jack bumped into a pretty girl and lapsed into gawking admiration as she graciously offered to help, the time span was but a few seconds before he happily announced to her, with familiar movie-romance ardor, "To sum it all up, I love you!"

Later, the two found themselves on a bridge spanning a river. "I love you," Jack avowed for the tenth time. She smiled and coyly told him, "In Klopstokia there's another way of saying that."

"In public?" Jack gasped in amazement.

Whereupon the girl reached into a handy trash barrel, pulled out a rolled-up scroll, and handed it to him. "Here is the song of love," she said. "It's in the old Klopstokian language we spoke before we learned English." (Pre-sound?)

"What's it printed on?" asked Jack as he unrolled the scroll.

"My grandfather," the girl replied.

And with that Jack began singing a fearful garble of words to the tune of "If I Could Spend One Hour With You."

Soon becoming impatient, Jack tossed the scroll off the bridge. Swiftly the girl leaped upon the rail, told Jack "Don't go away!" and easily executed a beautiful swan dive into the river. When he later rejoined her, he remarked in breathless wonder, "I'll bet if they laid all the athletes in this country end to end it would stretch . . ."

"Four hundred and eighty miles," she caught him up.

"How do you know?" he asked.

"We did it once," was the reply.

In addition to continually browbeating and threatening his cabinet ("What this country needs is money, and it's up to you to get it for me. If you don't, I'm gonna take it out of your hides! The country starves and here you are with gold in your teeth!''), the President held his power mainly because he was the best one-arm Indian wrestler in the land. His closest and most aggressive rival was the Prime Minister, played by stuttering Hugh Herbert, and the sight of these two, struggling, hands locked, at the cabinet council table with the other cabinet members gathered around, was an absurdity derived from slapstick farce.

Finally, abandoning hope of overthrowing the President by physical prowess, the Prime Minister and his group of highly conspicuous conspirators called upon a sensational vamp, Mata Macree, to assist them. Her assignment was to vamp the members of the Klopstokian Olympic team and reduce them to jelly, thus foiling the plans of the boastful President. Mata, played by Lyda Roberti, was the perfect travesty of the traditional movie vamp—the type that was being imported from Europe, such as Vilma Banky, Greta Garbo, and Marlene Dietrich. A sign on the door of her mansion advised ''Not responsible for men left over 30 days,'' and she herself was universally famous as ''The Woman No Man Can Resist.'' When she made her entrance before the delegation which called to enlist her services, she came down a long flight of stairs in a slinky gown like a burlesque stripper, swinging her hips and singing a throaty song, ''When I Get Hot!''

Without further explanations, the Klopstokians were on a train in America, pulling into a station.

''San Francisco,'' the Pullman porter called.

''I thought this train went to Los Angeles,'' someone complained.

''So did I,'' wailed the astonished conductor. ''We haven't made a mistake like this in years!''

Leap-frogging, then, to Los Angeles on the night before the opening of the games, Mata wrought havoc with the runners by vamping them one by one and egging them on to fighting ferociously among themselves. The next day, when they marched into the Rose Bowl along with contestants from other lands, the Klopstokians were swathed in bandages, some on crutches, seemingly crippled beyond repair, causing Oakie to moan, ''We might be able to get some money if we sold these guys for souvenirs.''

Nonetheless, when the contests started, the Klopstokians burst forth. The indomitable little majordomo, Andy Clyde, raced around the track at a superhuman speed (possibly because he was being paced, through Oakie's connivance, by a beautiful girl on a motorcycle). Others were equally triumphant in their running events. And when it came to the crucial trial of weight-lifting, Mr. Fields was supreme. A threat of competition from Mr. Herbert—who heroically hoisted 900 pounds, inspired by a sinuous dance by Mata—was countered by Mr. Fields. He became so annoyed at Mr. Oakie for accidentally stepping on his toes that he grabbed up a 1,000-pound weight and flung it at his escaping councilor. Indeed, so supreme was this endeavor that it won for Mr. Fields not only the weight-lifting medal but the shot-put award as well.

Thus did the Klopstokians triumph, but the puffing and boastful Mr. Fields was brought low in a private post-game encounter at Indian wrestling by the genial Mr. Baldwin, who had, it turned out, financed the trip. Tumbled to the ground, the chagrined President meekly and apologetically exclaimed, ''It must be the climate. I've been drinking too much orange juice.'' And that brought the picture to an end, like that of a suddenly deflated balloon.

As we've seen, there was little structure or organization in this tatterdemalion *Million Dollar Legs*. Sight gags exploded indiscriminately amidst clusters of nonsensical dialogue. Situation and geographical transitions were made with abrupt nonchalance. And over all reigned the abusive, bombastic, self-important Mr. Fields. His was and continued to be, in my estimation, a more engaging and surprising travesty of human aggressiveness and flamboyance than that which Groucho Marx spewed forth. It's a shame those two top-notch comedians were never coaxed to slug it out in the same film. I know which one I would have bet on. But I concede it would probably have ended in a draw.

It is interesting to note that this folly did not catch on in the United States until it had triumphed in France, due in large part to the endorsement of René Clair. When it was replayed here, with new promotion, it got the reception it deserved.

The elegant dancer, Jerry Travers (Fred Astaire), leads a chorus line in the musical number, Irving Berlin's "Top Hat, White Tie and Tails."

TOP HAT

1935

If you ask any older film fan what his or her favorites are among the films of the 1930s, I will bet that wonderful bubble-weight movie *Top Hat* with Ginger Rogers and Fred Astaire, will be named. That is as inescapable as Charlie Chaplin's *City Lights*. For *Top Hat* is one of those oldies that remain ever green in a viewer's mind and is today quite as vibrant and charming, for all its evident crudities, as it was when released in 1935. To be sure, its enchantment may not depend upon those exceptional qualifications we expect in outstanding films—an unusual or penetrating story, strong dramatic characters, some sort of philosophical intimations, and the creative use of cinema. Rather, it derives from the quite uncommon magic of projection through the mobile photograph of a quality that can best be described in mere words as *rhythmical personality*.

By that I mean the articulation of nature, impulse, and temperament through a combination of visible deportment, graceful movement, and the exuberance of dance. It is a way of projecting style and spirit, pronounced individuality, by conjoining the rhythms of the body with the basic personality proposed. The effect does not presume cerebration, nor does it demand a technical knowledge of film or dance. It simply flows from the liberation of one's own feelings and fantasies stimulated by the moving images on the screen. It is a matter of imagination exploded, of illusion dynamized by dance, and all continued and elaborated, with stretches of narrative dialogue,

through the normal running time of a film.

Such was the magic of *Top Hat*, a film of such airiness and grace, pseudo-sophistication yet corny simplicity, and danced with such skill and dexterity by the unaffected Ginger and Fred, that it could be understood and admired by *everybody*, from the society debutante to the dime-store clerk, from the Madison Avenue ad man to the fellow who drove a truck. The magic lay in the cadence and harmony engendered by these two, bantering romantic fiddle-faddle and dancing beautifully to dandy Irving Berlin tunes.

The story line was so slender, so fictitious, and so absurd that it appeared to be calculated that way, as though the purpose was to discourage viewers from taking the film at all seriously. Fred played an American stage dancer who had come to London to appear in a musical show, and there met a blonde American model who was conveniently registered at the same hotel. The maneuver to bring them together ("meet cute," as they used to say) looks as stagy today as a rubber chicken but was consistent with conventions of that day. Fred, full of joy and vigor, was doodling a minor tap routine in the suite of his nervous impresario (Edward Everett Horton) which happened to be directly above the bedroom in which the model was trying to get some sleep. Her annoyance produced the inevitable: she complained to the management and then, when the tapping continued, went directly to the suite herself, fuming with indignation—and wearing a fetching negligee.

Fred was immediately smitten, apologized profusely, and explained, "Every so often I just find myself dancing," which was his most profound

a montage of shots of "Cheek to Cheek"

Jerry contrives to meet the aloof American fashion model, Dale Tremont (Ginger Rogers), by posing as a London hansom cab driver.

comment in the film. But Ginger was not sympathetic. "It must be some kind of affliction," she snapped back. "Yes," he agreed with mock contrition. "I feel an attack coming on." Then, after she stormed off in anger, he sprinkled a bit of sand on the floor and mischievously glided into a slumberous sand dance that soon put everyone to sleep—the model, his impresario, and finally himself. The dance was done to a muted reprise of his earlier solo to "Fancy Free and Free for Anything Fancy," with which he introduced himself at the start.

This playful encounter led, next morning, to Fred's endeavoring to meet the young lady again. He disguised himself as the driver of a horse-drawn hansom cab she got into outside the hotel to head for a horseback ride in the park. His tapping a jaunty little signal on the coachman's box above her head revealed his identity to her. "Stop this horse!" she commanded huffily, and he cheerily responded, "I don't know how. I've never dealt with anything more complicated than a Dusenberg." That must be recognized as wit.

A sudden shower happily compelled them to seek shelter in an open bandstand in the park, and casually he drifted into warbling "Isn't it a lovely day to be caught in the rain," while commencing a sort of light-footed walk-around to the convenient accompaniment of an unseen orchestra. Soon she was lured into following, and gradually they drifted into a succession of tap-dance rival-

ries, he leading, she emulating, then compulsively stepping up the pace until soon they were spinning ecstatically in a superb simulated improvisation of tap and ballroom steps. This progressively intoxicating performance, which concluded with them plopping exhausted and happy on a bench and amiably shaking hands, is most likely the perfect image of Ginger and Fred that most of their old devotees have.

The story thenceforth grew even sillier: Ginger was off to Italy with her employer (Erik Rhodes), a prissy and starchy dress designer, to visit in Venice with the wife (Helen Broderick) of Fred's producer. Somehow Ginger got the idea that Fred was the lady's husband, which led to indignation and mix-ups galore when he, blithely deserting his stage show, pursued her to the city of the canals. (In those days, the height of impertinence was to be courted by your best friend's spouse; at least, it was in the etiquette invented by the arbiters in Hollywood.) But all was happily settled when the misunderstanding was cleared up and Ginger and Fred were united in an elaborate and complicated dance to the now familiar "Piccolino," done on an overdressed set which looked more like the amusement pier in Venice, California, than anything in Venice, Italy.

Meanwhile, before leaving London, Fred had

Madge Hartwick (Helen Broderick), wife of the producer of Jerry's London show, takes a jaundiced view of the budding romance between Jerry and Dale in a Venetian supper club.

All set up for the memorable dance number with Jerry and Dale, "When We're Out Together Dancing Cheek to Cheek."

superbly displayed his style and grace as a solo dancer to the classic "Top Hat, White Tie and Tails," presented as a big production number in his London musical show. He appeared wearing the specified haberdashery and backed by a chorus line of dancing gentlemen similarly attired—a display of sartorial magnificence as posh as any parade of Ziegfeld Girls. Fred and Ginger had also got together during the course of their Venetian contretemps to whirl gracefully on a handy dance floor, she in a sumptuous ankle-length gown of flowing marabou feathers which fell from her shoulders like Spanish moss, and he in his favored formal get-up, to the tune of "When We're Out Together Dancing Cheek to Cheek." (It might be noted here that the only perilous real-

Jerry and Dale wind up in a standard romantic setting on a Venetian Canal.

life disagreement between the two came when Fred intractably objected to Ginger's wearing that particular gown and she just as stubbornly insisted. He said the feathers made him sneeze.)

Although this was the fourth film that the couple appeared in together—the previous three having been *Flying Down to Rio*, *The Gay Divorcee*, and *Roberta*, in each of which they progressed markedly—it is generally agreed that in *Top Hat* they and their producers achieved the complete unification and culmination of their rhythmical personalities. A subtle combination of their own dancing dexterity and chic, the pace of Mark Sandrich's direction, the choreography of Hermes Pan, and the very special tricks of editing, in the camera as well as in the cutting room, all added up to an amalgam that totals out as the thing we call Class.

Fred had it more than Ginger. His way of walking with his torso flung forward, swinging easily from the hips, moving in a lithe and graceful fashion as though he were always about to snap into a dance, was inimitable. Add to this his always boyish and cheerful face (giving him an odd resemblance to a happy Stan Laurel) and you have the image—or the illusion—of utter self-confidence and charm. Ginger was usually somewhat peevish, even truculent at times, but that in itself was alluring. It was the posture of hard-to-get. This turned their encounters into crises of a fabulous courtship ritual. Their problems were never more urgent than finding ways to get together to dance.

This, in the 1930s, was a blessed release from a general social constriction under burdensome realities. And it is, indeed, significant that the team of Ginger and Fred became the most striking and popular dancing couple since the legendary ballroom team of Irene and Vernon Castle had been the rage before the First World War. Today few remember the Castles; everyone knows of Ginger and Fred.

Robert Conway (Ronald Colman) and his younger brother George (John Howard) look out of their mysteriously hijacked plane upon a mob of menacing Asiatics.

LOST HORIZON

1937

The most beloved and celebrated *adult* adventure-fairy tale to come out of Hollywood's dream factories in the decade before World War II was Frank Capra's *Lost Horizon*, which he made immediately on the heels of his pseudo-populist panegyric *Mr. Deeds Goes to Town*.** This super-romantic pictorial rendering of a James Hilton novel, published in 1933, was purely escapist fiction on a scale that could only compare with that of the surprisingly similar dream-fantasy *The Wizard of Oz*,** which came two years later. Yet it was quite as alluring and bewitching, for grown-ups as well as for youths, and it stuck in the minds of countless millions (including President Franklin D. Roosevelt) for years.

Why its immense popularity? That is not hard to understand when we consider the circum-

stances of the times in which it appeared. The world was moving out of the Great Depression, which had conditioned the mood for *Mr Deeds*, but it was passing into a fearful period of international instability and gathering threats. The Nazis were building up in Europe, the Far East was beset with war, and Russia loomed as a smoldering menace. There seemed to be no place of pure tranquility on the face of the earth.

Suddenly there appeared this lovely movie, magnificently adorned and well played, which excitingly transported the viewer into a luxurious fantasy realm, far off beyond the Himalayas, where there dwelled in vast contentment and peace a handful of fortunate intellectuals who were assembling a sort of eternal repository for the academic and cultural achievements of civilized men. Here there was no crime, no sickness. All of the learning and wisdom of the world was contained here, presided over by hand-picked scholars who had been brought from the corners of the earth to this super-MacDowell Colony with

The passengers—Robert, George, Bernard (Thomas Mitchell) and Lovett (Edward Everett Horton)—are met by a strange reception committee after their plane has been crash-landed high in the remote Himalayas.

its palatial buildings, and were generously accorded the benefit of living on and on for hundreds of years.

No wonder that this ideal haven, sheltered within a verdant vale behind snow-covered mountains so lofty and forbidding that they rendered it totally remote, seemed to the mundane movie-viewer to be the veritable land of milk and honey from whose bourne no traveler could possibly wish to return. No wonder a simple viewer could not understand why, even so, some of the party—a kidnapped group of goggle-eyed Britishers and Americans flown thither in a hijacked plane—should almost immediately have wished to leave.

But that was the question that provided fascination and suspense in this strange adventure. Here was this hodgepodge of people—Conway, a distinguished British diplomat (Ronald Colman); an "ugly American" (Thomas Mitchell); a tubercular show girl (Isabel Jewell); a prissy paleontologist (Edward Everett Horton), and the restless brother of the diplomat (John Howard)—fleeing out of a war-torn Far Eastern airport and mysteriously flown to this place. Naturally they were as bewildered and nervous as was the audience at this wholly inexplicable and harrowing turn of events. Harrowing it was because eventually they had to leave their disabled plane and be

led by a mystifying English-speaking gentleman and a group of porters into a vast realm of mountains and snow until brought through a pass to this haven, identified to them as Shangri-La. (A surging concord of sweet musical sounds, composed by Dmitri Tiomkin, helped to define it as serene.).

Needless to say, they all wanted to know where they were and why, when they gathered that evening for dinner in what appeared to be the world's most elaborate Chinese restaurant. And slowly the information was dribbled to them, mainly by the dignified Chang (H.B. Warner), the gentleman who had met their plane and brought them up through the pass. They were in Shangri-La, a lamasary which had been founded by one Father Pereau, a Belgian missionary priest who had stumbled into the valley some two hundred years before. It was totally insulated from the outside world, except for the train of porters which occasionally arrived from five hundred miles away. Yet it had all the latest information and scholarly knowledge from the capitals of the world. The group had been abducted because the High Lama had his eye on the British diplomat as a likely perpetual resident of this truly Hiltonian ivory tower.

Of course, the diplomat was fascinated, and it peaked when he found a beautiful and brilliant

The survivors of the crash, including an exhausted show-girl, Gloria (Isabel Jewell), are ushered into the amazing chambers of the secluded lamasary of Shangri-La.

lady resident, played by Jane Wyatt. (Her intellectual or cultural qualifications were never explained.) They rode out through the verdant valley on horseback, watched the happy natives working in the fields, idled by a brook, and generally grew quite romantic in a natural wonderland. The brother, too, found a charming sweetheart, played by Margo, to whom he became attached. But that didn't pacify him. He wanted out. Meanwhile, the others—the American, the professor, and the show girl—found assorted interests and were generally inclined to stay.

Then, with the issue pending, Conway was formally ushered in to meet the mysterious High Lama (Sam Jaffe), whose death was imminent. Conway was his choice to succeed him. "I've been a great admirer of yours," he told the diplomat, and quoted one of his impressive sayings: "There are moments in a man's life when he glimpses the eternal." What could be more profound!

However, the shock came when Conway realized that this feeble and shriveled old man with the strange eyes and the two front teeth missing was actually Father Pereau and that he had lived in this place of great tranquility for more than two hundred years!

"My son," the old man continued, "I am placing in your hands the future and destiny of Shangri-La . . . to care for the riches of the mind, while the storm rages without."

"Do you think this will come soon?" Conway asked him.

"You will live through it," the High Lama replied. "I see a new world starting in hopefulness." Then he lay back, and a candle on the table in the chamber sputtered and went out. The old man was dead. A spectacular torchlight funeral ensued.

Now was the moment of decision. A train of porters was due to arrive, and if anyone wished to go out with them, they had to be ready right away. The brother announced he was prepared and said his girlfriend was going along, even though there had been some dire foreboding that if she left Shangri-La she would die. In agony and desolation (because *his* girlfriend would *not* go with him) Conway decided to pull out. "The world needs you," his brother urged.

But the trip down the mountains was tormenting, and at one bitter stop for rest, the pretty girlfriend of the brother suddenly shriveled into an aged crone. Then the whole party, Englishmen and porters, was smothered in a thundering avalanche, and apparently only Conway and one or two porters survived. The last we saw of Conway

Deeply perplexed by their arrival and reception at the luxurious Shangri-La, the survivors seek explanations from the incredible English-speaking major domo, Chang (H.B. Warner).

The spectacular torch-lit funeral procession for the High Lama, the one-time Father Pereau (Sam Jaffe), winds through the promenades and gardens of the palatial Shangri-La.

he was struggling back up the mountains toward the pass, while a small group of British officials, dissolved to in their London club, were recounting a wild report on Conway which had somehow reached the outside world, telling of his strange adventure and wondering whether it could be believed. "I believe it," said one of them finally, "because I *want* to believe it. . . . I hope we all find our Shangri-La."

One might have supposed that such romantic fantasizing by adult men, not to mention by practical merchandisers in a Hollywood studio, would have been looked upon with skepticism, if not out-and-out contempt. Not at all. *Lost Horizon* bewitched and sent into transports of praise and thanksgiving some of the toughest critics and moviegoers in the world. The notion of such a sanctuary—a combined think tank/health farm, one might say—captured imaginations as did no other fantasy of the day. The name Shangri-La became proverbial. It was widely and proudly attached to anything from resorts in the mountains to Chinese restaurants. President Roosevelt, who was reported to have loved the picture, saw it several times. At a press conference, some four years later, when newsmen asked whence a flight of American planes that bombed Tokyo early in World War II had departed, he answered, "Shangri-La!" And he ordered a new American aircraft carrier given the name toward the end of the war.

Why shouldn't we all have loved it? The film was as spectacularly designed as was artistically and technically conceivable in those distant black-and-white days. The mountains, the Shangri-La settings—all were Super-Art Deco. And the performances, without exception, were impressive and credible, especially that of Mr. Colman, who was the then reigning romantic British aristocrat.

What was loved by a public less disillusioned and cynical than is the public today was the chance to suspend one's worries for a few hours in a remotely conceivable dream. Perhaps in deepest Asia, beyond the Himalayas, there *might* be some such idyllic sanctuary to which one's fancy, at least, might escape—where the spirit, if not the body, of the dreamer could luxuriate with music and good books, soft beds and beautiful people, for years on endless years.

That such an illogical and ephemeral fantasy seems wistfully naive today was demonstrated a couple of years ago when a Hollywood producer who was more extravagant than wise did a remake of *Lost Horizon*. He drenched it in money and music, soaring fountains and dancing *boys*. Shangri-La was a World's Fair pavilion. The picture was a dud. Too many spy planes have crisscrossed and photographed the Asian areas, too many hopes for a new world have been shattered in continuing holocausts. All that is left of that old vision is the original *Lost Horizon*, still gauzy but faintly perceptible in its distant valley that may be glimpsed for a flash or two on the screen of a rerun theater or (as a last, sad resort!) on TV.

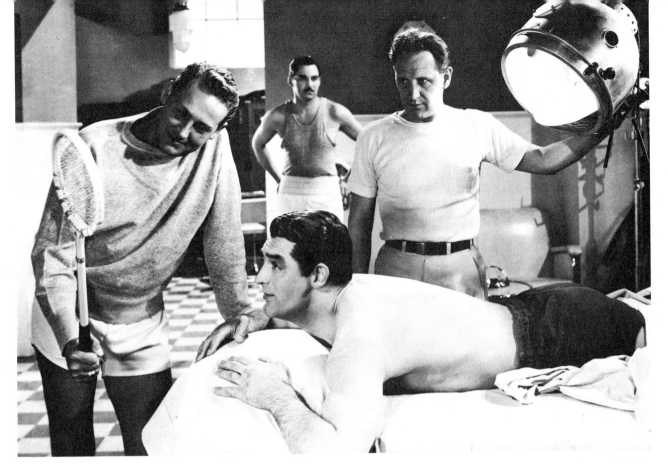

Jerry Warriner (Cary Grant) is given an impromptu squash lesson by a pal as he soaks up a "Florida tan" in the massage room of his New York club.

THE AWFUL TRUTH

1937

As with so many achievements of superior screen comedy, Leo McCarey's delicious and brittle *The Awful Truth* got to the screen through circumstances that were greatly affected by chance. Columbia Pictures, more by luck than by design, had got the reputation of the foremost comedy studio in Hollywood and had cast the thoroughly charming but somewhat serious Irene Dunne in a trifle entitled *Theodora Goes Wild*. This chancy endeavor came through as such a success and Miss Dunne proved so skillful and surprising as a comedienne that the studio was anxious to rush her into another light comedy.

Enter Leo McCarey, a director with an enviable string of comedy successes behind him that stretched back to silent shorts with Charlie Chase. Now, Mr. McCarey, departing from his customary frisky comedy style, had just done a

picture for Paramount entitled *Make Way for Tomorrow*. It had been a touching little drama about an aging couple—a classic in its way—but because of its disturbing subject matter (geriatrics) it was not a commercial success. For that and other reasons, Mr. McCarey was out at Paramount and was immediately available to Columbia to direct a film with Miss Dunne.

Likewise, by chance, completing a contract at Paramount at the time was a rising young male star whose talent for light comedy had been suggested by his performances in several modest roles. He was Cary Grant, and at the urging of Mr. McCarey he was picked to play opposite Miss Dunne. Thus three rather random talents were brought together at Columbia to make a film.

Selected as material for it was a ten-year-old Broadway play by Arthur Richman about an affluent married couple who were dancing on the verge of divorce—nothing very impressive, certainly nothing very profound, but presumably it was close to the kind of material that was then in

Jerry pleads fruitlessly for the custody of their dog, Mr. Smith, as he and his wife, Lucy (Irene Dunn), obtain a legal separation in a New York court.

Hollywood vogue. *The Thin Man*, an MGM creation with William Powell and Myrna Loy as a husband-wife team of smart detectives who wrangled charmingly and were the parents of a clever dog, was a notable box office winner in 1934 and set everyone to thinking about stories of husband-wife combos with dogs.

Several weeks of involved preparation went into shaping a script, during which a congeries of writers worked on the whole or parts of it. When the actors came together with Mr. McCarey on the set, they discovered that the script (which Vina Delmar was officially credited with) was of virtually no more use to them than would have been the telephone book. Mr. McCarey, who was famed for his eccentric and impromptu ways of doing his job, seemed to have tossed the script into a desk drawer and proceeded to make up scenes as he went along. The actors were simply placed in situations and told vaguely what they were supposed to do, without any specific direction from Mr. McCarey other than to play it the way they felt. Often he gave them slips of paper with freshly scribbled lines of dialogue at odds with what they had learned in preparation for the particular scenes they were about to do. Casually, he told them to forget the screenplay and come up with these new lines as best they could.

At the outset, the actors were befuddled, and both Mr. Grant and Miss Dunne were so completely irked at what they felt was lack of direction that they asked to be taken off the film. But as the days passed they discovered that Mr. McCarey's seeming hit-or-miss approach, his way of setting up scenes and improvising the flow of action and even dialogue, and above all his cheery disposition and his mood of spontaneity were bringing forth from them a kind of relaxation and effervescence that they had not felt before. Soon they came to the realization that their scenes did have fullness and shape and that they were accomplishing something quite unhackneyed in the way of light comedy. Needless to say, Mr. McCarey was confident of that all along. He was only extending into new realms the kind of improvisation he had learned in silent comedy.

This quality was quite apparent in the film when it came forth, exuding the ebullience and carefree spirit of something done in genuine fun. And fun was, indeed, the only substance and purpose of *The Awful Truth*. Its apparent concern for the social problem of divorce was absolutely nil. Some have detected criticism of the idle and frivolous rich in its outspoken representation of the extravagant behavior of this class. And the singular concentration of the story upon the marital ups and downs of a couple whose only bond of real attachment seemed to be their mutual affection for a dog was, if anything, a harmless indication of the superficiality of those who made the film. One would have to go far to discover any important social comment in *The Awful Truth*, which was based on a synthetic life-style, as much a fantasy as a Disney cartoon.

Lucy plays a clumsy accompaniment for her new and ardent suitor, Dan Leeson (Ralph Bellamy), an Oklahoma millionaire, as he insists upon warbling "Home on the Range."

But the value of it as entertainment—as pure diversion for those who unblushingly went to the movies to be "taken out of themselves"—reached an astonishing level on the Hollywood Richter scale, and many old-timers still recall it with affection as one of the best Hollywood comedies they ever saw.

Its essence was in the glib surprises of the light-weight complications as they unrolled, the wit and apparent spontaneity of the volatile dialogue, and the crispness and elegant timing with which it was played by Miss Dunne and Mr. Grant. The two were elastically able to make their frivolous characters appear attractive without being snooty, sympathetic without being gross. Although there was no particular reason for the body of a mass audience to sense a feeling of commonality with these glib, self-indulgent, got-rocks types, who were no more substantial or realistic as human characters than were those in the early plays of Noel Coward, the attraction was in the delicious casualness of their attitudes and the resilience with which they adapted to the screwy situations as they presented themselves. It was at about this time that the critics began referring to this sort of film as "screwball comedy." The term was slightly disparaging but it *was* commendably apt.

At the outset, the point was established that the characters of Mr. Grant and Miss Dunne—Jerry Warriner and his wife, Lucy—were what was then termed "playing around." He was caught at the start beneath a sunlamp and the ministrations of a masseur at his New York club being given the appearance of having just spent two weeks in Florida, while the clear implication was that Jerry had been holed up in some fair lady's bower. And Lucy, when soon we met her coming home to their apartment at noon wearing an evening gown and gingerly escorted by her singing coach, Armand, was nothing loath to explain that their car had broken down on the way home from a party the previous evening and they "had to spend the night in a country inn." The speciousness of the explanation was obvious to the group of sybaritic worldlings that Jerry had brought home to the plush apartment for some of his special eggnog drinks.

From this point of mutual suspicion, it was only a lapse dissolve until they were quarreling with one another and Lucy was calling her lawyer to inquire about a divorce. (The irony of the state of matrimony was counterpointed in this little scene. The lawyer, trying to discourage Lucy by reminding her that "marriage is a beautiful thing," then turning away from the phone to

Jerry is mortified by a tackily got-up Lucy, pretending to be his loud-mouthed sister, at a gathering of his high-society friends, especially his would-be fiancée, Barbara Vance (Molly Lamont).

Lucy tries to hide from the visiting Jerry the hat of a hidden gentleman caller which the amiable Mr. Smith persists upon bringing forth.

growl at his wife, who was ordering him to come to dinner, "Will you shut your big mouth!")

Jump to a courtroom where Lucy was stubbornly seeking a divorce and the judge was agreeing to give them a ninety-day decree nisi before making it final (an impossible ruling in the State of New York). The only hitch seemed to be the question of who would get custody of the dog, a cute fox terrier which had been known as Asta in *The Thin Man* and was known as Mr. Smith here.

This was a matter of great importance, Lucy explained, because it was really to have joint possession of the dog that she and Jerry had got married. They both had seen it at the same time in a pet shop window and found the only way they could resolve the question of ownership was by marrying and establishing a home. The judge tried to adjudicate the matter by seeing to which one's call the dog would respond. But Lucy cheated, getting the dog to respond to *her* summons by surreptitiously luring it with a favorite toy. Jerry, disappointed and bewildered (because the dog had seemed to like him more), was granted visiting rights.

So the separation was effected, and the two went their separate ways, Jerry to play the field as a gay bachelor and Lucy to take another apartment and live disconsolately with her aunt. But soon she was being courted by a big, clumsy Oklahoma goof, played by a cheerful Ralph Bellamy, from an apartment across the hall. One evening at a nightclub they happened to meet Jerry with a date. What an embarrassing situation—Jerry with his girl who talked, as he said, like Amos and Andy and was the vocalist at the club, and Lucy with her rawboned farmer-rancher who boasted he "could dance till the cows come home." To prove himself he grabbed the astonished Lucy for a whirl that left her breathless and dismayed. Of course, there were slyly cutting comments. Jerry glibly allowed that Lucy and her fellow should find it ducky living on that Oklahoma farm. "And if it gets dull," he assured her,

"you can always go to Tulsa for a weekend." And Lucy flashed her bit of sarcasm by expressing lifted-eyebrow surprise at discovering that the worldly Jerry called his sweetie by the quaint name of Dixie Belle.

The plot grew more complicated when the farmer brought his mother onto the scene to meet his intended. Jerry arrived in Lucy's apartment one day to find that a derby hat he thought was his descended around his ears when he put it on. This scene, with Lucy struggling to conceal the incriminating derby before Jerry discovered it and the dog persistently bringing it forth, was probably the high point of the picture—a running sight gag of classic inventiveness and renown.

One other scene matched it. Lucy, now shed of her farmer and his mother, having shocked them with her life-style and convinced her country suitor that she really loved Jerry and wanted to get him back, intruded herself into a formal party at the home of his highly social fiancée. She proceeded to humiliate him by pretending to be his sister Lola, a crude, gum-chewing tart. After calling for booze and talking loudly, she suddenly threw up her hands. "Wait!" she said. "Don't anybody leave the room. I've lost my purse!" And then she went into a routine simulating the flightiness of Jerry's friend Dixie Belle.

That, of course, was the killer. Having dragged her away and into his car, Jerry started off for the country, maybe to dump her in a lake. Their car broke down and, as chance would have it, they had to spend the night at an inn. There they occupied adjoining bedrooms but ended up happily at last in one bed together just a few minutes before their divorce was to begin. The playing of this scene, with the goings and comings of Jerry into Lucy's seduction-scented room in his pajamas, paced aptly by the cucking of a convenient cuckoo clock, provided an excellent sexy fade-out for this persistently suggestive film. Well, suggestive it was in those far days, when we didn't have to be shown *everything* to grasp what was cooking. And a lot more fun for all of us it was!

An incongruously amiable Tom Destry (James Stewart) is met on his arrival in Bottleneck by his astonished sponsor, Wash (Charles Winninger), who had expected someone much more formidable. His stagecoach companions are Janice Tyndale (Irene Hervey) and her brother, Jack (Jack Carson).

DESTRY RIDES AGAIN

1939

So many times has George Marshall's fine old comedy-western *Destry Rides Again* been shown on television in the past fifteen or twenty years that by now it must be as familiar in the American home as bubble gum. I would venture to guess it has been tube-run more often than any other film, with the possible exception of *Casablanca*.** Despite its overexposure, it still stands as one of the sharpest and most winning among the classic western films, and the elements that made for its preeminence merit reflection and thought.

Obviously the most important reason for its appeal to audiences as far apart in cultural orientation as today is from 1939 was the fact that it spoofed with great good humor most of the conventions and clichés of the standard western movie, which was then pretty much on the skids because of the slavish adherence of the makers to dull redundancy. Its story of an amiable young sheriff who tried to use reason rather than a gun to keep the peace in a thoroughly corrupted and lawless western town was such a novel departure from the usual picture of the sheriff as a man of stalwart and fearless disposition with six-shooters bouncing at his sides that the input of pleasant young Tom Destry was a charming and intriguing surprise.

Another obvious reason for this picture's unflagging appeal was the presence of Marlene Dietrich and James Stewart in uncharacteristic roles—she as a sultry "entertainer" in the town's monopolistic saloon and he as the freshly brought-in lawman who was supposed to put the kibosh on her sort. Neither—especially Miss Dietrich—was familiar in the kind of rowdy farce that Mr. Marshall put them to in much of this picture, and the shock was like seeing a courtly queen suddenly showing up in a low-life dance hall and doing the shimmy with a defrocked priest.

It's useful to recall that, before this, the famous Miss Dietrich had been seen in a progressively tedious succession of extravagant and ponderous films such as *Blonde Venus*, *The Devil Is a Woman*, and *The Scarlet Empress*, in which she played an assortment of serious sinners who generally drove men to their ruin. Inevitably, the public had grown profoundly weary of seeing her typecast as a destructive seductress. So weary, indeed, that Miss Dietrich was close to the top of a list of distinguished Hollywood performers who had been publicly tagged "box office poison" by a group of New York theater men. She hadn't appeared in a picture for two years before *Destry Rides Again*.

No wonder, then, that her emergence as the flashy Frenchie at the Last Chance Saloon, windmilling her feathered boa and virtually parodying Mae West, grabbed audiences where it tickled and set them up for the marvelous barroom brawl between her and the wife of a local nitwit whom she had fleeced of his pants in a blackjack game. This knock-down and drag-out catfight in which Miss Dietrich and Una Merkel jabbed and clawed, pulled hair, and violently wrestled one another all over the barroom floor, until the recently arrived Tom Destry poured a bucket of water on them, thus preventing inevitable slaughter, was one of the wildest slapstick scenes of all time. The fracas, followed by Frenchie taking out after Tom, throwing bottles, chairs, and punches at him, set the tone and the tempo for the film. From this scene on, the great Miss Dietrich was reborn.

And certainly Mr. Stewart's droll enactment of the drawling, slow-moving Tom, who had been brought in by a surrogate sheriff because he was the son of "old Tom Destry," one of the West's most famous lawmen, in the hope he would perform like his old man, was the all-time supreme personification of a misplaced pacifist. Imagine the shock of the surrogate sheriff—and of initial audiences, too—when they saw this long drink of water descend from the stagecoach that brought him to town gingerly carrying a birdcage and a parasol. No matter that these articles belonged to a young lady whom he was helping off the coach.

Tom politely confronts the town's wide-open saloon-keeper, Kent (Brian Donlevy), as Wash and the crooked mayor (Samuel S. Hinds) look on unbelievingly.

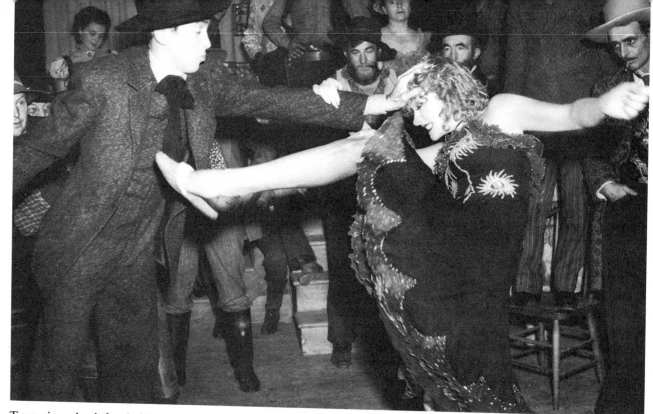

Tom gingerly defends himself against a ferocious frontal attack by the infuriated saloon-singer, Frenchy (Marlene Dietrich).

In his role of peace-maker, Tom resorts to a practical device for stopping a blazing barroom battle between Frenchy and a jealous vengeful wife, Lily Belle Callahan (Una Merkel).

nchy heats up the patrons of the ody Gulch Saloon with her throaty, gestive rendering of "You've Got That k."

Right off, all who witnessed this arrival—and they were, in addition to Wash, the hopeful surrogate sheriff, a goodly circle of the town's best reprobates—had the benign young fellow pegged. And, of course, their impression was compounded when Tom was invited to the bar to have a drink with the slippery proprietor whom Brian Donlevy played, and, incidentally, to hand over his guns, and they found that this fledgling sheriff didn't carry guns. "You see," he patiently explained to the proprietor, "if I had carried a gun, one of us might have got hurt—and it might have been me." That bleakly pusillanimous admission pulled the rug out from under Wash and caused everyone in the barroom to set up a guffaw. Even Frenchie, who had been a bit flirtatious when first introduced to him, fetched a broom and handed it to him with the taunting dig, "You can start cleaning up here!"

Later, berated by Wash in the quiet of his boardinghouse room and told by his desolate sponsor he "should have come in blastin' with shootin' irons," Tom gave the dumbfounding answer, "I don't believe in them." And to Wash's incredulous query as to what he did believe in, he replied simply, "Law and order." Then he patiently explained, "You see, you shoot it out with 'em and—I don't know why—they look like heroes. But put 'em behind bars and they look little and cheap." Such was Destry's philosophy, which was incomprehensible to Wash, as it was at the time the picture opened—and still is—to

many viewers. For the fact was that, by that admission, Destry revealed himself to be not only pacifistic but—infinitely weaker—impotent.

Although it wasn't carefully spelled out, Tom was a symbolization of western male impotency. And audiences, without analyzing what made him appear a ludicrous aberration, if not an outright freak, were unconsciously mystified and bewildered by this rare inadequacy. For, in the accepted mythology of the western, potency is represented by the gun, and any man who doesn't tote one and doesn't use it when it is needed is not a man.

Never mind that Tom Destry's posture was intellectually and morally good, that he took a philosophical position that, by most religious doctrines, was sound. The fact remained that he had abandoned the traditional western instrument of power, and by so doing had unwittingly castrated himself in the audience's eyes. And since a man who is devoid of his manhood is usually, in comedies, a joke, Tom's self-inflicted castration made him all the more amusing in a spoof. To be sure, he was not without ability to get off a scoring shot, as he proved when he took a six-shooter away from a noisy troublemaker and blasted some bits of ornamentation off a store-front sign. Nor was he unattractive to Frenchie, who took a progressively more protective shine to him. But for all his wit and homely wisdom, his dexterity with anecdotes (such as comparing himself to a stamp which, "like the man said, sticks to it until it gets where it is going"), and his ability at minor pacification, he remained an odd one almost to the end, when he finally did "come in blastin'" and brought the picture to a flawed but masculine close.

I say flawed because the ultimate recourse of Destry, the no-gun advocate, after failing to jawbone the rascals into abandoning their evil ways and especially after Wash had been murdered for helping him uphold the law, was to move in with a band of outraged citizens and bombard the Last Chance Saloon, he himself being the boldest and most agile in getting to and gunning down the boss. Against this aggressive maneuver, fearless Frenchie tried to intercede, not to assist her employer but to keep Destry from being plugged, and for this unselfish intrusion she was accidentally hit and died in Destry's arms.

It's a shame that a more original climax was not found for this uncommon film by the three writers and Mr. Marshall, who adapted it from a novel by Max Brand. Something clever and ironic should have been devised that would have let Destry follow through on his line of passive resistance in defiance of the western formula. A major satire instead of just a grand, superior spoof might have been achieved, but I strongly suspect the general public would not have liked it as much. The popular climax for it was that Destry finally proved his potency.

Miss Dietrich's splendid performance was notable in that her famous sexiness, so pronounced in her prior pictures, was skillfully parodied and mocked. Glints of the old eroticism in flashes of garters and bare thighs were revealed in that barroom catfight and, of course, the huskiness in her throat was used for guarded innuendo when she sang her celebrated barroom songs: "You've Got That Look," "Little Joe," and "See What the Boys in the Backroom Want (and Tell Them I'll Have the Same)." But her intimate encounters with Destry were significantly subdued, and her gestures in pursuing her occupation were bold but impersonal. Incredible as it may seem today, the brashest and then most shocking line in the film, which came when the businesslike Frenchie tucked a folded bill into her bust and one of the barflies chortled, "Thar's gold in them hills," was cut six days after the picture opened on order of the custodians of the Production Code. And, what is even more incredible, it is *still* out when the film is shown on TV!

No more need be said for the performance that Mr. Stewart gave. It was a masterpiece of underplaying in a delightfully sardonic vein—the freshest, most offbeat characterization that this popular actor ever played. It was, to my mind, even better than the rampant young senator he portrayed in *Mr. Smith Goes to Washington*, which was, by an odd coincidence, released simultaneously with *Destry Rides Again*.

Excellent, too, were Charles Winninger as the bibulous, volatile Wash; Mischa Auer as the spouse of Miss Merkel who yearned to be more than a buffoon; Donlevy as the "heavy"; Allen Jenkins as one of his hired killers; and Samuel S. Hinds as the laconic, dictatorial "mayor" of the town. There was a first-rate musical score by Frank Skinner, and Mr. Marshall's direction gave the picture energy and pace.

As an interesting study in western concepts, you might like to compare this film with the classic *High Noon*.** This should provoke some pregnant thoughts on western heroes and the perennial demands of public taste.

Seamen off the freighter *Glencairn,* Yank (Ward Bond) and Driscoll (Thomas Mitchell), carouse with the local ladies in a Caribbean port before setting out on "the long voyage home."

THE LONG VOYAGE HOME

1940

Of the three superior motion pictures that were directed by the versatile John Ford in the three successive years preceding the entry of the United States into World War II, I consider the most profound and poignant his rugged *The Long Voyage Home.* He and his writer, Dudley Nichols, adapted the film from four one-act plays of the sea by Eugene O'Neill.

Strangely enough, this haunting picture, which was sandwiched in between the cornucopian *Stagecoach***and the sentimentally inclined *How Green Was My Valley,* is not often cited by younger film fans as one of Mr. Ford's finer films. They and TV audiences seem to skip it, for reasons I do not understand—except, perhaps, because it presents them with a tragic and hopeless theme, that of little men eternally searching for the unattainable peace of their souls, and because it was rambling and unstructured and preoccupied mainly with men.

But those seem unreasonable objections to a film which had significance and scope far beyond the physical confinement of a handful of sailors in the fo'c'sle of a ship—a film which, indeed, bears close comparison to some of the more recent introspective films which have come from directors whose forte is "alienation" in the present troubled world.

The Long Voyage Home was based on four early O'Neill plays: *The Moon of the Caribbees, Bound East for Cardiff, In the Zone,* and *The Long Voyage Home.* All were originally no more than minor dramatic episodes linked together by their setting, the British tramp freighter *Glencairn,* and the same cast of characters. The time was around 1915, the midpoint of the First World War. But Mr. Ford and Mr. Nichols strung them together with loose connecting links, invented a few more appropriate incidents, arranged a change in the ending, and set the time in the first year of World War II.

The precarious continuity permitted the random contemplation of several intimate personal stories without any central story line—something

Members of the crew of the *Glencairn*, including Axel (John Qualen), Yank, Ole Olson (John Wayne), Driscoll and the mate (Douglas Walton), look down thoughtfully as they haul up the pilot's ladder, their last tie to the land.

roughly like what was done in *Stagecoach* or the prototypical *Grand Hotel*. By its nature, the form precluded the accumulation of intense dramatic action to form a strong climactic point, but it was right for the mood of poignant probing and inconclusiveness that was the spine of this film. For the stories were those of several sailors in the *Glencairn*'s crew who were making a long and endless voyage toward an elusive goal, sailing from an island in the West Indies to London, via an American port, and surrounded by a cargo of ammunition to be used by Britain in the war.

There was Driscoll, the tough Irish rowdie and unofficial leader of the fo'c'sle hands; Olson, the gentle, complacent, unobtrusive Swede who wanted nothing more than the opportunity to return home to his mother's farm; Smitty, the mysterious gentleman who carried a heavy secret in his heart; Yank, the iron-muscled farmer; Cocky, the comical steward; Axel, the chipper Scandinavian, and several more less apparent crewmen. And the symbolic voyage they were making was more than just a perilous wartime trip across the North Atlantic. It was a voyage toward a land which they all fantasized was better than the sea on which they drifted, but a land which in every case, save possibly that of Olson, received them cruelly and unrewardingly.

This was the essential idea, along with the consequential thought that man is a vagrant creature who must ever wander with a hungry heart. Even in the warm, luxurious tropics, these men were unable to rest or relax for a brief spell. They even fought among themselves when the evil influences of the land—booze and the native women—penetrated their blood. But at sea they always reverted to talk of a haven somewhere on the land. The dying words of Yank, a powerful, farm-bred deckhand afflicted with a punctured lung, were, "I dreamed I was 'way in the middle of the land, where you could never smell th' sea or look at a ship." But as they approached the land, the evils of it came out to meet them in the form of a German plane intending to strafe the ship. And when finally onshore in London's stews, they were bewildered by drink and tradesmen's trickeries until they ultimately crept back to their vessel, deflated and disappointed, to go to sea again.

Perhaps older readers remember Rudyard Kipling's disgusted seaman, Sestina of the tramp *Royal*, who ". . . out at sea beheld the dock lights die and met my mate, the winds that tramp the world." So it was with these sailors on the *Glencairn*. Only at sea did they find the balm of fantasies and longing for their restless souls.

Mr. Ford's comprehension of this concept could be observed in every detail, every mood.

He etched the whole picture with bold, realistic strokes, thus establishing the tough substantiality of the vessel and the men. The ship was of iron, dark and solid, and the decks rang when men walked on them. Every man of the crew looked like a sailor on a genuine cargo ship. The tough, dirty firemen wore sweatrags, the able seamen fairly reeked of salt and rust. And the presence of the sea, though seldom looked at (which is common with sailors), was as penetrating as the gloom of night.

Further, in several fine scenes, he captured and distilled the pathos in the lives of the men. In one magnificent sequence the body of Yank was buried at sea, without elaborate detail or heavy sentimentality. Just a forlorn group of seamen were huddled on the heaving deck, while the captain's reading of the burial service was lost in the wail of the wind and the crash of the seas alongside. Then the prayerbook was snapped shut, the mate shrilled a whistle signal to the bridge, the ship was slowed down, perfunctorily the plank bearing the shrouded body of Yank was lifted, and the body slid overside. The mate shrilled another signal, there was one long, deep blast on the ship's whistle, the group of sailors broke up, and that was all. Within a few passing moments, the solemn ritual was performed and the ship with its still living cargo went plowing on.

In another, more intimate sequence some of the men, suspecting that the quiet, seclusive Smitty was perhaps a spy, grabbed a letter from his locker. While a couple of mates restrained him, another read the contents aloud to the group. It was a heartbreaking farewell from the girl he had loved back home and whose cruel dismissal of him had obviously sent him to sea. Moved and understanding, they simply gave him back the letter and left him alone.

That was a gratifying aspect: the film was spartanly free of emotional sham or mock heroics. When the British agent who came aboard in the American port started driveling about "unsung heroes," he got a contemptuous rebuff. None of the men considered himself other than a hardworking seaman with a dirty job to perform. Even when Yank died in the fo'c'sle with his pal Driscoll hovering over him, the maudlin note was avoided, despite the painful length of the scene.

Men of the deck crew spot an approaching Nazi bomber as their ship plows on in the North Atlantic danger zone.

Ole Olson, Axel and Driscoll watch in dread and fascination as the Nazi bomber zeros in on their ship.

53

Yes, we might have been spared the embarrassment of that visionary Union Jack waving over the body of Smitty when he was shot on deck by the German plane, but that was just a touch of chauvinism, allowable at that time.

And the performances of all were consistently vibrant and restrained by a cast which seemed to come together so often thereafter that they were known as "the Ford stock company": Thomas Mitchell as the brawling Driscoll; Ward Bond as the seemingly indestructible Yank; Barry Fitzgerald as Cocky; John Wayne as the gentle Swede; and Ian Hunter as the quiet Smitty. Wilfrid Lawson was veritable, too, as the stolid British captain, and Arthur Shields made a colorful donkey-engine man. Suffice it to say that women appeared only marginally. They were merely gauzy and deceptive, creatures of the land.

To be sure, a lot of the credit for this picture went to O'Neill, whose poetic philosophy and conception were at the heart of it. But Mr. Ford, Mr. Nichols, the actors, and Gregg Toland, the brilliant cameraman, made it all cleanly cinematic and shared the credit for its lasting poetry.

A howl of contempt for their defrauders in a British port is raised by Davis (Joe Sawyer), in foreground, Driscoll and Cocky (Barry Fitzgerald) as they ruefully return to their ship.

In the Grand Tradition

Sportswriters Phil (Roscoe Karns) and Sam Craig (Spencer Tracy) look suspiciously at a gift sent to Sam by their paper's star female columnist.

WOMAN OF THE YEAR

1942

The entertainment values in George Stevens' urbane comedy *Woman of the Year* were manifold and conspicuous. But what assures the picture of special historical significance is that it marked the first time those worthies, Katharine Hepburn and Spencer Tracy, were teamed. Miss Hepburn and Mr. Tracy were certainly one of the great acting couples of the American screen, and the rapport they discovered in this picture, the perfect blending of their differing social types and comedy styles, led to a happy succession of nine memorable Hollywood films.

It is difficult to pinpoint precisely what this harmony between the two was—what compound of powerful personalities made for uniqueness and charm. Miss Hepburn was a positive individual in so many ways—a woman, yet more than a mere woman. She was a unique feminine force. Tall, slender, angular, and upright, she moved with a confident, fluid grace, emitting an air of vitality and assurance. She seemed always in full com-

Tess Harding (Katharine Hepburn) and Sam rush into an impulsive marriage which doesn't turn out precisely as expected.

mand of herself. Her voice and her bearing revealed her as what we call a thoroughbred, which evokes an image of equine perfection that is not inappropriate. For the simple fact is that Miss Hepburn was "horsey" in a beautiful, smooth, sleek way. You'd guess she carried more of an aroma of leather than of Chanel Number 5. "Sexy," in the sense of sweet compliance, is not a word you would have used for her.

In short, she had the aura of a person of authority and power, attributes that were generally regarded in those days as the fashionable distinctions of males. This was true of her personality off screen as well as on. She was the sort who wore slacks and tailored jackets when those garments were not the common feminine style. Louis B. Mayer, the absolute monarch of Metro-Goldwyn-Mayer, with which Miss Hepburn was associated under a strong contract for some twenty years, always said he had the kind of respect for her that he had for the toughest man. She was able to stand right up to him, which very few men or women were.

Miss Hepburn represented the independence of the female sex; she was a woman who would concede superiority or give ground to no man. She was by way of being a premature exponent of women's lib, a lady who clearly stood for sex equality. Indeed, her familiar screen image was that of a woman so competent and strong that she was tacitly superior to most ordinary men. She was above the conventional recognition of women as sex symbols, to use the familiar expression of the liberation movement in recent times. She was always up and doing, not staying at home tending the house and kids. And this was an image which, in those days, shocked a lot of women, as well as men.

On the other hand, Mr. Tracy was the model of the good old solid male—rugged, forthright, unpretentious, but thoroughly able and self-contained. He had his codes—of honor, courtesy, and responsibility, and likewise his code of making a proper match with a member of the opposite sex. He was not one to trumpet loudly that a woman's place was in the home, but he was certainly one to maintain stoutly that, in that area, she had a definite place. When a woman entered into marriage, she had clear responsibilities, he believed, and among them were being mutually helpful to her husband and caring for whatever children might ensue.

Some say the inspiration for bringing Miss Hepburn and Mr. Tracy together in a film came from Joseph L. Mankiewicz, who was then a burgeoning producer at Metro-Goldwyn-Mayer. He saw in these two contract players a chance for combining chemistries that could make for a cheerful addition to the then popular category of husband-wife comedies. So he got Ring Lardner, Jr., rightly regarded as one of the most clever scriptwriters in Hollywood, and Michael Kanin together to prepare a script, and he persuaded the versatile George Stevens to direct. (Mr. Stevens had previously directed Miss Hepburn in *Alice Adams*, one of her better films, in 1935, and had also done very successful pictures with Fred Astaire, Cary Grant, and Irene Dunne.)

There is a persistent legend that when Miss Hepburn and Mr. Tracy first met in Mr. Mankiewicz's office to discuss their roles, Miss Hepburn remarked to Mr. Tracy, "Aren't you a bit short for me?" He allegedly replied without hesitation, "That's all right, I'll cut you down to size." This makes a very good story, but has a slightly manufactured sound, as though it were carefully fabricated to suggest the interesting essence of the film.

For *Woman of the Year* was the story of a high-powered lady journalist and a nice, rugged, homespun sportswriter. They met, fell in love, and were wed. But, after their rather mismatched marriage, Sam discovered that Tess continued on her way of being totally involved with the pressures and demands that her singular profession imposed.

On their wedding night, indeed as they were preparing to consummate their marriage, their cozy bedroom was suddenly invaded by a refugee Yugoslavian premier and a horde of frenzied followers. The customary business of the nuptial evening had to be postponed while she dragged an exclusive interview out of these preoccupied visitors. Likewise, a short time later, when he had hurried home from covering a Notre Dame football game in Chicago in order to have a free Sunday with her, he found her busily engaged dictating her column to an autocratic male myrmidon. Bewildered, he relegated himself to the kitchen and prepared a pick-up supper for three.

But the crisis in their matrimonial setup came after Tess brought home a Greek orphan boy for adoption—a gesture in line with her exalted humanitarian principles—and then virtually abandoned the lad to Sam's kindly care while she went bounding off here and there. On the evening that she was to be honored at a huge banquet as the "Woman of the Year," he politely declined to go with her, a refusal which elicited her astonishment and hurt. He put it on the line without minc-

Tess spends her wedding night in her bedroom getting an exclusive story from a refugee Yugoslavian premier (Ludwig Stossel) while Sam sits by not too patiently.

Tess being honored with the Woman of the Year Award, which Sam considers a mockery because he says she is "not a woman at all."

ing. "It's too bad I'm not covering this story," he said, "because I have an angle that would be sensational. The 'outstanding woman' is not a woman at all!"

A few days later, she called him in his office to tell him she had a telegram for him. Both were reserved and remote. She asked if he wished to come and get it. He said no, so she brought it to him. It was a telegram assigning him to cover a big prizefight. She asked him if it was important. Coolly (as only Mr. Tracy could) he replied: "It's quite important . . . in an unimportant sort of way." And on that hint of the extent of his hurt, they kissed and said goodbye.

The lively urbanity of the picture derived from the cheerful environment of the New York newspaper world. Mr. Lardner, whose father was a famous sportswriter in his day, was glibly *au courant* with the ambience, as was Mr. Kanin. They were also fellows who could turn a nifty line. The fictional newspaper had the aroma of the *New York Herald-Tribune*, and the bar to which Sam and his cronies retired—and Tess, too, when he took her on a date—was recognizable to the cognoscenti as the famous old waterhole Bleecks. Yes, every little thing about this milieu had a

crisp and authentic ring, from the bartender, played by William Bendix, to the soft hat and softer heart of Sam.

We all of us loved the humor, the sharp and independent attitudes of the two newspaper people, and the clever juxtaposition of sports and international politics. Those were the topical subjects at the time the film was being made, in the months before Pearl Harbor. What escaped us at the moment was the looming shadow it cast of professional jealousy between newspaper people and the latent male chauvinism of Sam. No matter how patiently and tolerantly we look at it today, if we want to be realistic, he was pretty much of a "pig."

However that was a matter to which we were not too sensitive in those days, and the way of resolving the issue was along conventional lines. Sam was entirely in conformance with the sympathies of women and men when he stood on the platform that a woman should be attentive and considerate toward her spouse and that, having assumed the responsibility of being a mother, it was unacceptable to walk away from the job. His requirement that Tess be a woman and a wife to those extents was precisely what the public expected and applauded when the issue was drawn.

The writers and Mr. Stevens resorted with Hollywood dexterity to sentimentality and farce to break the impasse of these two indomitable wills. Tess, alone and strangely uneasy without the presence and companionship of Sam, was suddenly called to Connecticut to attend the simple wedding of her widowed father and a favorite aunt—two people she loved and respected, who were somehow "above marriage" she foolishly thought. And as she stood in a country living room, with snow falling silently outside, and listened to a minister reminding the older couple that they were "performing an act of faith," adjuring the wife that she should "sustain" her husband, Tess began to cry, the tears welling in her large, bright eyes and her chin quivering tenderheartedly, as only Miss Hepburn's could.

After the emotional scene, she made a nocturnal dash to the tiny apartment in Brooklyn, to which the wounded Sam had repaired. And there, in the early morning, while he was still asleep, she began fixing breakfast for him—a wifely service which, as it went along, became more and more clumsy and clownish and the comic high point of the film.

In this almost twenty-minute sequence the obviously unskilled but thoroughly confident Tess collided head-on with the gadgetry of a modern kitchen—coffee-maker, mixing machine, and such. Slowly she became entangled—setting the coffee-maker upside down, putting yeast into the mixer for waffle batter, splattering the room while trying to break eggs—her agitation increasing and confidence ebbing in one of the funniest sequences in sophisticated screen comedy. It deserves to be given a top position in any anthology of such.

In the midst of this confusion, Sam awoke. Aghast to see what was happening, he muttered unbelievingly, "What's *this*?" When Tess replied glibly, "I've come home," he answered with realistic candor, not to be taken in, "I'm afraid I can't agree with you. This is the top phoney of all." Whereupon he sat and watched with incredulity. No one could beat Mr. Tracy's expressions of wide-eyed disbelief. When the waffle-maker, filled with yeast and batter, began to rise until it appeared ready to explode, he blurted out a warning: "Fourth down! You'd better kick!"

At this point, Tess, crestfallen, gave up, and surrendered herself to his arms. She knew when

An estranged and sceptical Sam discovers Tess, full of contrition, trying to whip up a surprise breakfast for him in his lonely Brooklyn flat.

she was licked. The reconciliation was tacit. "Why can't you be just Tess Harding?" he asked, implying that she didn't have to be Mrs. Sam Craig. The picture ended with her secretary arriving to fetch her to rush off to launch a battleship. Instead Sam took him by the seat of his pants and his coat collar and showed him the exit. Returning with a look of satisfaction and a tone of triumph in his voice, he said, "I've just launched Gerald."

This ending admittedly was inconclusive. It offered no practical prescription for the future sweet concord of Tess and Sam. But it left audiences with a feeling of tacit agreement between the two and, most particularly, with a feeling of having been royally entertained.

Greatly contributing to this spirit were the characters with which the principals were involved—William Bendix making his screen debut as a porky Irish barkeep, and former prizefighter; Dan Tobin as Gerald, the secretary, who played the role in a nice shade of gay; Roscoe Karns as a dyspeptic sportswriter and barfly whose philosophy was that "women should be kept illiterate and clean, like canaries"; and little Ludwig Stos-

sel as the Yugoslav premier who came bursting into the wedding boudoir spraying indignation and alarm.

However, nobody, quite rightly, got in the way of the principals, whom Mr. Stevens kept generally front and center. It was a dandy combination and made for a winning formula—amiable conflict between the sexes which was usually concluded with some sort of draw. Although Mr. Stevens did not again direct them, the pattern was successfully carried on, with George Cukor frequently handling them, in such comedies as *State of the Union*, *Adam's Rib*, and *Pat and Mike*.

It is touching to note that their last film together was *Guess Who's Coming to Dinner*, a Stanley Kramer comedy, in which they played elite liberal parents who were thrown into some confusion when their daughter brought home a distinguished black gentleman whom she intended to wed. Mr. Tracy was mortally ill with cancer as the picture was being made and died ten days after shooting was completed. It was a sad but appropriately valiant termination for him—and them.

Woodrow Truesmith (Eddie Bracken) finds himself being hailed as a hero of Guadalcanal by Mayor Noble (Raymond Walburn) and all the people of his hometown.

HAIL THE CONQUERING HERO

1944

Preston Sturges was a unique filmmaker not only in the scope of his work but, indeed, in the whole sprawling landscape of American talking films, and his *Hail the Conquering Hero* is the last of his remarkable run of satiric comedies—seven within a span of four years!—considered in my books. This audacious and colorful satire made at the peak of his career, was not only the last great film made by him—everything after it was downhill—but it carried to a creative crest the elements of his ironic comments and the characteristics of his farcical techniques. In a sense, it brought to a climax the ferocity of his social mockery, and it concluded with one of his typical sardonic incongruities.

The conquering hero of its title was no conquering hero at all, but a mild little small-town American who had been medically discharged from the United States Marines because he had chronic hay fever (a dubious excuse, but let it pass), and was thwarted in his great ambition of participating gloriously in World War II. He was a favorite hero type of Sturges—a decent fellow either so naive or dumb as to be a potential sucker for all the greedy, guileful rascals around and a pushover for conformity with all the standard middle-class American ideals.

He wanted to be a hero, for instance, because his father had been one—a legendary Leatherneck idol killed in the First World War while moving forward with his comrades at the Battle of Belleau Wood. And his reverence for his mother (who revered the memory of his father) was such that he simply couldn't go home and tell

Woodrow and the hysterical chairman of the welcoming committee (Franklin Pangborn) almost come to blows in the excitement of the homecoming parade.

her that he had been kicked out of the Marines, that he'd been assigned for six months to a shipyard instead of the battle front (as he had written in his letters) on Guadalcanal. Quite a dismal dilemma for a fellow entrapped by bourgeois conventionality.

That was his plight as the picture opened in a San Francisco bar, the hero worrying over his problem and listening to a woman sing a maudlin "Mother" song.

Then six bemedaled Marines for whom he bought drinks bumped up to the bar alongside him, and soon he was pouring his story into their ears. When he gave them his name, which was painfully wormed out of him—Woodrow Lafayette Pershing Truesmith—they set up a howl.

"Not the son of old Hinky Dink Truesmith?" one of them hopefully exclaimed.

Woodrow nodded, and that was the clincher. There was nothing now they wouldn't do for him. And after several more drinks, they decided, in their ingenious military minds, that the thing they would do that would be most honorable would be to take him home to Mom. But not to comfort him in his embarrassment. Nothing so negative as that! They would dress him in a Marine uniform, cover his chest with *their* medals, and present him as a hero of Guadalcanal and themselves as his officially designated Marine Corps honor guard!

Against Woodrow's violent protests, they hustled him along, and arrived in his hometown ex-

Woodrow enjoys a moment of bliss as he is reunited upon arrival in his hometown with his uncertain fiancée, Libby.

pecting to see him merely fall into his mother's arms. But when they pulled into the station they found a welcoming committee comprised of the entire town—the mayor, the rival political leader, hundreds of cheering citizens, and several bands—which gave Mr. Sturges the opportunity for one of his incomparable frenetic mob scenes, compounded of countless comic details, and the homecoming party flying totally out of the parade marshal's hands.

To the dismay of poor Woodrow, now the local Ulysses S. Grant, he was compelled by his six solemn guardians to carry through with the outrageous sham. As played by Eddie Bracken, the little actor with the constantly astonished look, popping eyes, pursed lips, and frantic gestures, he was a miserable, hilarious sight. And William Demarest as the ranking topkick, a rugged rascal with a side-mouthed gravel voice, was a wickedly deadpan parody of military adaptability and authority. Freddie Steele was a smolderingly pugnacious defender of the sanctity of Mom; Jimmie Dundee, Stephen Gregory, and Len Henry were other lumpish Marine types.

So Woodrow obediently allowed them to march him off to the church where the townsfolk had arranged a ceremony which featured the burning of the mortgage on his mother's home. Subsequently his sweetheart, who had lately abandoned him for a disgustingly smug young man, swore her eternal devotion. As a capstone, a statue was dedicated to father and son in the town square.

"What do I do *now*?" Woodrow demanded at this latest embarrassment.

"You just let it all blow over," Mr. Demarest replied.

"Did you ever see a *statue* blow over!" Woodrow fairly screamed. The accumulation of mortifications had him a nervous wreck.

And then came the final challenge! The local judge turned up that night and, after some initial uncertainty in which the guardians grabbed for their guns, fearing he had come to arrest Woodrow, the jurist announced that his political party would like to have Woodrow run for mayor in the coming election. "There's something rotten in this town," he said, and allowed that Woodrow was the only person who could set it straight. So again, against the frightened young man's wishes,

Woodrow is compelled to go through with the hoax by his stubborn Marine Corps sponsors, Bugsy (Freddy Steele) and the Sergeant (William Demarest).

Woodrow, flanked by his mother (Georgia Caine), his fiancée Libby (Ella Raines) and her aunt (Elizabeth Patterson), bid farewell to the squad of Marines who have perpetrated the disconcerting hoax.

but with the total approval of the Marines, the judge nominated Woodrow at another great Sturges-staged rally. Demarest, inspired to oracular heights by the occasion, threw in his support with a rousing speech in which he told how Woodrow had saved his life in a brutal encounter on Guadalcanal. The judge observed that "a man who fought for you so bravely overseas will fight for you now—and win!"

The offhand mixture of rampant patriotism and

political flimflam was superb!

After some further fearful sweating and a weak attempt to break away by pretending to his wised-up guardians that he had been called back for "limited service," Woodrow got up before another rally and admitted that he was a fraud, not to mention all sorts of other low things. "The farce is over!" he announced, and therewith sneaked off to the railroad station to catch a train out of town. But again Demarest rose to the occasion and, in another spellbinding harangue, told the dismayed citizens that "what that kid just done took courage, more courage than fighting in a war." Whereupon they rushed to the station, grabbed Woodrow off the train, and, in response to his terrified inquiry, "What's this, a lynching?" lifted him on high and proclaimed they would make him mayor—which bore out the word of the judge: "Politics is a perilous business. When they want you they don't need a reason."

And with their good deed accomplished, the six Marines departed on a train with Woodrow and the town bidding them farewell and the band booming out the Marines' Hymn.

It took a great deal of audacity and Mr. Sturges's kind of impudence to kid with such patent cynicism the fatuousness of hero worship with the nation in the midst of a war. And it also took his taste for debunking to let fly at the pious cult of Mom, pursuing a theme he had kidded in his previous *The Miracle of Morgan's Creek*. But that is the sort of satirist that Mr. Sturges was. He seemed to be most delighted when he was giving the bourgeoise a jolt.

Many of the characters in this picture were of his familiar sort—the marshal of the welcome-home gathering, whom his much favored Frank-lin Pangborn played with a great sweep of wild-eyed confusion and eventual hysteria; the bug-eyed nincompoop mayor of Raymond Walburn; the sardonic political boss of Alan Bridge; and the reform mayoral candidate of Harry Hayden, who oozed piety and insincerity.

But Woodrow was a new one for Mr. Sturges—or perhaps an extension of the Henry Fonda character in *The Lady Eve*—because he was the first who was allotted a goodly measure of pathos and sympathy. To be sure, he was a typical Sturges innocent—a decent, well-intending, hapless chump—but he was also tender and considerate, the sort of noodle the audience could love. I think we all felt he *was* appropriate to be the mayor of a Sturges-cockeyed town.

And those Marines—they were absolute originals, particularly Mr. Demarest's! They revealed all the streaks of urban humbug, packed into a sacred uniform. They mingled the gullible and the crafty with such delightful openness that no one could take exception. But they were shysters you had to watch! And that sendoff for them, with flags waving and the band banging out the Marines' Hymn, was as close as anyone got to stating, in those years, the ironies of soldiering and war.

It was tragic that this fine filmmaker petered out so pathetically after that burst of creativity during the grim years of World War II. In his subsequent Hollywood productions, the old spark mysteriously died, and nothing more, save one dismal letdown, *The Diary of Major Thompson*, was heard from him after he moved in the 1950s to France. But he left a legacy of satires that are brilliant and viable to this day. He was a "conquering hero" in his own mad, precocious way.

Laura Jesson (Celia Johnson) and Dr. Alec Harvey (Trevor Howard) strike up a chance acquaintance in a grubby railway buffet.

BRIEF ENCOUNTER

1946

David Lean's *Brief Encounter*, by all the criteria of well-organized social drama and skillful utilization of techniques, might be judged on the level of the "washboard weepers" of long-ago daytime radio, but is, for several interesting reasons, one of the still endearing works of the British screen. This 1946 film adaptation was based upon a modest one-act play by Noel Coward (who produced the movie) four years after Mr. Coward's classic war film, *In Which We Serve.**

To compare this simple little picture with that towering drama of British people in the midst of war is like putting a graceful sloop beside a dreadnaught. The first was large in significance and scope. This successor was wholly individual and limited in time and place. It told a quite slim, emotional story of a short and tentative romance between a middle-class English housewife and a married doctor whom she secretly met on her shopping trips to a dowdy provincial town. The whole affair took place within that area and in a matter of only a couple of weeks.

Indeed, the one weakness of the plot was the speed—the breathless spontaneity—with which the very proper small-town housewife and the doctor fell in love. A chance encounter in the buffet of a railway station (during which the doctor graciously removed a cinder from the lady's eye), a casual meeting on the street a week later and a coincidental sharing of a luncheon table in a tearoom, followed by an innocent visit together to a movie, and then a planned rendezvous two weeks later, during which they went for a walk in a park—all very friendly and proper and, bang, they were suddenly in love!

But it was precisely the swiftness with which attraction and emotion overwhelmed these two that, while hard to believe, really carried the sense of hunger and poignancy of their reaching

65

out. For the very essence of this slight drama was the loneliness and the need of these two people—especially the woman—for some involvement that would take them out of the narrow and corrosive environments in which they passively lived. Some fresh stimulation of their emotions was called for to lift them, in approaching middle age, from the rounds of their domestic obligations and the bonds of middle-class morality.

I would say the effectiveness of this picture came wholly from the simplicity of the tale and the wonderful skill and sincerity with which it was directed and played. There was no question that Celia Johnson was a genuine middle-class housewife, wearing rather tasteless clothes, saving pennies, being proper with her neighbors, and dutifully taking care of her husband and two youngsters. And Trevor Howard, who played the doctor (he was just then coming into films), was gentle and deeply affecting (a trace of bedside manner, perhaps), always deferring to the lady, yet maintaining his naturalness and dignity.

It was, of course, a "woman's picture," in the common sense of that phrase—a tear-invoking reenactment of an average housewife's lonely fantasies. No psychological probing was attempted, nor any explanation backward (or ahead) as to the conditioning of the woman and her adjustments to domesticity. What was omitted could easily be imagined from the very banality of her life. Her husband, whom we saw on those evenings after she returned to her home from her secret rendezvous to sit brooding in her armchair while flashbacks ran through her head (and the radio—or simply the sound track—obliged softly with snatches of Rachmaninoff's Concerto No. 2), was a pallidly dull, unquestioning fellow, treating her too considerately and perhaps giving a vague impression that maybe he, too, was indulging in a bit of philandering.

Likewise, the doctor was a stock figure to generate and indulge the emotional inflammation that bewilderingly surged in her. We were not given any knowledge of him, other than that he had a wife and kids somewhere in the background, which we never were shown, and that he was professionally interested in diseases of the lungs. The implication was that he suffered from frustration as much as did she, that a passing meeting in a railway station and a casual date at the cine-

At home that evening, Laura refrains from mentioning her exciting encounter to her humdrum husband Fred (Cyril Raymond).

Alec and Laura slip away for an illicit (and embarrassingly interrupted) rendezvous in one of his friends' apartment.

ma were sufficient to excite his latent ardor and drag from him an impulsive admission of love.

That was all this picture, and all that Mr. Lean, required to create the illusion of his nobility and excitement for the heroine—and obviously for the millions of people who have seen and been moved by this film it was enough. He was, to put it succinctly, a proper gentleman, even though just a small-town doctor. And that was most gal-

At what they agree must be their last meeting, Alec and Laura are intruded upon by an unsuspecting and talkative friend (Everley Gregg).

lantly displayed in the crucial scene, when the couple went one afternoon to the lodgings of a friend of the doctor, obviously drawn by an urge to make love, and were shockingly interrupted by the arrival of the friend. The gallant deportment of the doctor, after this shabby contretemps, and the humiliated flight of the lady, were enough to show everyone that he was a splendid fellow, an ideal consort for a poignant fantasy.

Today, this little picture, so sexually bland and quaintly suffused with serious concern for rigid morals and forthright domestic dignity, may seem peculiarly old-fashioned to liberated young folks. It may seem a timid exposition of suburbanity and a simple repetition of an oft-told movie tale.

But, oh, it was striking when it came out! It was simple and direct, it was restrained and impressively devoted to the concept of loyalty. The word for it was "adult," a term that was warily used to describe such exercises suggestive of near-adultery from Hollywood.

And David Lean made it most effective in simple but quietly artful ways. He utilized excellently close-ups to keep his principals right before one's eyes, tactfully excluding the shabby backgrounds when proper concentration was desired. Equally brilliant was his sensitive use of the railway station to form a racking, satanic surround for the fragile little meetings of his couple, with trains roaring through officiously, shrieking their terrifying whistles and belching incredible clouds of steam. All the effects built up nerve-jangling tension and supported the mood of conscience-stricken dread. And, for those more philosophic,

a symbolic suggestion of transience.

It is interesting to compare this picture with some present-day films bearing a similar theme—the anxieties of married women and their feelings about loyalty and sex. The changes in attitudes and manners that have occurred in a mere three decades are nowhere more bluntly demonstrated than in a comparison of this romantic film with something like *Sunday, Bloody Sunday* or *Network*. Shadows pass swiftly on the screen.

The final moment of parting forever between Laura and Alex on the platform of the railway station where they first met.

A small party of fearsome Cheyenne Indians sweeps down upon their white enemies in the awesome and magnificent expanse of Monument Valley.

SHE WORE A YELLOW RIBBON

1949

Director John Ford once told me, after some mention of Art, as I recall, that there was nothing he knew of more beautiful and exhilarating than the sight of a horse in full stride. And I truly believe he was serious—assuming, of course, that the steed was suitably caparisoned and mounted by a United States Army cavalryman or a ululating American Indian and was racing across a western plain with a sweep of purple mountains in the background and a great bank of clouds in the sky.

For Mr. Ford's sense of magnificence reflected a genuine passion for the elemental splendor and vitality of the pristine American western scene.

His own deep, romantic Irish nature found aesthetic gratification in the unsullied natural beauties of the western mountains and plains, in the simple and direct motivations of the human beings who early inhabited—or invaded—them, and in the efficiency and dynamism of the animals and artifacts they employed. Most potent and essential to fulfillment were the weapon and the horse—the weapon for defense and survival, the horse to transport men with needful speed.

This predilection for the equine in association with man was thoroughly and fervently manifested to the point of being virtually choreographed in all of Mr. Ford's westerns, which were a major

Captain Nathan Brittles and his devoted Sergeant Quincannon (Victor McLaglen) inspect a ravaged stagecoach brought into Fort Starke by a Seventh Cavalry patrol.

Quincannon arrives to summon Captain Brittles as he muses upon a daugerrotype of his recently deceased wife on what is expected to be the day of his retirement.

category of his work. And nowhere was this more evident than in what I consider his best—alongside his classic *Stagecoach* — *She Wore a Yellow Ribbon*, starring his favorite cowboy actor John Wayne.

She Wore a Yellow Ribbon was not an attempt at history. Nor was it technically unassailable. (No Western that I know of ever was.) It did not try to dig beneath the surface of an offbeat soldier personality, as did its immediate predecessor, *Fort Apache*. (In the latter, Henry Fonda played a frontier cavalry officer whose hatred of Apaches was so vengeful that it led him and his command to vainglorious doom.) It was simply a vivid illustration, a composite of all the legends of the frontier cavalryman in the years of westward expansion after the American Civil War— all of it burnished freely by the imagination and style of Mr. Ford. It blazed with bold and dashing courage, unabashed sentiment, the grandeur of rear-guard heroism, and the blunt bravado of barroom brawls. And, best of all, it caught in literal *color* (it was Mr. Ford's second color film) the intensely dramatic scope and beauty of the western scene and of those legendary mounted soldiers as they ranged forth into silent "Indian country" and were swallowed in the vastness of the plains. Mr. Ford had said he wanted to make it comparable on the motion picture screen to the bold and

Captain Brittles, flanked by his lieutenants, Cahill (John Agar) and Pennell (Harry Carey Jr.), and the colonel's superfluous niece, Olivia (Joanna Dru), as they ride out with a cavalry company to circumvent the mystifying Indian raiders.

lustrous beauty of the frontier paintings of Frederic Remington. While he modestly feared he had not done so, I think he did.

From the moment that Mr. Ford assembled his rawboned troopers of Company C around the immortal guidon of the Seventh Cavalry at distant and lonely Fort Starke, thence to ride forth on a perilous mission under Captain Nathan Brittles' firm command, the rifles were held at the ready and the scouts were flanked wide on alert. For somewhere out there in the vastness a Cheyenne dog-party was ominously on the prowl. Custer was lately dead at Little Big Horn, his whole complement of troops massacred, and the buffalo were curiously ranging farther north than they had since '69. Someone was obviously making "big medicine" among the strangely emboldened braves. And it was up to Captain Brittles and his troopers to find out who and why.

But before they rode out on their crucial mission, there was ample activity at the fort—and on preliminary scouting forays—to acquaint the viewer with the muscular characters and the two slightly incongruous females who were resident on the post. In addition to Captain Brittles, whom

Mr. Wayne played with full command, whether barking orders to his troopers or secretly watering the flowers on his wife's fresh grave, there was Victor McLaglen as an Irish sergeant, Ben Johnson as a veteran cavalryman, and John Agar as a southern-bred lieutenant who loved the colonels' sprightly niece, Joanne Dru. There were numerous assorted buck-toothed rankers, mostly Irish and itching to fight, among themselves or against the Indians, and there was Mildred Natwick as another officer's wife.

Miss Natwick deserves a special mention. Her way of intermingling crinkled smiles and the tenderness of an older woman with waspish tongue and the courage of a lion contributed much to the mix of masculinity and supported a whim of Mr. Ford. He always favored the presence in his westerns of a sturdy, competent female, as encouragement to masculine pride and valor—but never a rival in beauty to the sight of a horse in full stride.

There was time to get in some tasteful spooning between the shavetail and the jaunty little lass who wore a symbolic yellow ribbon for him, as it says in the freely used old cavalry song. There

Olivia and Captain Brittles stand amid the burned-out ruins of a stagecoach relay station, grim testimony to the vengeance of the Cheyennes

was time for square dancing in the officers' mess room and for a smashing thunderstorm out on the plains, for the twilight death of an old Confederate officer who ended his days as a trooper in the Seventh Cavalry, and for an emergency surgical operation in a wagon at night far from the fort. As I say, Mr. Ford was not embarrassed by an abundance of sentiment, scooped up by his writers, Frank Nugent and Laurence Stallings, out of a rugged James Warner Bellah yarn.

But the essence of his film was the ballet of men and horses against landscape and sky, the magnificent movement of files of horsemen and supporting wagons snaking out across the plains, the onrush of hordes of mounted Indians, whooping and waving feathered spears in one of the most galvanizing "entrances" I have seen in a film. Henry James once said that landscape, well presented, was character. No director has ever made such "character" work better for him than Mr. Ford.

There are those who have challenged the director for his frank endorsement of martial aggressiveness as a driving dramatic element in his westerns and his advancement of militaristic panoply as an icon of "good guy" Americanism. And they have charged him with racial prejudice in making the Indians the "heavies"—though, of course, he reversed that postulate in his compassionate *Cheyenne Autumn* toward the end of his career. And, indeed, in this film, as in most others, the onus was somewhat taken off by having the evil white road agent who was selling guns and accessory war-waging material as the secret agitator of the tribes. But I always felt Mr. Ford's affection for all things having to do with the cavalry was a merely romantic outpouring—and a shrewd concession to an enduring public taste.

Anyhow, I challenge any viewer to resist a bit of a tingle down the spine even now when he sees those mounted troopers ride out from the frontier fort to the high-pitched, long-drawn shouts of "Yee-eoooo!" to the rattle and clang of saber sheaths, and the thump and agitation of wheeling horses' hoofs. Mr. Ford knew how to gild the old horse soldiers, and he did it magnificently in this film.

The scheming lawyer, Alonzo Emmerich (Louis Calhern), pampers and pets his naive mistress (Marilyn Monroe) during a comparatively relaxed moment in *The Asphalt Jungle.*

THE ASPHALT JUNGLE

1950

It is interesting to note, in passing, how the flow of Hollywood's crime and gangster films since the advent of sound has run in cycles—or in "generations," as it were. The first generation was projected by those venerable classics of gangster lore, the quasi-biographical *Little Caesar,*** *Scarface*, and *The Public Enemy*,* which reflected the years of Prohibition when the Chicago gangsters fought for pelf and power. For al most a decade thereafter, the characteristics of crime and gangster films followed pretty closely the format of those shattering gratifications for crime voyeurs, except that with time mobsters versus G-men (or T-men) replaced internecine gang warfare.

Then, in 1940, a conspicuous advance was marked with John Huston's crisp *The Maltese Falcon,** which improved the contemplations of crime with liberal admixtures of literary original ity, sophistication, and caustic wit. Now the old-time criminals gave way to more modern types—pursuers of new kinds of plunder and the tricksters who were out to plunder them. The crime itself became incidental to the diversity of the characters. In the cast of *The Maltese Falcon* the pivot for the action was the shady private detective whom Humphrey Bogart played—a fellow who was not himself a criminal but was wise to all the ways of beating the law. With this new kind of conniver, a second generation of crime films came, and it, too, ran roughly for a decade, marked by such outstanding works as Billy Wilder's *Double Indemnity* and Howard Hawks' *The Big Sleep*. And then, in 1950, came Mr. Huston again with his scorching *The Asphalt Jungle*, and a third generation evolved.

Looked at today, this classic movie may seem a bit commonplace in its well-paced, meticulous recounting of a spectacular jewel robbery, from the moment of its complex inception and the careful setting up of the job to its nerve-tearing execution and disastrous aftermath. The theme and the plot, which Mr. Huston and Ben Maddow derived from a novel by the famed crime-story writer W. R. Burnett, have been unabashedly copied or imitated so many times in later years, from Jules Dassin's tingling *Rififi* to Barry Pollack's 1972 *Cool Breeze* (an acknowledged remake of the Burnett story, only with blacks in the principal roles), that it is no wonder latter-day viewers, unfamiliar with the original and its time, may charge it with being "old-fashioned" or, at least, "like all the rest."

How undiscriminating and ironic such a potential charge is can be seen only by examining the more subtle aspects of this film. For there was something quite as fascinating in it as the documentation of a crime, something quite bold and penetrating that some viewers even today do not see. (Or if they see it, which, of course, is fairly obvious, they do not analyze it properly.) That was the basic social difference between the fellows who carried out the crime and the high-powered criminal lawyer who secretly financed it and intended to double-cross his partners when the stolen jewels were in hand.

Here was a new and subtle wrinkle in the arcane of fictional crime that presented the mind and emotions with a cleavage of sympathies. On the one hand, there were the working criminals, the familiar underworld stiffs who normally made their livings by doing illegal things—by running betting parlors, making usurious loans, "fencing" the goods from minor robberies, pulling their own small-time "heists" and occasionally getting involved in a big one when an opportunity

The shifty bookmaker Cobby (Marc Lawrence) is beaten and abused by a crooked police detective, Lieut. Dietrich (Barry Kelley).

came along. They were the technical experts, the professionals who knew the rules—how to pick locks and use firearms, blow safes and drive getaway cars, and accept the occupational hazards that went with such taut activities. And their leader was a scientific genius in the organization and direction of such work, a creative enterpriser who needed only financing to mount a job.

On the other hand, there was the banker, the essential financier who was able to summon the capital and invest it for a share of the spoils. He was, in relation to the workmen, the familiar capitalist whose hands were never dirtied and whose only considerable risk was that of losing his money if the enterprise went sour. He was the very model of a risk-capital financier—elegant, educated, endowed with an expert legal mind, swift to perceive an opportunity and turn it to self-advantage. While the workmen with whom he made a contract to rob an expensive jewelry store lived in virtual squalor and in the shadows of the underworld, he lived in a sumptuous apartment on what was evidently the good side of town, hobnobbed with city officials, and kept a mistress (played by Marilyn Monroe!). What more graphic depiction of class differences could be thought of than was evident in this film?

While, of course, there had been prior pictures in which elegant but crooked characters had been mixed up with working criminals—the blue-collar element, you might say—Mr. Huston's *The Asphalt Jungle* was the first to make the contrast so pronounced and to convey without a hint of moralizing the ugly irony in such a relationship. Here were the socially branded criminals who were only out to do a hard night's work, and there was the socially prominent lawyer who was only out to do them double-dirt. No matter how you looked at it, the moral balance in this film was heavily weighted against the lawyer. He was the villain in the piece.

Of course, every character in it, with the possible exception of Miss Monroe's pouty and cuddly little mistress to Louis Calhern's silken financier and the nightclub performing Jean Hagen, who aspired vainly to be Sterling Hayden's "moll," was a crook of one sort or another, each distinctive in the styles of movie thugs. Mr. Hayden was a tough, deadpan hoodlum who was quick and ruthless with a gun. His job was described as that of "hooligan," the lifter and lookout when the robbery was being carried out. Anthony Caruso was the "boxman" who drilled the hole and set the explosive in the vault. James Whitmore was a shifty hunchbacked barman who drove the get-

The jewel robbery team goes at its task under the expert supervision of Doc Riedenschnieder (Sam Jaffe), with the "boxman," Louis (Anthony Caruso) drilling holes in the vault door for the explosive charges while the "hooligan," Dix Handley (Sterling Hayden), stands guard.

Dix wipes out an interceding security guard while Louie and Doc wait impatiently to make their escape with the stolen jewels.

Emmerich and Doc gloat for a few euphoric moments over the richness of the haul before Emmerich makes the astounding announcement that he does not have the money he promised to pay for them.

away car. Marc Lawrence was a betting-parlor owner who was the "fixer" on the financial end. And Sam Jaffe was the brilliantly creative and efficient mastermind who put the whole enterprise together and was an expert appraiser of jewels. As an incidental annoyance, following the tradition of crime films, Barry Kelley was an occasionally intruding and inevitably bullying crooked cop.

In the main these crooks all had something to engage a viewer's sympathies. Mr. Hayden was a compulsive horse-player, an obvious "loser" in life whose great ambition was to get enough money so he could return to Kentucky and his parents' farm. Mr. Caruso was a dutiful and patient family man who got involved in robbery to support a wife and kids. Mr. Whitmore was a regular low-brow, generous and loyal to his pals. And Mr. Jaffe was a German ex-convict who commanded respect for his intelligence and skills.

Indeed, I would doubt that any viewer could avoid rooting for this team as they gingerly executed what Mr. Jaffe called "the biggest one yet"—entered the store through a manhole and passageway from the street, reached the vault through the salesroom, carefully circumventing the electric "eyes," set the explosives in an at-

mosphere of choking suspense, then beat it out through the passage after the charge had gone off, the jewels in their clutches, as distant alarm bells and sirens signaled the law being alerted and closing in. Mr. Huston's staging and pacing of the details of this sensational heist, the most pictorial ever done in a movie (up to that time), hit a cinematic high.

But all this, as I say, was prefatory to the more significant conflict which came when the burglars returned with the booty to the apartment of Mr. Calhern and were told by him that he didn't have the money he had promised to pay them off. This was the ultimate shocker, a dumbfounding slap in the face which the audience knew and Mr. Jaffe suspected was the beginning of a well-planned double-cross. And from here on the drama developed, heightened by the resentment of the thieves at being bilked. The progressive erosion, through disasters, of the participants ensued until all were gone. These included an immediate confrontation while the crisis was at its boiling point when a henchman of Mr. Calhern tried to grab the jewels for himself. He was dispatched by Mr. Hayden with a quick and impulsive pistol shot. Then Mr. Calhern, apprehended by the police when he bungled an attempt to dispose of the henchman's body, bid a tender farewell to his mistress and tidily killed himself. Mr. Jaffe, a closet lecher, was caught because he lingered too long with a little pick-up while trying to escape with the jewels. And Mr. Hayden died from a festering gun wound just as he finally got back to the Kentucky farm.

The thieves' unhappy fates seemed to be directed to proving that "crime does not pay," a conclusion rigidly demanded back in the days of *The Asphalt Jungle* by the stiff Production Code. (There was even dropped into this picture toward the end a pious little scene in which an upright police commissioner told a group of reporters that they shouldn't judge all policemen by the exposure now and then of one bad cop.) But a less conspicuous message was cynically filtered through and ultimately became on close analysis the new and significant social theme—namely, that felonious greed is not confined to the members of a so-called criminal class. It may be just as strongly felt and practiced by those who appear respectable. Indeed, under a silken cloak of probity, there is no end to what may be tried—and maybe pulled—by someone with social standing and a nice lack of moral principle.

Missed, by most, in the passage of one very brief and gentle scene may have been the soft remonstrance that Mr. Calhern gave to his invalid wife when she complained about his consorting with disreputable business associates. "There's nothing so different about them," he told her amiably. "After all, crime is but a left-handed form of human endeavor." So, he might have added, is graft or lying or welching on a bargain—or cheating one's employees. But the film said it adequately for him.

Stanley Kowalski (Marlon Brando) pursues his deliberate campaign to challenge, harass and abuse his sensitive sister-in-law, Blanche Dubois (Vivien Leigh).

A STREETCAR NAMED DESIRE

1951

Two very considerable anxieties nibbled at the minds of interested observers of the movies when Elia Kazan set out to make a film of Tennessee Williams' powerful stage play *A Streetcar Named Desire*. The first was what might be expected from the British actress Vivien Leigh, whom Kazan and his producer Charles K. Feldman, cast to play the tragic heroine, Blanche DuBois, a fading Louisiana spinster who was trying to keep her ego afloat by supporting it on the memories and/ or illusions of a considerably fantasized past was

so indisputably "southern" in so many of her ways and attitudes, so pretentious to a kind of gentility that was indigenous to southern ladies of a rapidly dwindling caste, that it was wondered how accurately and credibly Miss Leigh could handle the role, even though she *had* played Scarlett O'Hara in the more romantic rococo *Gone With the Wind*.*

The unease was of course unfounded, and abated perceptibly before the film was half completed. It was rendered ridiculous by the time the final take had been made. Her Blanche, while considerably different in histrionic style and emotional range from that performed by Jessica Tandy in the original production of the play, was

In an altered mood, Blanche attempts to exercise a bit of southern charm on the coarse and corrosive Stanley.

a harrowingly tense and slowly shattering revelation of a woman going mad under the pressures of her own long-drawn frustrations and the vicious aggressions of a resentful man. It was a terrifying and heartbreaking exposure of the ruin brought about by the collision of a self-deluding nature with a force—or fate—beyond its control.

The second cause for anxiety was that Mr. Kazan might not be able to make this drama "move" within the essential confinement of a four-room apartment in a New Orleans slum. But ingeniously and boldly, he used the strictures on physical movement as a tangible force in making the audience feel the slow and horrible claustrophobia and suffocation of his frenzied heroine. From the moment he walked Blanche through the doorway of that apartment in the Elysian Fields (the incongruous name of the neighborhood and an irony in itself) after moving her across the busy city and into the narrowing area on a streetcar named Desire, Mr. Kazan aggressively kept her within that confining space, which was both a painful constriction and a hopeful haven for her. Blanche had reached that level of defeat and despair when she arrived that made her yearn for a peaceful isolation where she could nurse her spiritual wounds and fantasies.

Only once did Mr. Kazan and Oscar Saul, who adapted the play, let her out of that apartment for more than a momentary spell. That was when she was taken to a dance pavilion beside a moonlit lake by a tentative gentleman suitor who had met her in the apartment by chance and had become infatuated with her. And it was a most significant release. For in that physical withdrawal from the apartment to a quiet, open-air, romantic place where she could feel herself free for recalling and reciting her wistful memories and, as important, have a gentle and sympathetic man to listen to her, Blanche was removed for a short time from the accumulating hell which her life had been in the apartment to the blissful enchantment of *her* Elysian Fields. Then back to the apartment it was for her and to the harassment which finally drove her mad.

While the preoccupations of audiences over the years have been largely with Blanche and the pathos of her deterioration, the core of the drama and the essential reason for its impact lay in the battle between Blanche and her brother-in-law, the notorious Stanley Kowalski, played with a rush of intense impersonation by Marlon Brando. This is a basic detail which many viewers have tended to underestimate. Because Stanley came on with such a line buck of arrogant masculine dominance, asserting immediate hostility toward his newly arrived sister-in-law and trying to give an impression of domestic authority, the tendency has often been to accept him as a two-dimensional brute, a cruel and vulgar roughneck whose only purpose was to bully Blanche out of sheer contempt. And with all the physical eccentricity and energy that Mr. Brando brought to the role— his bold and ferocious swagger, his dockwallop-

Stanley, driven from the apartment after a fight with his wife, Stella (Kim Hunter), is finally forgiven by her.

er's sweaty *déshabillé*, his curiously slurring way of speaking, and his brash social crudity—he frankly invited acceptance as just an ill-mannered foil to her, a clever and relentless deflater of her pretensions and tacit snobbery. Indeed, it was common for viewers who discovered Mr. Brando in this film (his only previous screen appearance had been as a paraplegic war veteran in the fine but comparatively obscure *The Men*) to see Stanley as a *macho* champion of the lower class and to laugh with animal enjoyment when he taunted and tormented Blanche.

But, of course, that betrayed a pathetic and disconcerting insensitivity to the subtlety and meaning of the conflict that was taking place. For Stanley was far from a powerful and self-assured individual. He was not a clear-headed assailant of the manifestations of the elite. He was a desperately insecure and muddled Polish-American workingman who was intuitively aware of his ethnic inferiority to his animalistically devoted and apparently better-born American wife. In truth he was terrified that she might be taken from him

by his exotic sister-in-law. Stanley, like Blanche, was motivated by a passion to survive, to hold on to what he had established in the way of a marriage through sheer sexual drive. To him Blanche was just as much a monster with vicious tendencies as he was to her, threatening to discourage his wife, Stella, from continuing to live with him. And Stella, played tautly by Kim Hunter, was his foundation, the illusion to which *he* strove to hold. He knew that if he lost her, he himself would be lost. Therefore, his sole determination in this battle was to do away with Blanche.

His first line of attack was to confront her with insulting suspicions about her sale of the alleged family property; he then escalated to desecrating the old love letters and mementos which embraced her fantasies. His final and crushing weapon was man's ultimate depravity, rape, which betokened the culmination of his hatred and subliminal lust.

One scene in particular captured the essence of Stanley's tactics of abuse and the effectiveness of Mr. Kazan's persistently close-up style. Blanche,

79

Blanche is caught in her increasing habit of secret tippling by Mitch (Karl Malden), a friend of Stanley, who has taken a romantic interest in her.

Mitch examines the ravaged face of Blanche in disgust after he has been told by Stanley of her far from lady-like past.

alone in the semidarkness of her narrow and cluttered room, was lost in a pretense of dancing with an illusory gentleman and babbling some elegant gibberish while dreamy music played. The music went into "Goodnight Ladies," and she whispered polite regrets. Suddenly the spell was broken by Stanley's ugly, mocking voice coming out of the darkness of the close-up: "Hello, Blanche." The music stopped. For a moment there was silence. Then a withering light came on and the poor woman's face loomed before us, a shocking image of torment and ruin. It was pale and haggard in the white light, a map of ravaged beauty and famished pride. And the eyes—those large, distinctive features of Miss Leigh's countenance which she used so superlatively in the close-ups—were full of hurt and fear. A prisoner confronted by a torturer would not express more agony of the soul. In this one shot was stabbingly compacted the tragedy of Blanche DuBois.

The counter to Stanley's tormenting was, of course, the brief, pathetic interlude of clumsy coquetry and a tentative outing with one of Stanley's bumptious poker-playing friends. The sudden and starry-eyed attraction of middle-aged Mitch to Blanche, on whom he superimposed all his stereotyped romantic dreams, and the meager opportunity this gave her to unburden her sentiment-laden heart, was a tiny, tenuous glimmer of hope within the darkness of her life. But it was nipped in the bud when Stanley found out some ugly aspects of her past and triumphantly confronted Mitch with them. It was the end of that impossible romance. It was also a side-bar revelation of the poverty of poor Mama-ridden Mitch, who was made by the writing of Mr. Williams and the fine performance Karl Malden gave into an unforgettable image of castration by middle-class morality.

In my book, one of the saddest, most cathartic scenes in film history was enacted at the culmination of this picture. The attendants had arrived to take Blanche away to what was tacitly acknowledged an asylum. Compelled to pass by the sullen, self-conscious poker players hunched over their cards in the front room, she said, "Please don't get up," in a last flash of valiant sarcasm for their savage treatment of her, "I'm only passing through." And then to the aides who were obviously trying to be solicitous toward her, she said, with a trace of awful loneliness in her voice, "Whoever you are, I have always depended on the kindness of strangers." And with that she was led away. The wrench was too much for Stella. She ran weeping after her with Stanley in pursuit, trying to stop her. She eluded him and rushed up the outside stairs to the apartment of a neighbor, screaming, "I'm never going back in there again!" The last shot was of Stanley bawling, "Stella! Stella!" at the foot of the stairs.

To be sure, there were many questions that were not precisely answered by the film and there were also many meanings that might be found in it. Were Blanche and Stella really remnants of a genteel family? Had Blanche indeed been gravely wounded by a hapless marriage with a sexually blank young man? Had she, in desperation, made a living of late as a prostitute? Did she unknowingly lust for Stanley, as was vaguely implied? Never mind. For all its unanswered questions, minor lapses and ambiguities, *A Streetcar Named Desire* was even more powerful as a film than it was as a play, and Blanche DuBois was a character to set alongside Anna Karenina and Tess of the d'Urbervilles.

Two things I think are significant: no one has tried to remake *A Streetcar Named Desire* in the more than a quarter of a century since it was released, despite the fact that it presents one of the classic tragic women in American literature. And second, it has come in for some nasty and sarcastic putting-down by advocates of women's liberation, for reasons that are plain. Blanche is a perfect example of a woman who let herself be used—nay, prided herself on being a sex object—and Stanley is by now a legendary prize-winning male chauvinist pig. I wonder if there is any connection between these two interesting points.

Rose Sayer (Katharine Hepburn) kneels in prayer with her bewildered brother, Rev. Samuel Sayer (Robert Morley), after an attack on his tiny mission in Central Africa at the outbreak of the First World War.

THE AFRICAN QUEEN

1952

There were those who strongly suspected, at the time it was released, that John Huston's howling screen rendering of C. S. Forester's novel *The African Queen* was not only a strange departure from his accustomed type of solid dramatic film but very possibly was some sort of cryptic inside joke.

Here was a queer, satiric story of a wild adventure on a river in the African wilds featuring a lady missionary and a ribald, uncouth Cockney

drunk. The tale was fraught with such mammoth paradoxes in the characters of the woman and the man and in the irony of their social juxtaposition that it seemed conceivable Mr. Forester was being derisively satiric to the point of virtual surreality. Then along came Mr. Huston, who, in collaboration with his associate scriptwriter James Agee, turned it into an encounter so laden with hyperbole that it had the shifty, suspicious appearance of an international Hollywood spoof.

To support this amazing suspicion—or perhaps to initiate it—he had in the roles of these two characters a couple of his most familiar and companionable friends whose movie images and act-

Rose, bereft of her brother, is taken aboard the tiny launch, the *African Queen* by its captain, Charlie Allnut (Humphrey Bogart), for an attempted escape down a jungle river.

ing styles were so dissimilar, so much at opposite poles, that it seemed that he—and they, too, with his needling—were parodying themselves. They were Katharine Hepburn and Humphrey Bogart, she usually a sophisticated social type and he an invariable example of the cynical, self-serving American stud. To have found these two acting together in any sort of film might have seemed a perilous miscalculation. Finding them in Mr. Forester's story seemed a gag.

I thought so, at first, but on reflection (which meant considering it for a few days) I began to be of the opinion that Mr. Huston was remarkably shrewd. He had seen the incredibility in Mr. Forester's bizarre tale and had decided, with the help of Mr. Agee (or possibly with his abrasive resistance, as I have sometimes heard), that the only way to adapt this monstrous fable of class confusion and accomodation to the graphic color screen was to make it *conspicuously* outlandish and thus even more incredible. And then, on thinking about it further and re-seeing it over the years, I have come to the conclusion that it was really, inter alia, a crafty and not too subtle put-down of popular myths about the potency of sex.

Why do I come to this conclusion? Well, con-

Charlie, given to guzzling gin, warns the prudish Rose not to try to discourage him.

After countless perilous adventures in their flight down the river, Charlie and Rose, now romantically involved, try to hack a way for the launch through a tangle of delta swamp grass.

sider the aspects of the film in which this straight-laced, old-maidenish female and a filthy rumpot developed a severe lust for one another while perilously isolated on a river in Africa, had sex several times amidst their ordeals, and then decided that they wanted to be wed.

She was the sole surviving sister of an English missionary whom she had helped and who died under somewhat inconvenient circumstances at his pitiful post in darkest Africa. He was the dirty outcast skipper of a wheezy steam launch that customarily plied the muddy waters of the jungle river on which the mission outpost stood. The two were haphazardly thrown together when a German patrol came through at the outbreak of the First World War, and they, as a couple of British citizens, were forced to try to escape downriver in the launch.

Here was as clear a pair of misfits as anyone could conceive—she in a long linen duster, a high choke-collar, and a floppy cloth hat, burbling her endless prissy charges from beneath an incongruous parasol, and he ragged, grease-stained, be-whiskered, booze-sodden, with a sweatrag around his neck and sullenly spitting back his protests while a soggy cigarette hung from his lips. Her clear evangelical purpose at the outset was to proselytize him, to force him to clean up his clothing and his language and especially to give up guzzling gin. And his was—as much as one was able to perceive any purpose in him—to keep the launch's engine going so he could soon get out of there and rid himself of this bothersome dame.

In one early confrontation, after she had poured out his stock of gin and banished him by sheer force of willpower to the open bow of the lonely little launch, she held to her resolution so righteously and stubbornly that his flabby resistance was finally broken and she charitably allowed him to come aft out of the rain. It was in this apparent moral victory that she conceived a bit of tenderness toward him.

Unable to put ashore at the town of their destination because the Germans had occupied it, they were forced to the dangerous extremity of shoot-

Captured and taken aboard the German gunboat, *Louisa*, which he and Rose have incredibly tried to blow up with a home-made torpedo, Charlie faces execution under the supervision of the First Officer (Theodore Bikel).

ing some wildly surging rapids that almost swamped the launch. The excitement and exhilaration evidently created a bond and brought them together, for suddenly, after their battered launch was clear, they gave way to lust in what was probably the most unlikely and least lustful seduction scene ever filmed. The surprise and absurdity of it were turned into a straight-out burlesque the next morning when she coquettishly asked him, "Mr. Allnut dear, what is your first name?" and he triumphantly beamed, "Charlie!" That was the beginning of love.

That was also the end of the bantering about the different social statuses of the two and the beginning of their increasingly grotesque struggle for survival. For her patriotic impulse to compel him to build a crude torpedo with which they might attack a German gunboat in a large lake for which they were bound resulted not only in an ordeal for him but in a heavier burden upon the small craft when they got snarled in impassable reeds and shallows. And their struggles to free the ancient vessel from this impenetrable morass became less amusing than painful when he, trying to pull the launch forward, got hideous, clinging leeches on his bare back.

To watch Miss Hepburn and Mr. Bogart, two of Hollywood's most carefully nurtured stars, enduring a sort of movie torture that wouldn't have been foisted upon Errol Flynn—she sodden, ragged, and dirty, with her hair streaming down in strings and he looking more than ever like the unholy wrath of God—was peculiarly disconcerting and almost embarrassing, for one still felt the characters they were playing were temporarily dislocated caricatures.

And then, of a sudden, they were out of it and back onto a level of *opéra bouffe* that might have been familiar territory for a slambang Marx Brothers farce. A last-ditch prayer for mercy by her brought a deluge of rain and the launch was miraculously floated out onto the lake, there to make for the gunboat and be swamped by high winds and heavy seas. Mr. Bogart was hauled upon the craft and slated to be hanged. But then she too was discovered and the German captain obligingly agreed to marry them before Mr. Bogart had to swing. While the wedding was taking place, however, there was a shattering explosion in the bow. The gunboat had hit the torpedo. That was the last devastation of the "African Queen."

For all the complete exaggeration and absurdity of the film as a spoof of social conventions and the artificialities of class when people are confronted by the perils of nature and of man, it was a delightful entertainment. There were beauty and excitement in its scenes of an African river, foaming white rapids and falls and the assorted birds and animals that live on the banks and in the stream. Mr. Huston and his producer, S. P. Eagle (now the Sam Speigel of multiple renown), went directly to a river in Africa to photograph much of it, under the fine camera eye of Jack Cardiff.

The advantage of this preciseness clearly showed.

Likewise, the gusto and abandon of the principals, who had it all to themselves—only Robert Morley showed briefly in the beginning as the English missionary and Theodore Bikel and Peter Bull at the windup as officers of the German gunboat—endowed it with a unique prankishness. It was dumbfounding that two Hollywood Bourbons should have thrown themselves with such elaborate zest and such readiness for deglamorization into such a grotesquerie. It was, in addition to being funny, a triumphant tour de force for them.

As for my feeling about it being a crafty putdown of the overblown ideas that Hollywood movies have generated about the infallible therapy of sex, I maintain that serious acceptance of belief that an afflatus of lust could have overcome these two characters is intellectually impossible. She was obviously a congenital virgin whose sex equipment had become so rusted by disuse that it was inconceivable that it could be stimulated and mobilized in such a short length of time. And he was so obviously saturated and emasculated by booze that only a romanticist could imagine that he could think of and achieve successful intercourse.

No, I'm sure Mr. Huston and Mr. Agee had their tongues in their sophisticated cheeks when they piled the Pelion of *their* conception of this encounter upon Mr. Forester's more restrained Ossa and thereby achieved the ultimate high point of absurdity in their spoof. And I maintain it is because of this extension of the grotesque into sheer fantasy that *The African Queen* is a classic of Hollywood kidding its own established myths.

Sergeant Milton Warden (Burt Lancaster) lays down the rules for a secret liaison with Karen Holmes (Deborah Kerr), wife of his commanding officer.

FROM HERE TO ETERNITY

1953

James Jones' powerful novel *From Here to Eternity* ran to 850 printed pages—some 430,000 words—when it was published in 1952, and it spanned an extensive panorama of life at an American army post—Schofield Barracks in Oahu, Hawaii—in the months preceding the Pearl Harbor attack. So it was no mean feat of compression that Director Fred Zinnemann and his scriptwriter, Daniel Taradash, performed in making a film version whose running time was little more than two hours. And it was nothing short of a miracle that it came out to be a great film.

The measure of this achievement was that the movie adequately contained all the essential char-

acters and their involvements that were in the book, while preserving the vehemence and ferocity of the original. To be sure, a certain amount of prudent cutting and purifying had to be done to satisfy the then existent censors and the custodians of the Production Code. The shocking chapters in the novel describing the sadistic brutalities that occurred in a typical army prison, known as "the stockade," were eliminated entirely, and some of the more startling obscenities that Mr. Jones tossed about freely were considerably toned down.

But the dominant muscularity of the basically all-male group that peopled this cryptic barracks story, the pathos and futility of the love lives of its soldiers, and the cruelty that was imposed by a stupid and inhuman officer upon his more susceptible men were all here in pressing abundance.

Determined to restrain his proven skill at boxing, Private Robert E. Lee Prewitt (Montgomery Clift) is nevertheless goaded into a bare fist fight with one of his hectoring company companions.

It was a gallery of portraits etched in truth. And it stands as a shining example of professional moviemaking at its best.

Foremost in its muster of soldiers was Private Robert E. Lee Prewitt, a quiet, hard-headed young Kentuckian whose only real interests in life were the army and playing the bugle. He had been enlisted as a bugler, in fact, and had once played Taps at Arlington Cemetery—a distinction of which he was most proud. But he had been busted from bugler by his captain as punishment because he refused to devote his equal talents in the ring to the company boxing team. The reason: he had accidentally blinded an opponent in an inter-regiment bout and he didn't want to risk a repetition, no matter what the consequences.

Then there was his tormentor, Captain Dana Holmes, a passionate boxing enthusiast who thought the triumphs of his company team reflected his own superiority. He was a stupid, incompetent man who left the running of the company to his top sergeant while he devoted his energies to philandering. And there was this remarkable topkick, Sergeant Milton Warden, a "thirty-year man," a rough-hewn professional soldier who kept everything under control, even his incidental dallying with the captain's bored and lonely wife.

Further there was a genial and sinewy enlisted man, Angelo Maggio, whose brash revolt against the rules of army life led him to run afoul of "Fatso," the brutal sergeant in command of the stockade. This unpleasant encounter was to snowball into tragedy.

And then there was Lorene, a B-girl, whose charms were politely purveyed at Mrs. Kipfer's New Congress Club, where Prewitt met her and became so amorously entwined by her innocent looks and evident loneliness and longings that he inevitably fell in love. It was to her that he fled for sanctuary when he himself went "over the hill."

It is fair to say that frustration was the central theme of the film—the smoldering frustration of Prewitt, whose one ambition was cruelly circumscribed by the ruthlessness of the captain, who himself was frustrated and enclosed by his own warped set of values and his helpless inadequacies; the frustrations of Maggio, the street kid, who was never meant for army life; and certainly the frustrations of Lorene and the captain's pitiful wife.

The only one to escape frustration was Sergeant Warden, who had gotten wise to the nature of his profession, to the immaturities of men, and to the incompetencies of officers, a caste which he despised. He might easily have gone up the ladder and the rise in rank might have changed his relation with the captain's wife, but he was honest enough to avoid it. He was tough—but he was sad.

Fortunately every member of the cast of this composite was superb, beginning with Montgomery Clift as Prewitt. He made this lonely soldier who endured the open contempt of his captain and the hazing—"the treatment"—received from his fellows in stoic silence to uphold a principle—a fetishistic one, beyond question, but one in which his youthful mind believed. When he was shot down at the end, while trying to get back to his company during the Pearl Harbor attack, dying with a scream at the Jap bombers, one was moved to mourn a minor hero in this simple hardheaded young man.

Burt Lancaster played the topkick to the military manner born, a fellow of strength and self-assurance who abided by his own unwavering code. When the captain's wife, Karen, remarking on his clipped formality toward her as she obviously moved to test his juices, said, "You seem very confident," he looked her straight in the eye and answered, "It's not confidence, ma'am, it's honesty." Anyone as experienced as Sergeant Warden was not going to cheat—at least, not on the captain's wife. He told her exactly the conditions of a possible relationship with her; and when, on a soft night, later, he took her swimming on an empty beach and made love to her with boiling passion at the water's edge (a scene, incidentally, which was famous for lush eroticism at the time), he did so with a clear understanding that neither he nor she had any strings attached.

As the lady, Deborah Kerr was excellent—and something of a surprise. Known previously for her performances of generally cool and genteel roles, she was all the more startling and effective as the sex-starved adulteress. "The lady's a washout, Sergeant," she meekly and self-pityingly confessed to Warden shortly after their first meeting, and her conduct thereafter carried through this drab and pathetic characterization of a dull, neglected "army wife."

Donna Reed, too, was effective as the muchly sanitized B-girl who desperately wished to be "proper" and get out of the cheap "profession" she was in. Wistful and lonely, like Prewitt, it was inevitable that they should fall in love—or, at least, what might seem the grand passion to two

Enraged by the taunts of Sergeant "Fatso" Judson (Ernest Borgnine), keeper of the dreaded stockade, Private Angelo Maggio (Frank Sinatra) attempts to battle the knife-wielding bully with a chair.

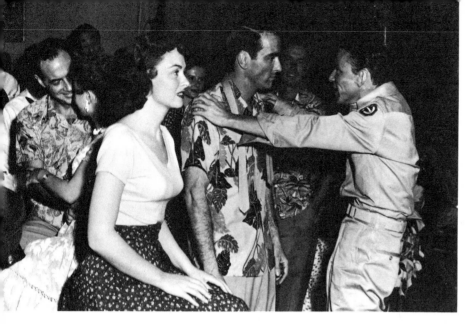

Prewitt and Maggio, on liberty, greet one another in the company of Alma (Donna Reed), one of the amiable B-girls in Mrs. Kipfer's New Congress Club.

such patently immature kids. Their fumbling confessions to one another and her pathetic pleas to him at the end, when he was leaving his hideout in her apartment on the morning of Pearl Harbor to rejoin his unit after being AWOL, were the sputtered disclosures of virtual children who were caught in snares thy could not understand.

"What do you want to go back to the army for?" she uncomprehendingly wailed when she saw he was really going to leave her. "I'm a soldier," was all he could reply. And that put the final void between them. Her fate was as clearly cut as his.

Other strong performances were given by Ernest Borgnine as "Fatso," a vicious and uncompromising brute; John Dennis as another thickskulled sergeant, and, in a more muted key, Philip Ober as the narrow-minded captain who represented all that was petty and weak about the peacetime officer class.

But the most surprising performance was that given by Frank Sinatra as the New York Italian kid, Maggio, whose bubbling good nature and intrinsic inability to live by discipline got him into the kind of trouble with the hard-heads that led to inevitable doom. The slashing scene of his tangle with "Fatso" in an enlisted men's bar when he scoffed at that dunghill tyrant who was lining him up for the stockade was one of the several explosive and memorable scenes in the film. As a consequence of this sure-fire performance, Mr. Sinatra graduated to a dramatic star.

And, in a way, he was the focal figure in the dramatic action of this film. For it was Maggio's defiance of "Fatso" and his subsequent brutalizing in the stockade—a high point in Mr. Jones's novel that had to be omitted from the film—that led to a vengeful knife battle between Prewitt and "Fatso" in a dark alley at night. The outcome left "Fatso" dead and compelled Prewitt to go "over the hill." This hideously violent confrontation, which so clearly ran counter to Prewitt's previous obsession against personal violence, was agitated by Prewitt's deadly loathing of "Fatso" after the brutally beaten Maggio, escaped from the stockade, had come to him, described his torture (at some length), and died in his arms. The boldness of Prewitt in seizing a bugle and blowing Taps at Maggio's funeral was sufficiently aggressive and emotional to prepare the audience for the battle with "Fatso" that was to come.

And, finally, it was the death of Maggio and the regimental investigation it brought on that resulted in the degrading of the captain, his being forced to resign, and an order that boxing tourneys, with their overemphasis, be banned.

But this dramatic resolution was redundant, for the climactic holocaust of the attack on Pearl Harbor followed close upon its heels, and in that historic culmination all the small dramatic crises were submerged.

I must note that Mr. Zinnemann did manage to describe the shock of this titanic event with appropriate confusion and excitement, terminated with a splash of sentiment, even though, by the 1950s, this phase was considerably *déjà vu*. The Jap planes roared in on a Sunday morning, mistaken at first for friendly aircraft. ("Sure look pretty over them mountains," Prewitt casually remarked to Lorene.) Schofield Barracks was alarmingly blasted by falling bombs, someone blew Cavalry Charge on a bugle, and Prewitt was killed by machine-gun strafing as he ran toward the barracks across an open field. His simple epitaph was spoken later by Warden to the new captain, as they looked at his body among the dead: "He was always a hard-head, sir, but he was a good soldier." That, for Prewitt, would have been sufficient praise.

At the time it was released, we were still enough captured by our conviction of the need for World War II to accept as military aberration the shameful evidence of injustice and waste in this film. But now, with our knowledge of corruption and inefficiency in the Korean War and especially with our hopeless awareness of the futility of our military establishment in Vietnam, we can feel only indignation in the lessons of *From Here to Eternity*.

This is not an anti-war film, as some have taken it to be. This is one that dumbfoundingly proclaims the inevitable dehumanization of the individual imposed by the military system and mentality. Like *The Bridge on the River Kwai* ** four years later, it stunningly revealed how men—and their women—can be captured, bored, and homogenized by the built-in defects and distortions of a military machine. For the aspects of human stagnation and sterilization that it revealed, *From Here to Eternity* might, with some slight changes, have been a prison film. Though it told of another era and another set of imperatives in our national life, this remarkably well done movie might be a mirror of what essentially is happening today.

Having killed "Fatso" in a back-alley fight and prudently gone "over the hill," Prewitt is finding sanctuary in the apartment of Alma on the morning of the Pearl Harbor attack.

Newly married to the eldest brother, Adam (Howard Keel), and finding herself the sole woman in a houseful of vastly untidy bachelors, Milly (Jane Powell) tips the dinner table to show her authority over her boorish brothers-in-law.

SEVEN BRIDES FOR SEVEN BROTHERS

1954

For reasons unknown, Hollywood, despite all the tempting material that could be found in the legends of the settlement of our country and the expansion of the frontier, has only infrequently undertaken the celebration of American folk themes in musical comedy. This is surprising in light of the fact that western dramas have been a staple since the earliest silent films and the musical medium has been, until lately, one of the most popular in the sound-film repertory. With the exception of *Oklahoma* (1955) I cannot recall a major musical that featured cowboys on a western ranch locale—and I am not overlooking (as much as I'd like to) those old "singin' cowboy" banalities with such favorites as Gene Autry, Roy Rogers, et al.

Indeed, the only first-rate musical movies on strictly American folk themes have been Marc Connelly and William Keighley's *The Green Pastures* made from the stage show back in 1936, and Stanley Donen's *Seven Brides for Seven*

Brothers, which surfaced in 1954. The latter, I'd say, was not only the better of the two but ranks in my estimation as one of the all-time great musical films.

The most conspicuous and enjoyable features of this combination spoof of male chauvinism and puritanism were the energy and lusty impudence which exploded far beyond the prim conventions and inhibitions of the standard musical, which had become rather formula-ridden during the years of and after World War II. Aside from Mr. Donen's prior *Singin' in the Rain*** and Vincente Minnelli's *Meet Me in St. Louis*,** there hadn't been anything to date as novel and full of delicious *joie de vivre* as was this musical tale of a farming family on the Oregon frontier. And significantly, like those predecessors, it was not lifted from the Broadway stage but was properly constructed from an original written for the screen.

Well, let me amend that slightly. It was, as they

say, "inspired" by a short story called "The Sobbin' Women" by Stephen Vincent Benét (which in turn was based on the tale of the rape of the Sabine women, one of the livelier and sexier fables of ancient Rome). Adapted for the screen by Albert Hackett, Frances Goodrich, and Dorothy Kingsley, who were among the more creative "adapters" in the "golden age" of Hollywood, it told a story about a group of farmer brothers eager for mates with whom to bed. Moved by the tale of the Sabine women, which had been related to them by their singular sister-in-law, they hitched up the wagon one late fall evening and hied themselves off to a frontier town where they kidnapped six likely young females and hustled them back to the farm. Fortunately for them, as they were going through a mountain pass on the way home, an avalanche tumbled down behind them, filling the pass, and blocking pursuit.

Thus these six lusty brothers, along with their oldest brother, his wife and the abducted girls, were stuck on the farm for the winter. The prospect of joy-filled nights seemed boundless. But they hadn't reckoned on the temper and the righteousness of their sister-in-law. Outraged by the arrogance of these fellows and her husband, who had gone along with them—indeed, had encouraged the foray—she pulled the Lysistrata bit and denied him her bed beyond recall until the brothers and the girls were properly wed. With pre-women's-liberation fervor, she proclaimed, "He's got to learn he can't treat people this way!" And since there was no preacher handy and the girls were still miffed, anyhow, the prospect of cozy winter evenings swiftly gang agley. The husband, as stubborn as his lady, took off for a cabin far in the woods, the girls were lodged in the upstairs dormitory, and the fellows were banished to the barn. Thus they passed the snowbound winter in agonized celibacy.

However, their boredom was dissipated by a providential happening: the wife soon found herself pregnant and, in due time, gave birth to a child. This called for much prenatal excitement and assumption of household chores by the girls, and later for a bustle of midwifery and female solicitude when the baby was born. The fellows were properly excluded and shoved into the background like a clutch of male chauvinist pigs. Nonetheless, they were restless and edgy all through the sacred ordeal, and they sighed as one

Six of the seven lusty brothers await their turn to show their prowess at country dancing with a sextet of local farm maidens in the memorable barn-raising jamboree.

Feeling lonesome and badly in need of female companionship, the brothers perform the magnificently rhythmic wood-chopping ballet, "The Brothers' Lament."

with vast relief as surrogate fathers when they finally heard the baby's first squawk. Suddenly the youngest (Russ Tamblyn), awakening to the full magnitude of the event, leaped up and shouted, "I'm an uncle!" then flopped over in a faint. Later he was designated to carry the earth-shaking news to the husband to fetch him back from the cabin when the snow had sufficiently thawed.

The coming of spring also brought an outraged posse of fathers and other townsmen through the pass to fetch home their innocent daughters and wreck vengeance on the rapacious kidnappers. But to their surprise they found the maidens quite content and ready to stay on. In addition, the fellows were ominously resistant to letting them be taken away. Happily, the tension was broken by the sound of the baby's off-screen cry. "Whose baby is *that*?" yowled an apprehensive father, to which the girls shouted in unison, "Mine!" The crisis was cleared when a preacher stepped forward to face the quickly paired-off couples and intoned, "I now pronounce you men and wives."

Beyond any question, this picture, like all musicals, was contrived, notably in the craftsmanship with which it was plotted and played. When

the oldest brother went along to town in the opening sequence and found for himself a willing bride in a discontented waitress in a hash-house, it was readily discerned that this was not a literal romance, that Howard Keel was not a real-life frontier farmer or Jane Powell an authentic frontier wife. They were strictly characters for musical comedy—handsome, trim, and melodic—and that was completely verified when they flexed their vocal cords on the way home through a pretty stage-set countryside with the lively "Goin' Courtin'," one of the eight memorable Gene de Paul–Johnny Mercer songs.

That night, after arriving home, Jane balked at going to bed with her husband, having become overwhelmed with despondency at finding the place such a male-cluttered mess. The musical artifice resumed with the frustrated spouse climbing a tree and singing to his wife through a window the heart-melting "When You're in Love." This was musical comedy, with no apologies.

But the best indices of fabrication and homage to a genuine folk theme were in the modern improvisations on traditional American folk dances. Comparable to—or even better than—the splen-

94

did "ballets" that Agnes de Mille contrived for the cowboys and the farmers in *Oklahoma* were the dances that Michael Kidd devised for the passel of highly athletic Oregon farm folk in this film. Most wonderfully spirited and agile was the so-called barn-raising ballet in which the brothers matched their skill at acrobatics with other lads in the farm community. Such brilliantly intermingled showoffs by fellows, either singly or in groups, leaping on and off saw horses, Indian wrestling on elevated planks, and doing other dazzling demonstrations of terpsichorean dexterity, had never before been presented in movies, not even by Busby Berkeley's troupes. Anyone of suspicious disposition might well have guessed this number was designed deliberately to surpass in ingenuity the *Oklahoma* dances of Miss de Mille, which, since that show was still on Broadway, had not yet been allowed to reach the screen. As a matter of fact, one might have suspected that *Seven Brides for Seven Brothers* was itself designed to get the jump on *Oklahoma* as a movie, which it most certainly did!

Another magnificent number in *Seven Brides for Seven Brothers* was the dance—or perhaps one should call it a slow-motion rhythmic ballet—done by the six agile farmboys to the music of "The Brothers' Lament." This had the lads out in the back lot in the first fall of snow, chopping stove wood for the winter and complaining about their loneliness. Immediately following this lamentation they decided to make that fateful trip to town and relieve themselves of feeling like "ol' polecats" by gathering suitable companionship.

Among the dancing brothers, Marc Platt and Russ Tamblyn stood out, with the latter, as the youngest and most limber, winning the greatest applause. But, lest one suppose that the fellows

Led by the understanding Adam and bent upon fulfilling their needs, the brothers go to a nearby town and kidnap six lovely but vigorously resistant companions.

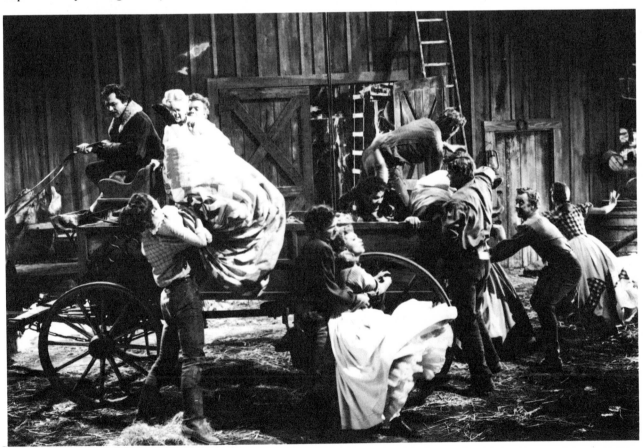

After a snow-bound winter on the farm and a change in their attitudes, the maidens resist their parents arriving to rescue them and are eager to be pronounced brides by the conveniently accompanying pastor (Ian Wolfe).

ran away with dancing honors, be assured that the girls came in for their share and had the added advantage of pulchritude. Along with Miss Powell, they chorused grandly on the lyrical numbers, "Spring, Spring, Spring" and the joyous salute to Hymen, "Wonderful, Wonderful Day." They were definitely more than sex symbols, although that feature was not overlooked in their delicate indications of feeling the urges of youth. One of the charming evidences of it was their nocturnal lolling on their beds in the upstairs dormitory from which the fellows had been dispossessed, each voluptuously wondering in whose bed she happened to be.

Of course, a "family picture" under the strict rules of the old Production Code would not be permitted a more explicit demonstration of the girls' concupiscence. Regardless, the girls' bedroom yearnings, coupled with the fellows' unmistakable indications of lustfulness, made this as raunchy a picture as one could see in a theater in those days. How genuinely innocent and healthy it seems when looked back upon now—as innocent as a Grandma Moses painting and almost as artificial, too! But it was a superior entertainment, bursting with vitality and the gusto of great athletic dancing. To paraphrase one of the lyrics, bless its beautiful hide!

Bick Benedict (Rock Hudson) shows off his huge Texas ranch to his recently acquired Maryland-bred bride, Leslie (Elizabeth Taylor).

GIANT

1956

No one is likely at this late date to nominate George Stevens' *Giant* as one of the all-time indisputably great American films. In a running-time of three hours and seventeen minutes, it was unconscionably slow. Its writers had obvious difficulty twisting several stories into a smoothly-flowing skein. After its central theme had reached a climax, the film lurched on for another half-hour, picking up and tritely completing a lesser theme. Some scenes which should have been crisp were overextended, and others which should have been fuller were not. Likewise, the performances were uneven. One was brilliant—that of the sensational young James Dean, playing a surly Texas ranch hand who became an oil

millionaire. Three or four others by actors who were well known for standard character roles came up to expectations but were disappointingly brief. And the two leads, played stiffly by Rock Hudson and Elizabeth Taylor as a Texas cattle baron and his wife, were heavy and embarrassingly revealing of the indulgence of the two as Hollywood stars. Altogether, this screen adaptation of Edna Ferber's novel had its faults.

So why, you may wonder, have I picked it to take a place in this book as a memorable representative of achievement in cinema? The explanation is simple. For all its unevennesses and flaws, its drifts into Hollywood ostentation and occasional distressing clichés, it was an outstanding example of a difficult kind of American film, the regional-sociological saga that has often been butchered in Hollywood. It was thoroughly replete with exquisite and significant visual images

An old-fashioned Texas barbecue is arranged by Bick to introduce his new wife to friends and neighbors on the "lawn" of his family mansion.

spread on the large screen in excellent color. And it did catch vividly the dramatic essence of its major theme—the massive incongruity and vulgarity of the twentieth-century Texas rich.

Indeed, its very crudities and ostentations, which looked so artless to the critic on first view, contributed inadvertently to supporting the fundamental theme. This was a film about Texas and that swatch of its society that had become rich beyond the bounds of credibility on cattle ranching and oil. It was a society which, in its basic ignorance and insularity, had no idea of how to spend its wealth except by lavishing it excessively on Bigness, with a maximum of bad taste. Everything was massive: the thousands upon thousands of acres of the famous Reata cattle ranch which was owned by the family of Bick Benedict (the role Mr. Hudson played); the furnishings in the family mansion, which itself was huge and hideous; as well as an outdoor barbecue held to welcome Bick's Maryland-bred bride (Miss Taylor) when he pridefully brought her home. Likewise Big was the self-proclaiming banquet that Jett Rink, played by Mr. Dean, threw in his spacious and ornate new Waco hotel to vaunt his as-

cendency to oil wealth and power, which later became the locale of his abasement in the major climactic episode. Their behavior and their social attitudes ceaselessly displayed the arrogance and vulgarity of neo-Bourbons who ran in plutocratic herds as perfunctorily as the herds of white-faced Herefords roamed across the endless grazing lands. As Bick explained to his bride on arrival, "My papa built it to show the cotton crowd he was just as big as they were." This summed up the major theme of Giant.

The film was most exciting and absorbing when it was closest to the subject of the life-style of the cattle plutocracy and the feudalistic philosophy of Bick and his friends. For the most part, the whole scheme of Texas ranch living in the wonderful pre-World War II days, before oil inundated the country, was fascinatingly imaged—from the "big house" point of view. There was that great, gaunt Victorian mansion with its high-ceilinged, ornate entrance hall, a huge longhorn steer's head beetling from the lintel of a second-floor balcony and a mammoth painting titled "The Roundup" above a horse-hair sofa big enough for a recumbent giant. There was that barbecue for hundreds of people, the miles one had to travel to reach the gate, Bick's Silver Cloud Rolls-Royce, the skies above—everything was immense.

So was the showoff country funeral of Bick's old maid sister, fatally injured when she was thrown by a big Maryland-bred stallion which she recklessly undertook to ride. "I never had a sick day in my life, except when I got throw'd and tromped on," she muttered before she pitifully passed away literally with her boots on, in one of the more eloquent scenes. Her departure was sad not only for the family and multitude of friends, but for the film, because she, with her rangy Texas stride and her brusque candor, a portrayal which Mercedes McCambridge made strong and appropriately individual, had set up a smoldering resentment to Miss Taylor's elegant wife which bid fair to burst into dramatic flame.

But her place as an irritant to the harmony of her brother and his "Eastern" wife was unspokenly taken over by the "white trash" ranch hand Jett, who had already shown his hatred for the husband and his distant admiration for the wife.

Indeed, it was vaguely hinted that he had secretly served as lover or just plain stud to the domineering sister, for she left him a section of land in her will. It was on this inherited property, a few years later, that he made his initial strike of oil.

Thus Jett, in his sullen, arrogant fashion, became the symbol of the "new" Texas rich who swiftly assailed the ranch lands and the social bastions of the cattle aristocracy, personified symbolically by the stubborn, resentful Bick. Graying gracefully through this progression which covered a span of some thirty years was his wife. She had taken up, against her husband's wishes, the cause of civil rights by trying to be helpful in advancing a poor looked-down-upon Mexican-American family. Then, because of Bick's sullen disapproval, she had picked up her children and gone back to Maryland for a spell. Thus there was casually intruded a secondary theme of bigotry, which was built up more in the screenplay of Fred Guiol and Ivan Moffat than it was in Miss Ferber's novel.

After setting the stage for a collision between the two diverse themes by going into complicated

Leslie lends a sympathetic ear to the halting, self-revealing disclosures of Jett Rink (James Dean), a loner "hand" on her husband's ranch.

Bick and a couple of his buddies try unsuccessfully to talk Jett into selling a parcel of the Benedict land which had been willed to him by Bick's old-maid sister—land on which Jett was soon to strike oil.

details describing the growth of the Benedict family, the divergencies of their three children, and the parallel happenings in the Mexican-American family, Mr. Stevens brought the two together on the occasion of the "grand opening" of Jett's new hotel in Waco. It was a tribal ritual that passed belief! Hundreds of Texas Croesuses, got up in excessive finery and representing what someone described as a full spectrum of the "cotton rich, the cattle rich, the oil rich, and the filthy rich," gathered in that plushy hotel to pay idolatrous and grudging homage to the state's greatest multimillionaire. And it was during these vulgar proceedings that Bick and Jett finally clashed in a private fistfight in the wine cellar because Jett's security goons had pointedly denied admission to Bick's son and his Mexican wife. Bick gave Jett a thorough thrashing which, on top of his already drunken state, rendered him ignominiously powerless to continue as the lordly host. As a conse-

quence, the party quickly broke up. "Old" wealth had metaphorically won, (though even Bick, by this time, had used a lot of his land for pumping oil.)

That should have been the finale, with Bick salvaging his pride, at least, and striking a blow indirectly for elimination of the rule of Jim Crow. But, unfortunately, Mr. Stevens and his writers felt they had to go on to get more dramatic mileage out of this increasingly popular theme. So they added a cliché confrontation between Bick and a diner manager over the right of a Mexican family to sit down and have a meal in the place. And again Mr. Stevens resorted to a bone-crunching slugging match to resolve the immediate disagreement. This time, significantly, Bick lost, conveying the implication that civil rights still had a long way to go. But the evidence of Bick's conversion gratified his onlooking wife. After the battle, she told him tenderly she was never so proud of him. And back home, beneath the painting of "The Roundup," they solemnly agreed to give up the pursuit of Bigness and let Texas go its way. "My saddle is just turning right out from under me," was the reconstructed Bick's last word.

Regrettably, their promise of deflation seemed more submission to a popular platitude than a statement of sincere conviction. Likewise their thrust for civil rights came over rather feebly. Both Miss Taylor and Mr. Hudson performed as though they possessed only a minimal comprehension of the thesis. Nor was Mr. Stevens' dramatization of it much more than perfunctory. The aspect of fabrication is even more apparent today, after all we've seen of the realities and brutalities of the civil rights struggle in the South. The chief device used by Mr. Stevens to impart strong emotion to the theme was to show the military funeral for the son of the Mexican-American family who was the first man in the county killed in World War II. The staging was stark and sentimental, like that of the classic country funeral in Mr. Stevens' earlier *Shane*,* but it conveyed little more about the issue than to illustrate a poignant irony.

However, there were so many vivid pictorial images throughout that clarified precisely the drama of the major theme that praise must still go to Mr. Stevens for the visual eloquence of his film—images such as that of the Benedict mansion standing in the midst of an empty plain, or of the bringing in of an oil well "gusher" by the doggedly laboring Jett, or, in contrast to that, of Jett struggling drunkenly alone to deliver what should have been his triumphal speech to an empty banquet hall.

The strongest personification of the irony and absurdity of these Texas nouveaux riches was beyond any question Jett, whom Mr. Dean made both monstrous and pathetic in what was ironically his last film. For all the arrogance and meanness that he showed in the man as a tycoon, he still carried through the flabby languor, the slur of speech, and the air of bitterness that characterized him as a ranch hand. A memorably spooky character!

Others, too, were commendable—Chill Wills as an old Texas type, Jane Withers as a plump and tacky heiress, Carol Baker as a Benedict debutante, Dennis Hopper as the son who studied medicine and married the Mexican girl, and Sal Mineo as the slightly too obsequious Mexican lad who was killed in the war.

There were certain people in Texas who sternly disapproved of *Giant*, but it went over big with general audiences. That should tell you how effective it was.

Bick and Jett, now an oil multimillionaire, come to an ultimate showdown of their hatred for one another in the wine cellar of Jett's new Waco hotel.

The aging Swedish professor, Isak Borg (Victor Sjostrom), pauses for a few moments of reflection and reverie at the summer home where he spent his early years.

WILD STRAWBERRIES

1957

In the twenty-odd years since Ingmar Bergman's *Wild Strawberries* was released in Sweden in 1957 under the title *Smultronstallet*, this exquisitely poetic picture has acquired, as a consequence of its theme, an ever greater relevancy to our contemporary interest in geriatrics. It was a film about an old man and his reflections upon his life, with particular concern for his relations with younger people, including his middle-aged son and the latter's wife. Thus it has become, with respect to our expanding sophistication and concern about old age and the attitudes of younger people toward the elderly, a moving discourse for enlightenment and thought.

This is not to say that it wasn't—and isn't—an artistic entity apart from whatever contemporary effectiveness as social illumination it has. The blunt yet compassionate introspection of its focal character, a seventy-six-year-old Swedish medical scientist, occurred during the course of one long day as he made an auto trip from central Sweden to the university town of Lund where he

was to receive an honorary degree, and it was sensitively conceived and constructed to juxtapose his own harsh misgivings about himself to the estimations of those around him and those of his professional peers. Significantly, his self-criticism reflected his doubts about the benefits of his life and probed a frequent concern of older people as to whether their lives have really been worthwhile.

It opened with a morbid dream sequence in which the old man saw himself strolling alone and bewildered through the empty streets of a silent city. Then he encountered a slowly passing hearse which broke a wheel against a lamppost directly in front of him and dumped the coffin out into the street. To his horror and mystification, the old man saw that the body in the coffin was his own, conveying the implication that his mind was troubled with a sense of loneliness and, of course, by fearful premonitions of the approach of death.

However, no such anticipation seemed to bother his old housekeeper as she awoke him from his dream and lovingly bossed him into making ready for the trip to Lund. From her affectionate attitude toward him and from that of his daughter-in-law, who was accompanying him on the journey, the audience was led to suppose he was a kindly, relaxed, slightly fretful, and considerably spoiled old gentleman, worthy of the honor to be paid him and serene in his regard for himself. This image of him was supported by the wonderfully benign eyes and looks of the fine old actor Victor Sjostrom, one of the great Swedish directors of silent films, who played the role—Isak Borg—with such submission to the cruel reproaches of his thoughts and memories that he blunted his self-criticism with inducement of his audiences' sympathies.

Shortly after starting out, Isak and his daughter-in-law, Marianne, played with quiet reserve by Ingrid Thulin, stopped off at an old house on a bay where Isak and his family had spent the first twenty summers of his life. There, wandering thoughtfully around the old place and reminiscing nostalgically about his youth, Isak found himself recollecting a long-ago meeting with his lovely cousin, Sara, in a wild strawberry patch. He remembered how he had clumsily spilled her basket of berries and she had reproached him for his shyness and prudishness.

His reveries were interrupted by a very lively and hippyish young woman, also named Sara. She was the image of her namesake, not surprising considering both were played robustly by Bibi Andersson. She and two young male companions were on their way to Italy and in need of a lift,

which Isak kindly agreed to give. So off they went, with the young folks on the back seat.

Suddenly an oncoming car swerved, forcing both autos off the road. Though a fatal accident was avoided, Isak and Marianne had to pick up the passengers from the other badly damaged vehicle. These turned out to be a married couple who quarreled so tediously and disagreeably that Marianne, thoroughly disgusted, finally ordered them out of the car. They were left standing subdued, humiliated, and looking quite pathetic beside the road. Such was Mr. Bergman's annotation on the shabbiness of a marriage gone sour, which nevertheless held the two people in a kind of bondage neither had the strength to break away from or correct.

Soon they came to a filling station. The proprietor, whom Max von Sydow played, tremendously pleased to see Isak, was loud in his appreciation and praise of what Isak had done for him, his parents, and the neighborhood when he was the resident physician here. The flattery and attention was gratifying and lifted the spirits of the old man, as was evident when over lunch at a lovely lakeside inn he told his companions amusing stories of his younger years hereabouts. A brief and pleasant visit to his aged mother in her nearby home ensued, along with more wistful and amusing reminiscing about the old days in the house by the bay. Surrounded by children's toys and other

Isak drowses beside his critical daughter-in-law, Marianne (Ingrid Thulin) on the day-long auto drive to Lund, where he is to be honored.

Isak is affectionately greeted by three youthful hitchhikers—Anders (Folke Sundquist), Viktor (Bjorn Bjelvenstam) and Sara (Bibi Andersson).

relics of the past, the old lady (Naima Wifstrand) was content to be a relic of those happier days herself. The thought that this imparted to the mind of the viewer was the grace of resignation to old age.

Continuing on the journey, the young people sulked in the back seat, the boys having quarreled over Sara in a burst of jealousy. Isak recalled a similar row between him and his brother over the earlier Sara. The old gentleman grew drowsy in the quiet afternoon and soon was dreaming again of the past. In one of these self-revealing reveries, he saw himself at his present age reaching futilely toward the youthful Sara, who slipped away to tend an infant child. In another, he was called before an audience of young people, including the present Sara and her hippy pals, to submit to a medical quiz conducted by the nasty husband

they had picked up on the road. Identify a certain specimen, the old man was ordered, but when he looked at it through a microscope all he could see was his own eye, greatly enlarged, staring back at him. What is a doctor's first duty? Isak was peremptorily asked. As hard as he tried, he couldn't remember. It is to ask forgiveness, he was told.

Then the inquisitor led Isak alone into a forest and forced him to look upon a scene that had occurred years before. It was his own wife, a woman other than the Sara of his previous dreams, being raped by a brutish man and then remarking ruefully, when it was concluded, that her husband would not be disturbed when she told him about it. He would accept it coolly and rationally, she said, indicating he did not love her. And in an extension of the inquisition, it was implied that Isak had committed an abortion on his wife, from

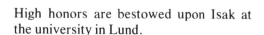

High honors are bestowed upon Isak at the university in Lund.

Before he goes to sleep at the end of an exciting day, Isak is reassured as to their marriage by Marianne and his son, Evald (Gunnar Bjornstrand).

which she may have died. In any case, this humiliating memory of events about which only he knew was clearly what was most disturbing the old man on this supposedly triumphant day.

When Isak awoke, he found himself alone in the car, parked beside the road, with Marianne. She wanted, she said, to tell him that a crisis had been reached in her marriage. She was pregnant and wished to have the child, but Evald, her husband, was against it. He was cold and distant toward her, she said. And then she surprised the old man by saying that Evald was much like him, that Isak's marriage was loveless and lonely and his son had grown up in that atmosphere. But providentially, at that point, the youngsters returned to the car, bringing a bunch of wildflowers for Isak as their tribute to "a wise and venerable old man."

That was the plateau of the picture—that conjunction of the old man's secret thoughts about himself and his attitudes toward others and the attitudes of others toward him. Thus the irony of the drama was most sharply interjected and drawn—the proposition that a seemingly fine person may be other than he appears. At least, he may be something other than he privately appears to himself.

Thereafter the picture gently wound down. The travelers reached Evald's home in Lund, where Isak's housekeeper had arrived to tend him; he joined the academic ceremonies and received his honorary degree in the old cathedral, along with several of his ancient friends, then returned to

the home of Evald to prepare for some much needed rest. But just as he was about to doze off, he heard singing outside his window and looked out to see the young friends of the journey enthusiastically serenading him and bidding him a fond farewell—again a tribute to the image of respectable old age. Later Marianne and Evald (played by Gunnar Bjornstrand) came to him, dressed and ready to go on to a university dance. Evald confessed to his father that he could not live without his wife and that he was content that she should have the child. Whereupon the old man, relieved and grateful, was ready to drop off to sleep. But before he did he saw again in memory that old summer house beside the bay, with Sara there as the wife of his brother, and his mother and father placidly fishing off a pier.

Wild Strawberries may have seemed dramatically thin, a conveyance of an idea which bordered on banality. The degree of Isak's self-estimation was neither exceptional nor profound, and one might say that his real regret boiled down to the fact that he had not been able to marry Sara. But the glints of human nature and feeling that were thrown off in this film, the perceptions of an old man's disposition in a world he knew he soon must depart, the serenity and comfort of the beauty of the Swedish countryside, caught in the camera of Gunnar Fischer, and filtered through Isak's (and the audience's) eyes, all added up to an experience drenched in poetry and tender sentiment, critical yet fundamentally gentle. It was a film to soothe the mind and warm the heart.

Lonely and hungry for romance. Emily Ann Faulkner (Kim Stanley) lures a shy friend, John Tower (Steve Hill), into marriage, which lasts only briefly before her flight to Hollywood.

THE GODDESS

1958

One of the few movie persons about whom movies have been made—without their being named in some cases but leaving little doubt as to whom the authors had in mind—was the voluptuous sex symbol and controversial Marilyn Monroe, whose sensational career and sad conclusion are among the great legends of Hollywood. The most perceptive and touching picture in probing the irony of the life of this star was John Cromwell's *The Goddess*, which was made four years before she died.

Its author, Paddy Chayefsky, insisted at the time and repeats that it was not conceived or intended to be a drama *about* Miss Monroe. But the parallels to her life that were drawn, the character of its leading role, and the key performance by Kim Stanley, an appropriately busty blonde, left little doubt that the image of the famed sex symbol was passing through his mind.

As a matter of fact, an endeavor was made to get Miss Monroe to play the role, and it is said that she was tempted, but her then husband, Arthur Miller, steered her off. He feared that the painful resemblance to her own life might prove embarrassing.

Whether that is true, it is regrettable that Miss Monroe did not take the role, which might well have finally let her attain the eminence of a serious dramatic actress to which she aspired. For *The Goddess* was far from the sort of drama that would have cheaply exploited her, since it was neither so personal nor voyeuristic that it would have appeared to invade her privacy. Its grand theme was the anguish and pathos of deep-down loneliness, an affliction that can cause emotional traumas and obsessive endeavors to achieve. It is a primal psychotic condition that can motivate the life of anyone who needs public recognition and adulation to give them the illusion of being loved—a pop singer, a politician, an athlete—not just a movie star. And it was the suffering so evidently experienced by Miss Monroe, even after she had reached the pinnacle of stardom as a glamorous, sex-vaunting type, which would have

Emily Ann, with her name now changed to Rita Shawn and married to a fading prizefighter, Dutch Seymour (Lloyd Bridges), is still inconspicuously lonely and unfulfilled in her quest for fame as a movie star.

given her a total identification with the role.

Significantly Mr. Chayefsky divided his screenplay of *The Goddess* into three "acts," each marking a major transition in the life of his desperate heroine. The first act, tenderly titled "Portrait of a Girl," began with her as a lonely youngster in a shabby southern town, dragged around by a selfish widowed mother who had no love or concern for her and only wanted, in her aimless, brainless thinking, to "have a little fun." And the act concluded with the sad, neglected youngster, now grown to young womanhood, hysterically entrusting her own baby by a brief wartime marriage to her fading mother's care and taking off for that one ephemeral mecca she had dreamed of through her girlhood—Hollywood!

How different was this presentation of the background and dreams of a girl who aspired to be a movie actress from those romantically put forth for little Esther Blodgett in the classic Hollywood film, the original *A Star Is Born*! No gentle upbringing in a comfortable farm home was visioned for this restless girl, no sweet and sentimental grandmother to finance her trip to

Hollywood. Two decades after that historic story of how the Hollywood bug bit and bemused young women with futile dreams of glory. Mr. Chayefsky put in focus the kind of pressure that more likely moved the majority of restless young women to make that hopeful but hopeless trek to the Golden Coast.

Likewise he had no Prince Charming in the form of a famous movie star waiting in the wings to fall in love with and generously promote the career of his callow Emily Ann Faulkner, whose name was glibly changed to Rita Shawn. In "Portrait of a Young Woman," the second act of his saga of a star, no one more charming or romantic to fetch her out of a luncheonette booth was provided than a punchy and declining prizefighter as lonely and drab as she. Together these two distracted persons wrangled and groped their helpless ways through a kind of connubial vacuum that gave them neither comfort nor strength. And, when the exhausted Rita saw no profit or hope in this affair, she made the conventional thrust toward stardom: she slept with a studio boss.

The traditional step to stardom is taken by Emily Ann as she is introduced to a desirous studio executive (Donald McKee) by a perceptive and accommodating producer (Bert Freed).

Ordinarily, as in other backstage movies, this recourse would have led conveniently to a sequence of diverting descriptions of the steps in a starlet's rise to fame. But Mr. Chayefsky and Mr. Cromwell did not choose this conventional route. They opted to jump right to the story of Rita as a star, for it was her continuing distraction and suffering in this preeminence that carried through the theme of the drama and presented its tragic irony. And so, in "Portrait of a Goddess," which was the conclusive act three, they gave us a grim and ruthless picture of a woman who, though outwardly a star and enjoying (?) the perquisites of stardom, was inwardly lonely and distraught, living in a vast and tasteless mansion (like Norma Desmond in *Sunset Boulevard*) immured by her own neuroticism, even though she was still young and beautiful.

This was the line of contemplation that Mr. Chayefsky and Mr. Cromwell pursued, this cheerless and ironic prospect of the emptiness of a life that was blighted from the beginning by lack of the nourishment of security and love. And even though Rita's aging mother did come at last to visit her after she'd had a "nervous breakdown" and, for a brief time, did seem to soothe her with some weird dedication to God—a solace that was clearly not as helpful as the momentary illusion that she had finally won her mother's love—the comfort of this illusion was suddenly withdrawn when the mother, herself bored and lonely and again unwilling to stay and play nurse, pulled out and left a screaming Rita loveless and alone.

The final sequence of this drama was set again in the southern town from which Emily Ann had departed for the dream of Hollywood. She had returned for her mother's funeral, elaborately draped in mourning clothes and breaking into an hysterical outburst at the graveside service, when she caught a quick glimpse of her first husband and a solemn little girl who was obviously their child. The image was unmistakable—the mother who had deserted her child brought to a symbolic confrontation with the evidence of her own complicity. But later, when the solicitous ex-husband came to see her in her darkened room with the request that he might bring the daughter for a reunion, the suggestion was peremptorily turned down by a tough and efficient female secretary who had Rita rigidly in charge. "I'll take her back to California," she told the ex-husband conclusively, "and she'll go on making movies because that's all she knows to do, and whatever happens after that happens. But I kind of love her and I'll take good care of her."

Thus we took leave of "the goddess," shut up in a curtain-shrouded room and prophetically sneaking oblivion from a bottle of sleeping pills, while her ex-husband picked up their daughter outside the house and walked silently off down a hill.

To be sure, certain questions went unanswered. Whence came the strength in Emily Ann that allowed her to make the bold hegira to Hollywood that other girls with her same pressures would not have dared? What was Rita's apparently unique qualification that made it possible for a studio to promote her into an outstanding star, besides "a quality of availability" which someone noted in her appearance in a bit role? And why did her poor, exhausted mother so abruptly leave her luxurious home, when it was obvious that she had the opportunity to settle comfortably for the rest of her life?

These were lapses in disclosure that were troubling but easy to excuse in the light of what had to be covered and the essential concentration on the theme. Loneliness and insecurity, those were the dark forces that moved the murky drama forward to its inevitable and ironic end. And so much that was revealing and moving in those areas was detailed along the way that gaps in attention to logic could be reasonably overlooked.

There was the early incident of little Emily Ann coming home from school with the thrilling news that she had been promoted and being paid no attention to by her indifferent mother, so that she had to whisper her childish pride to the cat. There

were the sleazy encounters of the blossoming youngster with the small-town boys who wanted her only for sex and with the lonely GI whom she inveigled into marriage and who soon deserted her. Likewise there were her ugly squabbles with Butch, the callous pug, who was as pitifully lacking in capacity for the felicities of marriage as was she. And there were those pathetic séances in which she kneeled with her poor mother on the parlor floor of the hideously vulgar mansion and cried out to a country bumpkin's God. There was so much that was sad and downright gruesome that the picture of pain required no more.

Perhaps this was but one man's conception of the mythological mockery of Hollywood or but part of the explanation for the psychological shape of Miss Monroe, who died, incidentally, as portended, from an overdose of sleeping pills. I was able to glimpse through this drama and through the brilliant performance Miss Stanley gave, so restless and delirious, what I could credit as the tormented heart of Miss Monroe. And so, for all the prevalent stories of her cruelties and eccentricities, I was able to conceive for that sad woman a strong understanding and sympathy.

Excellent, too, was the characterization of the mother which Betty Lou Holland gave and which covered a remarkable range of frivolity, frustra-

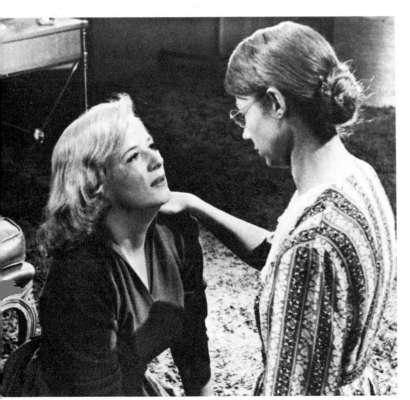

Emily Ann, now a star and living in a gaudy Hollywood mansion, still begs the love and approval of her ever cold and remote mother (Betty Lou Holland).

109

tion, and resignation through the years from the comparative youthfulness of the woman to her desiccated middle age. As the pug, Lloyd Bridges was doltish and clumsy in precisely the right key, and Steve Hill was touchingly poetic and unbalanced as Emily Ann's first spouse. Mr. Cromwell's direction stayed close to the personalities, rather than reaching for action or the glitter of the Hollywood scene.

The Goddess was a low-budget picture, shot almost entirely in New York and in the shabby environment of a small town near Baltimore. Lacking "production values" and a cast of familiar "names," it appeared to be a predestined loser when it was first shown around in a few key spots. Indeed, so grim appeared its prospects that it was practically given away to a small art theater for a token premiere in New York. Hailed by the majority of New York critics as an outstanding film of that year, it went on to be a limited but deeply appreciated hit.

But I still wonder what would have happened if Miss Monroe *had* played the lead. Could that have given her the sureness and satisfaction that might have changed her disintegrating life?

Now, returned to her old hometown in Maryland for the funeral of her mother, Emily Ann makes a hysterical scene at the graveside while her secretary (Elizabeth Wilson) tries to calm her as her ex-husband and their twelve-year-old daughter stand silently to one side.

C.C. keeps book on the dates for use of his apartment by the "top brass" along with his ordinary chores of simple housekeeping.

THE APARTMENT

1960

It is sometimes whispered by critics that Billy Wilder is the *spiritual* natural son of the legendary Ernst Lubitsch, so similar in so many ways have been the outstanding films of Mr. Wilder to the best of the famous satirist. The allegation is not far-fetched. Both spent their formative years in the bitter and cynical environment of pre-World War II Berlin. (Mr. Lubitsch preceded Mr. Wilder by a couple of fateful decades.) Both came to be respected for their "sophisticated" styles by Hollywood. Even further, Mr. Wilder joined ranks with Mr. Lubitsch when he helped to write the script for Mr. Lubitsch's *Bluebeard's Eighth Wife* and *Ninotchka*.* So it was plausible that Mr. Wilder should have been in direct line to receive the mantle of Mr. Lubitsch and inherit the patent to his notable "touch."

In none of his films has Mr. Wilder come closer to a Lubitsch theme and style than he did in his brilliant *The Apartment*. In my estimation, it is one of the finest comedy-dramas that has ever come out of Hollywood. Here Mr. Wilder, well established and comfortably settled in with his new scriptwriter, I.A.L. Diamond, achieved that rare thing in cinema culture, a funny movie containing a serious statement. And he helped to advance Jack Lemmon, the picture's star, as one of the truly fine actors of our time.

Through the first forty or so minutes, *The Apartment* seemed a casual comedy about a breezy young accountant, who, hoping to get ahead in a large New York insurance company, had fallen into the practice of secretly loaning his apartment to the company's top executives to use for sexual activities with some of the firm's more compliant girls. Though the arrangement was cheap and convenient for the sexed-up executives, it was wearying and wearing for the young man, C. C. Baxter. But he dutifully abided the inconvenience, buoyed by the vision of promised advancement it encouraged.

Then one night—by not so rare coincidence, it happened to be Christmas Eve—he came home to find his bed preempted not by the usual rutting pair but by one of the company's attractive elevator girls to whom, in his diffident fashion, he had taken an innocent shine. Only she wasn't there to give him a Christmas present. She, in a fit of despair at having been brought to the apartment for the usual purpose and then ditched by the company's chief executive, had taken an overdose of sleeping pills.

That called for fast and skillful action, which Baxter fortunately was able to get from a good-hearted Jewish physician who lived next door. After vigorous resuscitative measures, they were able to bring the girl around, but it was necessary and prudent that she stay in the apartment for a couple of days, and during her convalescence good old Baxter fell totally in love with her. But that wasn't the end of the story. She still went on carrying the torch for the top-level skunk who had deceived her, and Baxter went on playing the dupe, until yet another well-timed crisis. New Year's Eve found the girl on the verge of succumbing again to the seductions of the boss. Suddenly perceiving his baseness, she went flying to Baxter's waiting arms (though it was noticeable that wily Mr. Wilder didn't let them actually clinch at the end!).

As one can see, the tone and texture up to the suicide attempt was that of light and lively satire built around the popular game of sex. Baxter's frenzies and confusions in trying to apportion the time for the use of the apartment to suit the whims of the executives were lunatic and hilarious, like the bursts of speeded-up action in old-time farce, and Mr. Lemmon's simulations were deliciously inventive and true. Likewise, his efforts to dissemble with his solemnly watchful and suspicous neighbors and landlady were fine bits of ethnic comedy, especially his hallway encounters with the neighboring doctor, who assumed that all the action he knowingly overheard in the adjoining apartment was Baxter's doings. He had his neighbor pegged as a super-stud. Every night, he observed, he was doing it, with "a twi-nite double-header" now and then. "Do me a favor, Baxter," he told him, "when you write

C.C. Baxter (Jack Lemmon), the office fall-guy, is awakened out of a sound sleep by one of his superiors who wants the use of his apartment for a few hours of amorous activity.

your will—and you should do so *soon*—will you leave your body to the university?"

But underlying this humor ran a suggestion of the loneliness and shame of poor Baxter, whose eyes were always roving but whose own sex life was nil. Caught in the trap of the arrangement, he patiently and painfully endured the presumptuous and condescending treatment he got from the brash executives who dangled their bait like promised *pourboire* and patronizingly called him "buddy boy." One of them even grumbled that the stock of liquor in the apartment was running low and wanted to know "whatever happened to those little cheese crackers you used to have around?"

A particularly poignant example of such shabby indifference was an episode late on a rainy night. Baxter, roused from sleep by one of the office Lotharios, was virtually ordered to vacate the apartment while he brought up a very promising number who "looked like Marilyn Monroe."

At the office Christmas party, C.C. is the fellow who cheerfully fetches and carries while others have a good time.

Miserable and pathetic, the poor young *schnook* complied, going to brood on a park bench while his own warm bed was used for another's lust.

As this aspect developed, there emerged in a low-key way a sense of the cruelty and cheapness of such office shenanigans and the vulgarity and cynicism of corporate executives who engaged in them. Especially through the personality of the chief executive, J. D. Sheldrake, whom Fred MacMurray played with sleek and icy aplomb, was the essential corruption of such private aggrandizement exposed, and the meanness of cheating not only on employees but on wives and families was remarked. But all of this was accomplished by Mr. Wilder without preachment or piety. He put his ugly situation with easy sight gags and verbal wit, which was precisely the trick that Mr. Lubitsch pulled in his glib "sex comedies."

Even the long and painful sequence of the reviving of the elevator girl was done with sardonic humor. Dr. Dreyfuss and his Jewish-mama wife were wonderfully human people whose compassion for the girl on the one hand and on the other

their sarcastic digs at poor Baxter, who they thought had driven her to the act, gave this whole sequence an inverse aspect. There it was—the "Lubitsch touch" again.

Rewarding, too, were bits of business, comic and otherwise, which Mr. Wilder (and Mr. Lemmon) intruded to get laughs and point up character—Baxter's demonstration of digital acrobatics with a card-index file; the telephone scenes wherein he feverishly "booked" dates for his clients; his embarrassed pulling forth of wads of used Kleenex from his coat pockets while fishing for the apartment key to give the boss; or his thoughtful turning on of an electric blanket to warm the sleeping elevator girl.

The Apartment was full of humor, but its deeper implications were the potential flaws in a social system that puts a premium on "getting ahead," that allows the process of advancement to be not always determined by the efficiency of a worker but by the deceit and self-interest of those at the top. In this case, the worthiness of Baxter was not to be considered upon the basis of his achievements but on the proof of his docility. In

Aware at last of his shameful gullibility, C.C. shifts his benefaction to Fran Kubelik (Shirley MacLaine), the office elevator operator, who has been jilted and left to attempt suicide in the apartment by the top executive (played superbly by Fred MacMurray).

essence, *The Apartment* made its comment upon the ethical standards and moral conduct of big corporation executives, as represented by Mr. MacMurray and Ray Walston and David Lewis as lesser ones. While the latter were amusing fast-talk artists, Mr. MacMurray was the smooth and crafty one, as able to deceive a girl with promised romance as he was to dupe a bookkeeper. He was, indeed, a personification of knavery, a shameless exploiter of gullible employees. Mr. MacMurray's performance was perhaps the best he ever gave.

Shirley MacLaine was also excellent as the elevator operator, Fran, who presented herself as a lousy speller and a perpetual loser in the rough-and-tumble with men. Her voice had a tone of resignation and apology that suited the role, and she got off her casual witticisms with diffidence and even despair. In the scene of her worst humiliation, when her lover cruelly walked out on her in the middle of their assignation on Christmas Eve, leaving her with a "Christmas present" of a $100 bill, she was able to make the tearful comment, "When you're in love with a married man, you should never use mascara," sound both trivial and profound.

Jack Kruschen as Dr. Dreyfuss, Edie Adams as an ex-mistress condemned to sit as Sheldrake's secretary and watch the parade of her successors go by, Hope Holiday as a philosophical B-girl whom Baxter picked up briefly in a bar on that fateful Christmas Eve, and Johnny Seven as Fran's pugnacious brother-in-law who mistakenly gave Baxter a black eye were colorful and sardonic in the true vein of the film. And Arnold Deutsch's music was appropriate New York regional.

The big mistake made by some critics was to judge this as a "morality play." It was *not*, and I don't think Mr. Wilder would have remotely conceived of such a thing. It was a clear-eyed and realistic put-down of corporate exploitation of such *schnooks*, male or female, who were so eager, naive, and lonely as to let themselves be taken in—indeed, in a way, to be made whores of, which is what many honest people do. No punishment or pious moral judgment was passed upon the rascals at the end. The little people merely got wise—and Sheldrake apparently lost his wife. Whether Baxter and Fran could make it together was not Mr. Wilder's concern. He had made a wise and witty picture, and that was most certainly enough.

After all their disillusionments and disappointments, C.C. and Fran sit down to a contentious game of cards and a possible happy future together.

Fleeing with $40,000 which she has spontaneously stolen from her boss a secretary, Marion Crane (Janet Leigh), is filled with nervous dread when she is unsuspectingly stopped by a traffic cop.

PSYCHO

1960

Alfred Hitchcock's *Psycho* is surely among the foremost all-time great "scare" films. Nothing before nor since, including the latter-day monster movie *Jaws*, which has apparently imbued a generation with a mortal fear of sharks, has done quite as much as *Psycho* to scare people out of their wits and leave irremovable splinters of disquiet in their memories.

Everyone who ever saw this picture must remember with exquisite horror that whirlwind attack by a mysterious knife wielder upon a vulnerable young woman while she was taking a shower in a motel. The beautiful buildup to this key scene—the establishment of the woman's criminality and her tacit peril, the setting of the eerie surroundings, the suggestion of possibilities of those who might wish to harm her—followed by the sudden violent onslaught of the killer looming monstrously behind the cloudy shower curtain and slashing wildly and powerfully at her made for an unexpected trauma that caused some viewers to scream and even faint. And the subsequent representation of the fury and frenzy of the attack with rapid, split-second glimpses of sections of the woman's flesh ripped by the knife, of arms thrashing and blood splattering the white bathroom tiles, and then of a part of the dead body lying over the edge of the tub and bloody water gurgling down the drain made for as painful and gory a half-minute as has ever been played on the screen. It was no wonder that patrons were reported to have been made literally ill by this scene.

Likewise, the scene in which the private detective, hired to solve the mystery of the victim's disappearance, met a similar fate was equally shocking. As he approached the top of a stairway, he was suddenly and violently attacked by a knife wielder, grotesque in appearance, and sent tumbling backward to his death. The violence and virtuosity of staging is still awesome and macabre.

But those and other juicy bits in *Psycho* were not the only reasons why this film clobbered the minds of its viewers and left them strangely, morbidly disturbed. The basic reasons, not always realized, was that the questing Mr. Hitchcock here devised a kind of monster deft at violent depredations that could not be defined or controlled. This mystifying demon emerged from his keen interest in morbid psychology and was fattened by his fascination with the weird twists that determine men's fates. Simply, it was the creeping influence that can take over an innocent person's mind and render him uncontrollably lethal—or "psycho," to put it in a word.

True to the Hitchcock tradition, no foreshadowing of this menace appeared in the early stages of the film. And, indeed, full disclosure was withheld until technically explained at the end. At the start, *Psycho* shaped up as a caper movie. A young woman, sexually involved with a man who could indulge her only with lunch-hour trysts in a cheap hotel, found a fortuitous opportunity to make a getaway with $40,000 in cash which had

Stopping for the night in a remote motel, Marion is attracted by the very courteous, shy and accommodating manager, Norman Bates (Anthony Perkins).

been entrusted to her for placement in a bank safe deposit box. After a particularly frustrating "matinee," she rashly took off in her car without informing her lover, her sister or anyone else.

At first, Mr. Hitchcock played adroitly with this commonplace incident of crime—the nervousness of the inexperienced woman; the pressure induced by the knowledge of her guilt when she was stopped by a highway patrolman and suspiciously questioned by him; the desperation of her endeavors to elude him by buying a second-hand car and then, during the transaction, almost losing the money by momentarily forgetting her bag. All of this Mr. Hitchcock maneuvered into a sequence of tingling suspense.

When he had run that out, however, he took off on another tack by landing his fugitive woman at a lonely side-road motel which seemed to be utterly deserted when she arrived on a rainy night. In response to her honking horn, a young man came running from a strange old Gothic house atop a hill behind the motel. After registering and being shown to her room adjacent to the office, she was kindly invited to have supper with the youthful proprietor. His seemingly shy, courteous manner helped to reassure her, and she set about putting her things in order while he went to the house to fetch food. Most noticeably she wrapped the money—all in $100 bills—in a newspaper (which incidently contained an account of her disappearance) and put it on a table in the room. At this point, Mr. Hitchcock was deceptively attentive and kept the audience riveted to that wad.

After her host left, the young woman heard loud voices coming from the house on the hill, especially that of a perceptibly older woman irritably abusing the young man. Suddenly he shouted, "Shut up!" whereupon the voice of the scold stopped. When he returned with a tray of sandwiches, he apologetically explained that the irascible woman was his mother, but that everything was all right.

As they ate in the parlor behind the office, elaborately decorated with stuffed birds (he said his hobby was taxidermy), the two fell into friendly talk. She told him she was bored with the life she was living. "I am looking for a private island," she said. "All of us are trapped," he countered, and guardedly remarked that he could not desert

Norman is aghast when he later discovers the mangled body of Marion in the bathroom where she has been brutally murdered by a mysterious attacker.

his aged mother, though he loathed what she had become. "I hate the illness," he said. But when she asked why he could not put his mother in a home, he became angry and upset, and was dark and remote for a spell. After regaining control, he covered with the observation, "We all go a little mad sometimes." This she took as applying to herself also, and, after more conversation, she said she had decided to return home the next day. The thoughtful talk had led her to repent.

But all was not thus serenely settled. When she went to her room to retire, he secretly watched her through a peephole, then, disturbed, he went up the hill to the house, looked up the stairs as though pondering, then went into the kitchen and sat in a chair, all to the faint accompaniment of menace music which Bernard Herrmann skillfully composed.

Back in her room, the young woman had leisurely undressed and had got into the shower, symbolizing purification, when suddenly there

appeared that grotesque figure behind the curtain and the slaughter previously described began. The grisly scene was concluded with a close shot of the dead woman's face, limp against the floor of the bathroom, and a lingering shot of one blankly staring eye.

Here was indeed an enigma. Not only was the viewer mystified as to the identity of the murderer—the old woman, as it appeared, or her son—but in what direction was the drama headed now that Mr. Hitchcock had killed off his heroine—and, more bewilderingly, his star! Janet Leigh, who played the young woman, was hardly one you would have thought expendable.

Characteristically, Mr. Hitchcock did not choose to tell all at once. Instead he switched to a long shot of the old house, from which there were suddenly heard anguished cries, followed by the young man bursting forth and running, as if in alarm, down the hill. He went to the room of the young woman, looked aghast at the slaughter, then, without doing anything about it, turned out the lights and shut the door. Was he truly overwhelmed by the prospect? Was he going to call the police? The enigma was carried into the next scene, when the young man returned with a mop and slowly, deliberately, opaquely, went about cleaning up the blood. He mopped down the walls, and after wrapping the knife-slashed body securely in the shower curtain, washed his hands. All was contrived to milk the mystery and maddeningly stretch the suspense. Next the young man fetched his car, and after backing it up to the door of the room deposited the covered corpse in the trunk. Then he returned to the bedroom, stuffed all the woman's effects into her bag, all except the bundle of money, which still lay on the table, and threw the pocketbook into the trunk. When he went back for one last inspection, he spotted the cash and casually tossed it into the trunk as well. So that at least was significant: murder for material profit was ruled out. The cleanup was concluded with the young man driving the car into a nearby pond, where it slowly sank under the water. The primary evidence was thus destroyed.

Now came the second and completely nonsequential twist in the film. A private detective, hired to find the missing woman, had traced her to the motel and confronted the evasive young manager with the evidence of her name on the register. Then the detective noted the old house and remarked, ''There's someone sitting up in the window.'' ''My mother,'' the young man said. Could he talk with *her*, asked the detective. The reply was an emphatic no, and the detective was sent away. But later in the evening, he returned secretly to the house and, without anyone to stop him, started up the stairs to the second floor. Just as he reached the top of the stairway, that curious creature, wearing an old-fashioned woman's dress, came screaming out of a bedroom and attacked him ferociously. After his tumble down the stairs, the strange knife wielder leaped down upon him and stabbed him several times more.

The mystery was now truly throbbing. What sort of fiend was in this house, moved to murder an innocent woman and a detective who dared intrude? At this point, the young woman's lover and her sister, who had been informed by a phone call from the detective of his whereabouts before he met his unfortunate end, arrived to do a bit of sleuthing. They also went to the sheriff to inquire about the young man's mother and were startled (as were audiences) to hear him say, with an edge

Without revealing the murder to anyone, Norman stuffs the body of Marion and her belongings (including the undiscovered money) in the trunk of a car and runs it into a nearby swamp.

Norman is surprisingly confronted by a detective (Martin Balsam) who has deviously followed the trail of the missing woman to this motel.

of suspicion, that the mother had been dead for ten years!

So back to the motel went the couple, registered in a room as man and wife, and started looking for clues. (Why they didn't call the police at that point was not explained; the assumption was that they did not wish to expose the missing sister to the law.) Meanwhile Mr. Hitchcock's roving camera had overheard behind a closed bedroom door the young man trying to urge his mother to let him take her down and hide her in a cellar room. When she refused, the camera caught him in a fascinating overhead shot carrying the unresisting mother down the stairs.

Now the elements were assembled for the trap to be sprung. And it was, a few scenes later, when the lover, distracting the attention of the young man, made it possible for his companion to rush up alone into the house. Entering the now empty bedroom, she found it furnished in quaint Victorian style. She then proceeded into a smaller boy's bedroom, obviously the haven of the son. Suddenly the viewer was confronted with touching evidence of an effort to preserve the past. An aura of pathos and perversion uncomfortably seeped into the house. Then, in exploring the cellar, the sister walked into a bare room and saw the figure of an old woman sitting in a chair with her back turned. Slowly she moved over to it and turned the figure around. With a terrified scream, she saw the figure in the dress was a skeleton! At that breathless moment, a still louder and agonized scream rent the air and the previously seen murderer in an old dress leaped through the door. But before the attacker could plunge the knife into her, the lover rushed into the room, disarmed the would-be assailant, and knocked a wig off its head. There, unmasked and demolished, was the young man!

With such a generally unexpected denouement, it was no wonder that Mr. Hitchcock insisted that *Psycho* be advertised with a notification that patrons would not be admitted after the film had begun. He wished to keep that shock ending a surprise as long as he could. But, of course, it wasn't long before the secret was out. Even so, the startling deception was not sufficiently conclusive in itself, and Mr. Hitchcock was forced to end his picture with a pedantically explanatory scene. At the coroner's inquest into the murders, a psychologist explained that the obsessed knife wielder had a split personality and continued to be dominated by his mother even after her death, so that he lived not only his own life but that of his mother, who was racked with jealousy. Thus it was in her persona, dressed in her old-fashioned clothes, that he committed the murders and then, as himself, tried to cover up for her.

At best, this scene was anticlimactic, but Mr. Hitchcock did top it off with a brilliantly sharp and moving suffix—a medium shot of the anguished young man sitting alone in a cell and facing the camera, listening to the voice of his mother talking to him and then hearing his own voice explaining for her, "Why she wouldn't even harm a fly." Thus this drama of a psychopathic killer concluded on a note of sympathy and a hint of despair and frustration that we are powerless against such ironic twists of fate.

In the hands of a lesser director, this story could have been absurd, shot full of implausibilities and studied suspense-film tricks. But Mr. Hitchcock, with his strong command of camera and his metronomic sense of pace, was able to keep his viewers hypnotically engrossed. As the killer, too, Anthony Perkins contributed much, with his air of perpetual instability and his fascinating shifts of mood. Miss Leigh as the hapless absconder (one of the most expensive red-herrings Mr. Hitchcock ever pulled across a plot), Martin Balsam as the detective, John Gavin as the lover-turned-sleuth, and Vera Miles as the tag-along sister did what they had to do well, and Bernard Herrmann's precise cue-music was some of the smartest ever done for a horror film.

Members of the boisterous gang of Jets explode with animal energy in a running and leaping Jerry Robbins ballet on the streets of West Side New York.

WEST SIDE STORY

1961

West Side Story was and continues in the estimations of many, to be the high-water mark of ingenuity and aesthetic accomplishment in musical films. All others, before or since, from the superlative *Singin' in the Rain*** to the latest (but lesser) large achievement in film-cum-music, *Cabaret*,** have had their particular distinctions and their appeals to individual tastes. But this film from Robert Wise and Jerome Robbins qualitatively and quantitatively took the prize.

In *West Side Story* the quintessence of the adaptation and assimilation of dance as a major element of storytelling and emotion-building in the cinema medium was achieved. Many earlier films were conspicuous for using dance creatively to generate excitement and fulfillment of audience identification with the plot. Some of the early sound musicals, being novel and fresh, moved audiences to wonder and sheer intoxication with the elegancies and trickeries of dance: the Fred Astaire–Ginger Rogers frolics, the famous Busby Berkeley displays of kaleidoscopic show-girl

groupings beginning with *42nd Street*, the memorable solo dances of Ray Bolger in *The Wizard of Oz*,** the later *Seven Brides for Seven Brothers*, *The Red Shoes*,** and *On the Town*.

But in *West Side Story*, modern ballet, athletic and muscular, with its prototypical ensemble numbers and its explosions of exuberance and energy did as much if not more for the narration of a tragic story than did the straight plot-carrying scenes and the individually expressive and always lyrical songs. In the opening sequence, for instance, after the camera had brought the viewer in from a stunning helicopter panorama of lower and middle Manhattan to a group of restless, agitated tough kids in an actual playground on the West Side, the momentum suddenly exploded into a terrifying cascade of youths breaking up into small groups and patterns, racing across the playground yard and out into the street, tangling with a group of Puerto Ricans, dancing and leaping high into the air, spewing youthful energy and passion in a characteristic Robbins ballet.

Or there was the beautifully developed and spontaneous sequence in which a mass of trigger-happy youngsters at a West Side school-gymnasium dance betrayed the smoldering tensions of their ethnic rivalries by moving around in rhythmic patterns which would suddenly coalesce in separate groups making aggressive gestures at one another in the idioms of athletic ballet. Then out of this mass of seething teenagers, trying to remain well behaved but ever ready for an outburst of hatred, two innocent, first-sight lovers, an American boy and a Puerto Rican girl, found one another, danced together, and in the blissful isolation of a golden haze forgot there were others around them and knew only the innocent joy of falling in love.

To be sure, *West Side Story* was constructed on a base of traditional plot. It was, as they say, a "modern telling" of Shakespeare's *Romeo and Juliet* with the clash of two contiguous New York street gangs, the native Jets and the Puerto Rican Sharks, replacing the ritualistic rivalry of the Montagues and the Capulets. The two lovers were the leader of the longer established Jets and the sister of the race-proud head of the stubbornly invading Sharks, and the violences and disasters of their star-crossed romance carried through to the familiar tragic end. Plotwise, it did have the boundaries of a traditional theatrical form.

It was also an adaptation from the original highly popular stage production of *West Side Story*, also under the direction of Mr. Robbins, one of the outstanding American choreographers, with music and lyrics by Leonard Bernstein and Stephen Sondheim, of Broadway note. And to the extent that the dances and song numbers were performed within well-confined sets—all except that opening ballet, which roamed the literal streets of the West Side of Manhattan—the ambiance was that of the stage.

The differences did make for contradictions. The literal look of New York, so vividly and exhilaratingly captured in the expansive opening, gave way to the perceptible look of scenes shot on sound stages, studio rooftops and fire escapes. Most notably, the great climactic sequence of the deadly rumble between the two gangs, a superlative all-male ballet, performed under what was

The Jets and their girls match their dancing agility with members of the rival gang, the Puerto Rican Sharks, in a high school gymnasium.

Tony (Richard Beymer), a member of the Jets, having fallen in love at the dance with Maria (Natalie Wood), the sister of the leader of the sharks, enacts with her a modern simulation of the balcony scene in *Romeo and Juliet*.

supposed to be the towering vault of the West Side Highway, bore the distinct appearance of the stage. As powerful and effective as this dance was, it did lack the full graphic illusion of an actual rumble between juvenile killers armed with knives, clubs, and lengths of chain.

But *West Side Story*, after all, did not aspire to the style of realism of, say, the classic drama *On the Waterfront.** This was a musical movie with a serious and tragic theme which aimed at exciting the viewer with interpretive music and dance. Accepting that understanding, it is difficult to conceive how the story demands of the picture could have been more aptly achieved.

Once the star-crossed romance of Tony and Maria had been launched in the sometimes uneven youthful persons of Richard Beymer and Natalie Wood, the subsequent course of that liaison swirled through a maze of vicissitudes generated by the community prejudices of their ethnic differences. Maria's best girlfriend, Anita, whom

Rita Moreno played with the bustle and gusto of a proper hot-blooded Puerto Rican girl, constantly warned her younger playmate and sister of her own betrothed of the peril of being in love with a boy who was not of her ethnic group. And Tony's pals in the Jets were bewildered that he should lose his heart to a "P.R." So as the complication peaked with the killing of Maria's brother in a fight with one of the Jets, the retribution of Tony for such hostility was pre-doomed.

But the energy and meaning of the picture were conveyed in those spinning ballets and in the melodic spontaneity of the lively and lovely songs. Anita's sardonic "Puerto Rico," sung and danced to by her and a group of girls who had got together at night on a tenement roof, was a wonderfully exuberant expression of transplanted enthusiasm for life in America. And her tender duet with Maria, "When Love Comes," was a sensitive salute to an eternal miracle.

Similarly the musical statements of the rival

124

A group of the Jets, with Riff (Russ Tamblyn) in the center, badger their nemesis, Police Officer Krupke (William Bramley) in front of the neighborhood candy store.

Anita (Rita Moreno), sweetheart of the leader of the Sharks, flees from the candy store after being abused and assaulted by members of the increasingly aggressive Jets.

gangs were excitingly integrated with the flowing course of the romance. The Jets' jolly "Officer Krupke," a choral jibe at the cop on the block, was a great bit of sarcastic humor set to music, and the ominous violence contained in the pre-battle antiphonal singing of "The Jets Are Going to Rumble Tonight" went with the boastful "Play It Cool, Boy" as a manifestation of the bravado and braggadocio of these too self-intoxicating youths.

It would be as wrong to regard *West Side Story* as an urgent plea for brotherhood as it would be to categorize it as merely a picture about street gangs in New York. It was a wholly romantic adaptation of the material of ethnic rivalries into a lovely and expressive comprehension of the wastage of the energies of youth. Like the movement of Bizet's *Carmen* or, indeed, Shakespeare's *Romeo and Juliet*, it made no pretense at being historical or sociological. It was simply a sensitive telling of a tragic story in a cinematic-operatic form. When Tony sang "Tonight" to Maria as she leaned toward him on a fire escape, it was a haunting reminder of the classic balcony scene, with all its Renaissance implications, in *Romeo and Juliet*. Or, after the tragic rumble when Tony and Maria, solemn and subdued, chanted the poignant "A Place for Us," it was an eloquent protest against the kind of stupid bigotry that kept them apart. And Maria's final singing of

the wistful "Hold My Hand," as she walked behind the body of Tony, held high by his grieving friends, was just the duplication of a traditional heroic ritual.

In addition to Miss Wood, Miss Moreno, and Mr. Beymer to a lesser degree, other performers were much to be commended: George Chakiris as the leader of the Sharks; Russ Tamblyn (a superlative dancer, as he had been in *Seven Brides for Seven Brothers* and many subsequent films) as one of the principals in the knife fight; Sue Oakes as a skinny little tomboy hanging around trying to be accepted as one of the Jets; Simon Oakland as a hard-boiled detective who tried to keep peace between the gangs; William Bramley as Officer Krupke; and Ned Glass as the keeper of a corner candy store. It was he who pronounced the ultimate judgment on the ritualistic battling of the gangs: "You kids make this world lousy! When will you ever stop?"

Sadly, in all the years since *West Side Story*, it hasn't stopped. It has only grown worse as street-gang feuding has expanded into more violent street crime. Bigotry and hate in the city are as ugly as they are throughout the world, and prayerful expositions such as this one can do little but move the heart. Even so, *West Side Story* stands as splendid and eloquent as the day it was released, a deeply moving entertainment and a sad memorial to a humane sentiment.

Toward a New Cinema

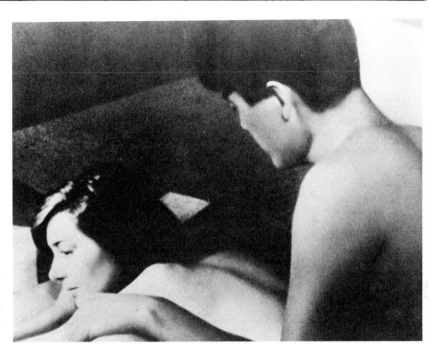

The Japanese lover (Eiji Okada) caresses the back of the French actress (Emmanuelle Riva) with whom he is having a strange, morbid affair in post-war Hiroshima.

HIROSHIMA, MON AMOUR

1959

Close on the heels of Francois Truffaut's trend-setting *The 400 Blows*,** which along with Claude Chabrol's *Les Cousins* marked the first rush of the famous French "new wave," there came from France a surprising, ambiguous, and intellectually challenging film which made an even further departure from the deadening orthodoxy of most of the postwar movies of France. It was Alain Resnais' elusive, disturbing *Hiroshima, Mon Amour*, which derived from a screenplay by Marguerite Duras, and was Mr. Resnais' first feature film. Beginning with its title, which was a puzzle in itself, and continuing on through a labyrinth of allusions that were densely interwined to a curious exchange of ambiguities by its two focal characters at the end, it taxed the immediate comprehension of its initial audiences and, even today, it provokes confused emotions and unsettled judgments in those who see it for the first time.

On the surface it seemed a strangely ponderous and deliberately obscure attempt to convey a plotless story of a young Frenchwoman trying to exorcise herself of painful, guilt-ridden memories of a secret romance with a Nazi soldier during World War II by having a love affair in postwar Hiroshima with an accommodating Japanese. Somehow a sense of her new lover as a catharsis for the guilt of the atom bomb was entwined with her nightmare recollections of her girlhood affair with the shadowy Nazi, who was shot near the end of the war. The interrelation of these two burdens of violence and shame seemed to be the complication and the reckoning of the film.

Essentially it was. But the import of the drama slowly emerged as something more—perhaps not too clearly on first viewing, but on reflection and on seeing it again. For the issue that Mr. Resnais was laboring to resolve and which he dared to assume that his audiences were able to comprehend was that memories have no fixed positions in the

The lovers lie together on her hotel bed communing with their thoughts and letting the vibrations of their mutual transient attraction pass between them.

vast surrounding sea of time, and that they and illusions and sheer imaginings all become mixed in the conscious as well as the subconscious mind. Indeed, the mind of each individual is a private world all to itself, and the way it sees, feels, and stores impressions and casts out those which it does not wish to have is conditioned by its own sensitivity, anxiety, and loneliness.

Obviously this was a difficult and devious idea to get across, and the fact that it intruded a new dimension—that of abstract time—into the conventional framing of the psyche challenged those who were accustomed to routine psychological plots. Who was prepared to perceive or imagine that a present experience could be the emotional reaction to an experience one had years ago? Or that the intensity of an experience that one was having now could be totally suffused and conditioned by one's accretion of the experiences of others from the past? It was not a metaphysical concept, but one very physical and real.

An intimation of this idea was made by Mr.

Resnais at the start. The viewer was presented an image of what appeared to be mounds of putrefying flesh, oozing into changing patterns by movement through slow dissolves. Then as these images focused into clear, close-up pictures of healthy flesh, the voices of a man and a woman were heard in quiet argument. "You saw nothing at Hiroshima," the voice of the man remarked. "I saw everything," replied the voice of the woman. "I was four times to the museum." "You saw nothing," his voice insisted. Then we were shown that the two were a Caucasian woman and a Japanese man who had just concluded a sexual embrace. The flesh was theirs, and the montage suggested that the mind of the woman was impregnated with images of horror and death while involved in the living act of sex.

This mental obsession with the horror of the Hiroshima blast was further magnified by a long succession of literal photographs of the gruesome relics of the nuclear detonation in a museum at Hiroshima and a sequence of a parade of local

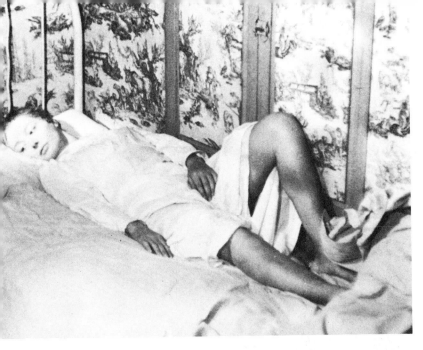

In a memory flashback, the actress sees herself hidden in her parents' home in Nevers, France, after she has suffered a nervous breakdown from seeing her Nazi lover slain in the street.

The lover and the actress find themselves trying to resolve their emotional and intellectual dilemmas in a Japanese house which seems a symbolic prison cell.

people elaborately memorializing the monumental destruction. Thus two significant observations were independently made: first, that the memory of the holocaust was perpetuated as a living agony by the people of Hiroshima, and second, that the visiting Frenchwoman had steeped herself deliberately in the arcane of this event, to the point where she was convinced that she had actually experienced it.

From this conception, Mr. Resnais took the viewer, via flashback, to a haunting description of the tragic experience of the young woman with her German lover in her hometown of Nevers—how, going for a rendezvous with him, she found his body still quivering, shot by a sniper, and how she lay with his body all night before it was hauled away—an experience which was pictorially related to the picking up of the Hiroshima dead.

Then the ever probing camera reconstructed how the traumatized woman had "gone mad"—a nervous collapse—and had been hidden in the cellar of her home by her humiliated parents to prevent the townsfolk from torturing her further than they had, then later had been forced to leave town.

In the flow of these recollections, Mr. Resnais was also much concerned with the conscious present—the fact that the young woman was an actress who was playing the role of a nurse in a film, set in Hiroshima, on the theme of peace. The man was an architect. Both were married, and the implication was that their involvement stemmed from a casual pickup that flared into an upsurge of sexuality.

The span of time in the picture was approximately twenty-four hours, during which the couple made love (several times) and she more and more revealed the agony of her trauma-troubled mind. In arguments, separations, and reconciliations, the uncertainty of the woman, her isolation and loneliness in her despair, were made tangible and moving. And, at the end, after the two had had what was evidently their last consummation of sex before the actress was to return to France, the matter was brought to a summation when she told him that in her mind he would always be "Hiroshima." He reciprocated by replying that she would always, in his mind, be "Nevers." Thus for these lovers the quintessence of their brief romance would always be associated with the interchange of emotional experience they had made in this passage of time.

The ambiguous conclusion of the film has led some viewers to believe that it implied the two would continue with the relationship. I don't see how that could be. The psychological effect of catharsis and fulfillment blended precisely with the imperative of art. The involvement had served its purpose. The intellectual point had been made.

But, of course, the attraction of *Hiroshima, Mon Amour* could not and did not depend only upon the solution of an intellectual apothegm. The intensity and moving quality of it came also from the hypnotic spell which Mr. Resnais created with his characters—especially with the woman, whose story it really was, since the man was but a sounding board for her bewilderment and questioning. The patina of it was nostalgia—a deeply wistful, intoxicating sense of the presence and ongoing importance of all the old experiences that are afloat in the mind.

This nostalgia was beautifully summoned by the sensitive use of music and sounds, along with images, overlapping the present and the past, so that for instance, the thought of Nevers was accompanied by the whisper of distant church-bells and country sounds before the image of the town came on the screen, or a musical strain indicated the wispy intrusion of a mood. Sensuous and sensual stimulation—and there was a fair degree of the latter—was tremendously important to the capture of involvement with the girl. It was the puzzlement and poignance of her problem

The actress, supposedly released, stands on a balcony overlooking restored Hiroshima on the last day of her sojourn there.

130

that compelled the viewer to feel deep concern and made this a film of uncommon and memorable urgency.

Also, Emmanuelle Riva was extraordinarily luminous in the role, conveying through her pained expressions and anguished thoughtful attitudes the depth and complexity of the turmoil in which her emotions were involved. Miss Riva had the ability to sit quietly with her lover—as, for instance, at a table in a restaurant where they were virtually alone late at night—both maintaining perfect silence, content to let their thoughts and feelings flow, and forcing into the mind of the viewer all the sorrow and confusion that were in hers. Since Mr. Resnais leaned heavily on the insinuations of such shots and scenes, the film, while seemingly passive, had a powerful galvanic quality.

Eiji Okada was likewise moving as the gracious and helpful Japanese, presenting himself as a solvent for the turmoil of the young woman rather than an ongoing irritant. Though his spirit was not benign and passive—he was actually strong and aggressive in a couple of scenes—he played the character to balance with understanding the internal convulsiveness of the girl. And this was a delicate responsibility, since the two were virtually alone throughout.

It is notable that Mr. Resnais followed *Hiroshima, Mon Amour* with his even more esoteric and puzzling *Last Year at Marienbad*, which again pursued a conundrum of tangled memories and fantasies in time. It was a so much more difficult challenge to processes of thought and so much less helped by a suggestion of emotion between its two principals that it stands today as a stylish but erratic manifestion of the "new wave." The outstanding feature of the exotic landscapes explored by Mr. Resnais in those years of assorted experiments and expansions remains *Hiroshima, Mon Amour.*

The hoodlum, Michel Poiccard (Jean-Paul Belmondo), surreptitiously takes money from the purse of one of his briefly used girl friends.

BREATHLESS

1959

Of all the early productions of the historic French "new wave" started by François Truffaut, Claude Chabrol, and Alain Resnais, certainly the most shocking and disturbing—to the stubborn traditionalists, at least—was Jean-Luc Godard's explosive *Breathless* (known in France as *A Bout de Souffle*). While previous French films had had their quota of seamy and vicious criminals, no Frenchman had turned out a character more completely without moral tone or concern for the prerogative of others than the casually anti-heroic, existentialist type conceived in the script of Mr. Godard and played to the absolute hilt by the fascinatingly ugly newcomer Jean-Paul Belmondo, in this essentially melodramatic film.

This brashly independent small-time car thief, mugger, shoplifter, and ladies' man whose obvious *modus operandi* was looking out for himself drew outraged howls of resentment from the solid Establishment, film industrialists, and others, when *Breathless* was released in France. Likewise some Americans were moved to dub it "Tasteless" when it opened in New York. The fact that its author was discovered to be one of the ardent young men who were caught up in the movement toward a "new" cinema in France went to brand him further in the eyes of the Old Guard and drew some critical observers to remark that this kind of moviemaking was corruptive not only to cinema but to youth. Also Mr. Godard frankly acknowledged himself to be politically radical and strongly antisocial, which again did not please the bourgeoisie but delighted that nucleus of students and young people who were quite as radical as he.

This kind of explosive reaction to *Breathless* may seem strange and absurd to present-day moviegoers who have witnessed some of the wild and vicious films of recent years. So often has the existentialist character that Mr. Belmondo played been copied and brazenly expanded by filmmakers all over the world that this once alarming creation may seem now a tepid prototype. And the startling innovations in filmcraft that Mr. Godard made—his characteristic trick of jump-cutting to hasten the transition of scenes, his elimination of conventional nonessentials, his quick shifts in lighting and locale—have been picked up by other young directors and made a part of latter-day styles. Like his friend and associate Mr. Truffaut, Mr. Godard shot virtually all of his film in natural settings—in the streets, bars, cafés, cheap hotels, even one scene in a men's toilet where the hoodlum blandly mugged a middle-aged man. Shooting time was thirty days, with Raoul Coutard, Truffaut's cameraman, filming much of it with hand-held cameras while virtually on the run, with no fixed setups or sound recording. Dialogue was dubbed in later on. The consequence was a picture which had a sharp, realistic look and conveyed a sense of the hectic, frenzied pace of the life of the punk.

The story, suggested by Mr. Truffaut, required no elaborate plotting or detailed laying out. It was a simple tale of a young hoodlum who, after stealing a car in a city in southern France, blandly ditched a girlfriend who had set up the theft for him so he might get to Paris and move into the

Michel further attacks and robs a garage attendant as he steals a car to flee to Paris.

"big time." Significantly, this petty crook frankly fantasized himself to be an American movie gangster, and in one celebrated scene he was shown gazing at a theater billboard of Humphrey Bogart in *The Harder They Fall*, quietly rehearsing the actor's mannerisms, running a thumb across his lips, smoking a cigarette in Bogart fashion, and reverentially muttering "Bogey," a

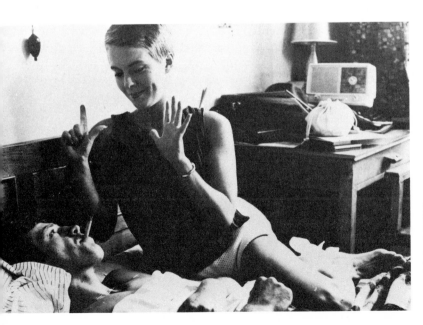

An ingenuous, oddly charming seduction in a cheap Paris hotel goes on between Michel and Patricia (Jean Seberg), a little American newspaper vendor he has picked up in the street.

sacred word! Indeed, Mr. Godard acknowledged that he, too, was a movie gangster fan and that he considered this film an updating of the spontaneity and candor of the old grade-B American gangster films, dressed up with modern attitudes and idioms. He even dedicated it to Monogram, one of the smaller Hollywood studios that specialized in the genre.

This reverence for the styles and traditions of another day did not prevent Mr. Godard, however, from reorganizing his film and abandoning the mythological criminal for the wanderer full of offhand savagery. En route to Paris, his car thief has casually shot down a policeman who appoached him in a parking lot as he would later walk indifferently past the body of an accident victim lying in a Paris street. There was no surge of emotion in his action; it was just a simple knee-jerk response. But it classified him in his own awareness—and that of the audience—as a killer on the lam.

So this was the threat that hung over his life in Paris, covering some five or six days—during which he casually filched some money out of the purse of a photographer's model he had been following around, rabbit-chopped the fellow in the men's room and took a couple of bills from him, met up with an American girl who was earning money hawking the Paris *Herald* on the Champs Elysées and made a stab at living with her in a shabby left-bank hotel. After a few days, however, she betrayed him by tipping a police informer as to his whereabouts while she was out of their room on the pretext of buying newspapers and milk. And in the end, realizing his peril, he made an attempt to escape and was shot and killed by policemen while fleeing down a crowded Paris street.

Audience feelings for this "anti-hero" were inevitably and intentionally mixed. Mr. Godard portrayed him as he saw him, a totally amoral sort, neither asking for the old-time "understanding" nor fishing for sympathy. After the callous betrayal of his girlfriend in the opening scene—an act done with such cool indifference it made the viewer start—he could drive away toward Paris along a lovely tree-lined country road and soliloquize almost sentimentally about his affection for France. He was less concerned about the ethics and the peril of having killed the cop than he was

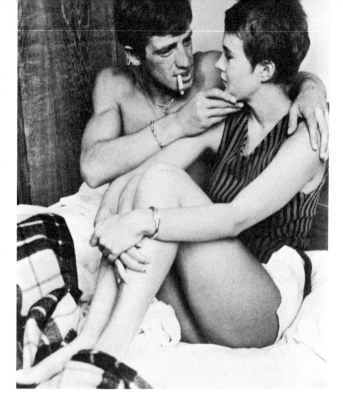

The seduction approaches fulfillment.

about the chance of his little American taking up with another man.

A further ambiguity was that, while the rogue had no moral shame, he was clearly insecure, uncertain, and lonely in his haphazard way. His pursuit of the newspaper vendor—a thin little boyish-bobbed blonde, whom Jean Seberg made quite as vivid as Mr. Belmondo made the punk—had a curious desperation about it. He was offhand when he took up with her but then tended to be sullenly possessive after she showed a modest interest in him. When he drove her to keep a date with an American journalist, for whom she covered small stories now and then, he lurked around in the vicinity so he could keep an eye on her. And later, when he feared she might leave him, he became alarmed.

The most interesting, touching scene in the picture was the seduction episode, with the two on a rumpled bed in her hotel room, he being amusing and nonchalant, although a trace of anxiety and impatience showed through his insouciance. She appeared sexily coquettish but also played girlishly hard to get. One could almost regard these street children as a couple of high school kids.

The hotel room, too, was significant, with its little touches of artiness—in particular a wall poster for a Renoir exhibition, implying that this youngster might have come from an average American bourgeois home, picked up a yen for Gallic culture, and was having a scrimpy fling in France. She, too, was obviously lonely, shallow, and immature, attracted to the offbeat Frenchman yet, deep down, distrustful of him.

"I'm undecided," she told him in a vaguely troubled mood, as they sparred for some resolution of their vagrant relationship. "What about?" he indifferently asked her. "If I knew, I wouldn't be undecided," she replied, which was a sadly ingenuous revelation of her irresolute mentality. Yet she also showed flashes of shrewdness and self-defensive cruelty, as when she casually informed on her lover because she had evidently become afraid of him. A touch that may have escaped some viewers was that she was wearing a conventional maidenly dress, not her usual news vendor's jeans and T-shirt, when she went out to throw the switch. And when she later rushed up to be with him as he lay dying in the street and he glanced at her with indifference, a filthy name for her on his lips, she drew back and innocently mumbled, "I don't know what that means." Yes, her kitten was a match for his old tom cat in a number of shadowy, opaque ways.

The facet of this picture that apparently caused so much alarm was its ruthlessly honest exposure of the reckless, amoral attitudes of a widening stratum of young people which the oldsters did not want to recognize. The very thought of such callous behavior had to be blotted out. Yet these two types of the postwar youth rebellion were as true to the rhythms of their day as were Scott Fitzgerald's models of the Jazz Age or René Clair's waifs in *Sous les Toits de Paris*. And because they were realized so truly, they came forth with terrifying power.

They still do, despite the dilution of their venom that the onward surge of youth into life-styles (and films!) more poisonous than those in *Breathless* has inevitably caused. They still stand—especially the hoodlum—as memorable cult prototypes, responding to random impulses yet finding no joy in being alive. Ironically their types have faded into the mists of time like that small cloud of smoke that the hoodlum puffed out of his dying lips. Yes, Mr. Godard was telling us something when he ended his film that way.

Patricia, fascinated but uncertain, places a girlish kiss on the cheek of the predatory, self-serving Michel.

In the cold light of a winter morning in wartime Genoa, the shifty con man, Bidone (Vittorio de Sica), who calls himself Colonel Grimaldi, vigorously and charmingly denies his association with any resistance activity to the commanding Nazi colonel (Hannes Messemer).

GENERAL DELLA ROVERE

1959

It was significant of the trend of film production—and of conditions—in Italy after World War II that Roberto Rossellini, whose famous *Open City*** and *Paisan** inaugurated the style known as neo-realism in capturing the literal feelings and looks of people caught up in the Resistance and other travails toward the end and immediately after the war, turned away from exploring that period of crisis following those films. He did not come back to it until a decade later, when he made his great *General della Rovere*.

In that decade, Italian filmmakers had drifted slowly away from recollections of the war as reasons for sober soul-searching and had moved along to more immediate concerns of postwar social problems, then further into frank "escapist" fare. In that period, the Italian producers, with their great Cinecittà studio, their traditional

wealth of talent, and low production costs, aimed to get into the mainstream of international film enterprise by making and assisting in the production of pictures with that market in mind. The result was such elaborate and fatuous spectacles as *The Queen of Sheba* and *Ulysses* (known colloquially as "sand-and-tits" films) and gay and showy American-sponsored fare like *Quo Vadis*, *Three Coins in the Fountain*, *Roman Holiday*, and *Ben Hur.*** "Hollywood on the Tiber," the cynics dubbed Rome, and, indeed, the tag was not inconsistent with the spirit of Italy. Industry was booming, workers were being hired, and the new-rich were vying with tourists to flaunt and indulge themselves. It was the period of "la dolce vita," to put it in one famous phrase.

Whether Rossellini was revolted by the gross materialism of this trend and wanted to flash a reminder to his countrymen of the ideals for which his old Resistance friends had fought and died, or whether he and his writers, the accomplished team of Sergio Amidei, Diego Fabbri, and Indro Montanelli, simply had in hand a remarkable true story certain to make a winning film, I cannot say for sure. But whatever their motivation, *General della Rovere* turned out to be a powerful film in the neo-realist tradition, as great as its predecessors in its special way.

The focus of it was a shifty and shameless small-time gambler and confidence man plying his shabby occupations in Genoa during the last ugly winter of the war, when the suffering and despair of the Italians were probably most acute. Poverty and privation were manifest, the Nazis were still in tight control, and only vaguely filtering vapors and vibrations of resistance were in the air. Yet this fellow was either blankly insensitive to the pandemic suffering or else too much preoccupied with his own selfish struggle to survive. Indeed, his principal source of income was selling what he pretended was his influence with the Nazis to help desperate and gullible people get their loved ones out of Nazi jails.

Such was the depravity of this character, whom Rossellini was able to persuade his good friend and fellow director Vittorio De Sica to play. And a finer and more fortuitous selection could not have conceivably been made. For De Sica oozed precisely the right air of false distinction and faked solicitude in the role of this fraud-ulent Colonel Grimaldi, which was a respectable old family name. Silver-haired, handsome, well-spoken, and commanding in his well-tailored clothes and his rakish black fedora cocked proudly and almost comically on his head, he was the perfect image of the type of mediary in matters of "making arrangements" with officials that Italians knew so well. He was also—and this is a detail that was not then too widely known, except by his friends and associates and most of the casino operators in Europe—addicted to high-stakes gambling, a compulsion which allowed him to comprehend and "feel" much more keenly than might another the passion and desperation of his poseur.

The crunch came when Colonel Grimaldi, caught in a shabby attempt to defraud a well-to-do woman, was imprisoned. But the Nazi commander who gleaned his personality also knew that his name was not Grimaldi but Bidone and that he was a deserter from the Italian army. He offered leniency if Grimaldi would act as an undercover man and keep him informed about the inmates in a big political prison in Milan. To cloak him with the highest credentials, he was slipped into prison in the guise of one General della Rovere, a famous hero of the Resistance

Bidone, pretending to be able to obtain release of civilian prisoners (for a fee), fraudulently presents an anguished wife (Anne Vernon) and her mother before a petty and powerless Nazi clerk.

On a deal with the Nazi colonel whereby he is put in the most formidable prison on the pretense of being one General della Rovere, a legendary resistance hero, to spy, Bidone is given a token beating and returned to his cell.

who was known among the prisoners and expected to arrive soon in that area to take command. But unknown to them, the General had been secretly captured and killed while attempting to make a nighttime landing from a submarine.

Thus installed in the prison, Bidone immediately became an awesome idol and confidential counselor via the grapevine to all the prisoners. (Apparently his resemblance to Rovere was sufficient to deceive the few who got close enough to see his face.) He gloried in the gratitude and deference, but he also was shaken and impressed by the bravery and devotion of little people to the cause of helping to free Italy.

Then two shattering things happened: Bidone was ordered to detect a particularly wanted Resistance fighter from among a newly arrived batch of prisoners—an order he vehemently protested because he said it called upon him to be an "executioner" and not just a "decoy"; and, second, he received a deeply touching letter and photograph from the wife of General della Rovere, who, of course, assumed he was alive. "We have told the children," said the letter. "We will try to be worthy of you. When a man has two choices of action, he should choose the harder one." The message reached him right after he had been beaten to support his disguise, and De Sica's silent show of reaction was one of the high poetic moments in the film.

The fateful time for decision came in a blood-chilling scene. A group of prisoners were sequestered in a guard room. Ten would be taken to be shot as retaliation for the killing of an important Italian Fascist by the underground. Bidone was placed among them, not because he was a candidate for execution but because pressure was being put upon him to identify the wanted man, which he had not yet been able to do with certainty. The tension was agonizing. The prisoners were racked with fears, not knowing whether they were to be placed against the wall or taken to a labor camp. The presence of the presumed Rovere among them led them to hope for the lesser punishment. One fellow, seized with hysteria, screamed his innocence. Others were calm and courageous. In a corner were five lonely Jews— only five because the rest of the Jews in the area had been taken to concentration camps. Their remote and dignified decision was to put their trust in God. In the clutch of this agonizing waiting, a prisoner came up to Bidone and quietly identified himself as the partisan intended to make contact with General della Rovere. Then he whispered the words to Bidone that solidified his resolve: "Knowing you gave me courage—and knowing so surely man will build a better world." Here was the clinching indication that this was the wanted man.

The rest was heroic resolution. The names of the doomed men were called. Bidone's was not among them. And as they were marched to the execution yard, Bidone was drawn aside by the Nazi colonel and asked if he yet knew the wanted man. Instead of answering directly, he requested a piece of paper, as if he meant to write the name on it, but instead he hastily scribbled a note to the Contessa della Rovere. "My last thoughts were of you," said the note. "Long live Italy! Long live the king!" Handing the paper back to the colonel, and asking that it be delivered to the contessa, Bidone broke away and ran after the doomed men, already lined up at the execution stakes, and took his place beside them, his head held high and his arms at his sides. In that moment, the order was given, the volley of the firing squad rang out, and Bidone dropped dead with the others. He had made his sacrifice for Italy.

In the corridor from which he had watched the execution, the Nazi colonel was confronted by a subaltern. "I think there's been a mistake," the officer whispered. "You were only supposed to shoot ten."

"I know," answered the colonel. "I take the responsibility."

It was interesting to note how closely and evocatively this picture compared with the historic *Open City*, yet how different it was in salient ways. It followed precisely the model of the neorealist style, with the cold, hard look of an Italian city and the authenticity of the people graphically reproduced. The dismal light of a winter morning, a dusting of snow on the rubbled streets, the bareness and harshness of interiors, the coarseness of a whorehouse to which the desperate Colonel Grimaldi went to try to fob off a worthless ring, the iron-barred enclosure of the prison and the shabbiness of the men within—all were so accurately imaged that they gave an unassailable illusion of truth. Except that Rossellini had the advantage of more sophisticated equipment and techniques in photographing this picture than were available to him in his previous films, the pictorial quality of it recollected *Open City* and *Paisan*. Likewise, he and his writers echoed such sharp analogies to the contents of those legendary pictures as the stealthiness of the underground, the steadfastness of Resistance fighters, the use of an informer as a catalyst, and the ultimate execution of the hero by a firing squad, that it might have been thought they were deliberately trying to stir up the spirit of the past.

But the major difference of *General della Rovere* from those earlier films was its intense and dramatic exploration of the principal character. Where all the multifarious patchwork of participants in *Open City* and *Paisan* was restrained to the point of austerity and conspicuously unadorned, delving no farther below the surface than was essential to *suggest* characters—or, let us say, characteristics—the surface of *General della Rovere* was arranged primarily as an environment in which to observe and probe the significant ambiguities of Grimaldi/Bidone. Here was a reprehensible person, a treacherous and villainous sort, who could be taken as a prime example of the worst kind of Italian during the war, worse even than the puerile puppets that stuck with the Fascisti to the end. He represented exactly the sort of rascal that looked out only for himself. Yet there were hidden within him human sentiments and strengths that would respond to the evidence of loyalty and courage. He had a measure of humor and pride. And he had, too, a flair for the theatrical, not uncommon in his nobler countrymen. All of these facets of his personality Rossellini and De Sica uncovered through the vehement rush of this fiction to its melodramatic

Alone in his cell but surrounded by the nearness and sounds of his brave and indomitable prison-mates, Bidone begins to realize the shabbiness and shame of his treacherous role.

end. He might, indeed, have been taken as symbolic of many Italians during the war.

Different, too, was the picture that Rossellini gave of a Nazi officer assigned to a dictatorial task. His colonel in *General della Rovere* was a tough and unrelenting type, plausibly authoritarian but not a hate-the-Hun cliché. He, too, showed a measure of humanity at the end, and he was properly played by Hannes Messemer so that he could be believed. To avoid a hint of political bias, which some detected in *Open City* and *Paisan*, Rossellini gave no indication of his partisans being Communist, and his Contessa della Rovere (Baronessa Barzani) was an ironclad Roman Catholic aristocrat.

Regardless of how much reflecting this film caused Italians to do or how much admiration it revived for the wartime Resistance, it was an absorbing study which left ringing in one's ears those ironic words of the leader whom Bidone refused to betray, "Knowing you gave me courage—and knowing so surely man will build a better world."

Rather than expose a crucial partisan, Bidone rushes out to join a group of prisoners being executed as examples and is cut down. His body lies on the ground at right of stakes.

Arthur (Albert Finney), a Nottingham factory worker, finds his main excitement and release in a secret liaison with Brenda (Rachel Roberts), the wife of a fellow worker.

SATURDAY NIGHT AND SUNDAY MORNING

1960

Virtually simultaneous with the surge of the "new wave" in France there emerged in Great Britain a similar group of young film directors. Like their colleagues on the Continent, their aim was to make less expensive pictures about people as they really were. Widespread social changes in the aftermath of World War II, the moral and economic enervation of the middle class, and the flowering of a school of writers who were hotly sympathetic, in novels and plays, toward the postwar grievances of working people were the fuel that fed this burst and propelled these cinema artists into the commercial stream.

Their thrust was initially evident in a program of documentary films that were launched at irregular intervals over a period from 1956 to 1959 at the National Film Theatre. Loosely labeled Free Cinema, these were films of a realistic sort that looked with humor and sympathy on various marginal phases of working class life, such as jazz and youth clubs, food markets and amusement parks. Their directors were still undistinguished, such as Lindsay Anderson, Tony Richardson, and Karel Reisz, most of whom were fledged by the Oxford University Film Society, just as most of their French "new wave" counterparts were fledged by the magazine Cahiers du Cinéma.

The first feature-length manifestation of this Anglofilial "new wave" was Jack Clayton's caustic screen translation of John Braine's popular novel Room at the Top. It was a stinging contemplation of the devices and deceits by which a brazenly cynical young fellow clawed his way up from the slums to financial and social status in a gloomy industrial locale. Soon to follow was Mr.

Richardson and Nigel Kneale's film adaptation of John Osborne's play *Look Back in Anger*. The principal character in it was a testy, frustrated young man who cried out against the boredom of a dull middle-class environment and took out his wrath on his mistress and his pathetically fear-frozen wife.

By virtue of their precedential status and certain strong dramatic qualities, too, either of these films might have been chosen for presentation in this book as the primary breakthrough example of the aptly called "angry-young-man" films. But for reasons of its thematic substance and its superiority as an entertainment I am moved to select as the exponent of this significant and absorbing genre Karel Reisz's *Saturday Night and Sunday Morning*, adapted by Alan Sillitoe from his own first novel of the same title.

Here the principal character was not a vicious, intractable sort like the cold, self-serving climber that the grim-faced Laurence Harvey portrayed in *Room at the Top*; nor was he a bitter, self-pitying dropout from the stultifying middle class such as Richard Burton acted (and distorted!) in Mr. Richardson's film. He was an amiable young lathe operator in one of the giant industrial plants that bespeak and befoul the environment of the great Midlands city of Nottingham. Fast at his work, not a shirker, he earned his fourteen pounds three shillings a week with no more than the average amount of grumbling and an occasional practical joke at the expense of the solemn foreman or some of the more pious factory hands. This fellow, whose name was Arthur, was seemingly set in the workingman's routine, guarded only by his self-invented motto, "Don't let the bastards grind you down!" Young Albert Finney, who had distinguished himself on the stage before this, his initial screen appearance, was beautifully expressive of the role—vigorous, casual, sarcastic, and with a fascinating North Country accent you could cut with a knife!

At home, where Arthur lived with his parents in a meager but tidy simplicity, he sometimes watched "telly" in the evenings, as the old folks did, and restlessly battled with boredom. But then, come Saturday night, he was off to the pub with the fellows to joke, get excessively drunk, and keep guarded company with a truculent, sexy married woman, Brenda, whom the pug-nosed Rachel Roberts tartly played. On dreary Sunday mornings, he might go fishing with a factory worker pal whom he constantly admonished not to "get ground down by trying to get ahead" and notified that he himself was being cautious not to get married "until I'm good and ready"—which he did not intend to be soon!

Such was the endless rotation in which Arthur was confined—the ambience of the factory with its deafening noises from the whirring machines,

Arthur and Brenda are confronted with a serious dilemma when she finds she is pregnant by him.

Meanwhile, the bored and restless fellow finds a new girl Doreen (Shirley Ann Field).

the dark pubs with their babble of voices, the shabby workmen's homes, the tiny parks, the grimy streets, the shallow river, and Brenda's conventional bed, from which he might have to flee of an early morning when her workman-husband came home.

If this seemed a cheerless cycle and Arthur, for all his casual charm, seemed a dull, complacent fellow, willing to go along, this was precisely what was wanted by Mr. Sillitoe and was studiously documented in the sharp, hard direction of Mr. Reisz. This was an insider's vision of the quality of a British factory worker's life in the mid-1950s and of the nature of a singular factory man (Mr. Sillitoe, when he wrote his novel, was a lathe operator in Nottingham). There was nothing political about him; he was neither supine nor militant, nor did he ever identify his bosses as other than "them" or "they." He was just a symbolic factory worker, without any positive sense of class or social responsibility. He was becalmed between the proletarianism of the 1930s workers' literature and the active unionism of the postwar period when the British Labor Party shook things up.

But two things happened to Arthur at just about the same time that thoroughly disturbed his self-containment. He met another girl younger and more interesting than Brenda, with whom he was already becoming bored, partly because she was beginning to be peevish and demanding with him and also because he got a signal that her husband was getting wise. The major impetus to disengage was provided by Brenda when she "ungraciously" let him know that he had carelessly got her pregnant and demanded that he help her out.

The sudden unsettling of Arthur under these unfamiliar assaults, neither of which was uncommon in the general experience of men but both of which, coming together, clearly taxed his emotional strength, made for the dramatically suspenseful and personally poignant crisis in the film. An "aunt" to whom Arthur took Brenda, taking the customary way of ignorant, superstitious people, could do nothing to help her "get rid of the baby," and she told him she would have to go to an abortionist, whose fee would be "forty quid." This he agreed to pay, thereby morally commiting himself to a social responsibility. (His only way of expressing his frustration was to try to defend a poor old drunk who had heaved a jug through a window and was being beset by the police.) At the same time, he was having trouble

143

Found out by Brenda's husband, Arthur is ruthlessly beaten by the husband's tough brothers at a cheap amusement park.

with Doreen, his new and now much liked girl, who charged him with being egotistical and arrogant, which perceptibly brought him up short.

On Saturday night, while larking with Doreen, his chum, and another girl at a typical lower-class amusement park, he met a venomous Brenda and learned that she was going to go ahead and have the baby, evidently with her husband's cold consent. A few minutes later, the husband and his "two tough brothers," about whom Arthur had already been warned, stalked him and chased him wildly through the incongruous playland into a rubbish lot, where they caught him and beat him to a pulp. There they left him thrashed and humiliated, barely able to drag himself home.

That was Gethsemene for Arthur. Deflated and painfully reviled, he frankly acknowledged his dilemma: "God knows what I am!" And though Doreen soon reconciled with him and he later let himself be advised by Brenda's now placated husband that he should stop "making trouble and take things as they come," he was clearly subdued and submissive to the moral and social trap in which he was snagged.

The last we saw of Arthur, he and Doreen were atop a hill on a quiet Sunday morning looking out across the dreary expanse of factories and workers' houses, talking about themselves and the likelihood of getting married. In a burst of resentment against the expansion of the great industrial complex, he flung a rock down the hill. Doreen said to him calmly, "You shouldn't throw things like that." He looked at her archly and answered, "It won't be the last one I'll throw." And on that ambiguous rejoinder, the scene and the film faded out.

A few American critics, particularly Pauline Kael, took strong exception to this picture. It was shabby and hopeless, Miss Kael said, as though she expected luxuriance and a tidy, happy end. Could she not see it was a film about entrapment, the encirclement of a man who was hobbled by lack of education, by the social ostracism of his class, and by the limits of his own ambition from achieving the sort of freedom he desired? Where others might escape from the snare by advancing themselves through deceit or by lapsing into do-nothingness, Arthur could protest only by cuckolding a fellow worker, throwing things, and shooting off his mouth. To be sure, he was weak and ineffectual, but he did have energy and charm, and, as Mr. Finney played him, he was cheeky, pathetic, and proud. There was no "happy" ending for Arthur. But he *was* wanted and loved. He and Doreen could make a decent life together and perhaps see conditions change so their children could have more advantages than they had. That was cause for optimism and hope. So it was a historic comprehension of a formidable slice of British life.

In all, there was solid fiber in it and the throb of genuine character, from the Arthur of Mr. Finney to the Doreen of Shirley Anne Field and on through Miss Roberts' caustic Brenda, Bryan Pringle's prim enactment of her spouse, and Norman Rossington's amusing realization of Arthur's lantern-jawed pal. Mr. Reisz's firm direction caught them truly within the gray and granitine grubbiness of the factory town, which Freddie Francis' camera turned into clouded poetry.

Later there were to follow in the sequence of "angry" films such fine ones as *A Taste of Honey* with Rita Tushingham, *A Kind of Loving* with Alan Bates and June Ritchie, and then the ultimate anger-protest film, *The Loneliness of the Long Distance Runner,* ** from Mr. Richardson and Mr. Sillitoe. In that, the hero, played by Tom Courtenay, was an out-and-out slum-bred anarchist who rebelled not alone against injustice but against the entire Establishment. But that was a bit too strong for the public. It marked the end of the important "angry" skein.

Subdued and sobered, Arthur and Doreen are left to contemplate a future together in the imprisonment of a working-class life.

Before bombs begin falling on Rome, the widow, Cesira (Sophia Loren), considers a convenient relationship with Giovanni (Raf Vallone), a modest artisan.

TWO WOMEN

1961

As was the case with Roberto Rossellini, who harked back to remembrance of things past with his war-set *General della Rovere* in 1959, Vittorio De Sica, an equally distinguished Italian director in the early neo-realist style, returned to the kind of material he had handled in his great *Shoe Shine*** and *The Bicycle Thief* * with his hauntingly similar *Two Women (La Ciociara)* in 1961. The coincidence of these top directors turning back to the end of World War II for reflections upon the Italian people in that period of grim transition and personal trial was a phenomenon that takes on an interesting significance when viewed in the full perspective of those years.

De Sica, advanced successfully after *The Bicycle Thief*, directing such notable achievements as *Miracle in Milan*, *Umberto D*, ** the brightly comedic *The Gold of Naples* and the less impressive drama *The Roof*. At the same time he was

compelled to earn his living as an actor in a long string of commonplace films, Italian, American, and British, the nadir arriving in a catastrophe called *The Millionairess* starring Sophia Loren. But *Two Women*, which Cesare Zavattini adapted for him from a novel by Alberto Moravia, signaled the revival of the De Sica of old.

It was the story of a Roman mother and her twelve-year-old daughter who sought refuge in the rural region of Fondi north of Naples from the bombings in Rome. But this was shown against the teeming background of local peasants and other refugees who were caught in the middle of the conflict between foreign forces waging their struggle for power on the peninsula of Italy.

It was not a flattering picture of those people. They were not brave and self-sacrificial, as the urban underground fighters were made to appear in Rossellini's *Open City*. They were selfish, petty, cynical, disgusted, and disillusioned by the dislocations and discomforts that the greed and ambitions of their Fascist leaders had brought upon them. They were much more concerned with the privations and the curtailments of their business deals compelled by their helpless state of limbo than they were in lending a hand to scouts for the Allied liberating forces that once or twice showed up in their midst. And they paid no heed whatsoever to the pious philosophy of endurance and self-examination that a gentle young student attempted to preach to them.

Yet De Sica and Zavattini, fetching their precept from Moravia, were not too harshly critical or unsympathetic toward these unfortunate folks. As in *Shoe Shine* and *The Bicycle Thief*, they presented these villagers as genuine victims of circumstances. And the ultimate demand upon the mother to bring herself to adjust to the hideously traumatic experience of seeing her daughter raped—and being raped herself—by a gaggle of wild Moroccan soldiers when the Allied liberation was at hand made for a haunting symbolization of the shock and bewilderment of a peasant people forced to accept the reality of a world turned upside down.

The approach of De Sica to the story was in his old familiar neo-realist style. The country and the people, caught by his camera's lucid eye, were denuded of all adornment and cloying sentiment. The shambles of a Roman slum in the wake of an air raid, the hard and dusty desiccation of the

Having fled to the country to avoid the bombings, Cesira and her daughter, Rosetta (Eleanora Brown), are caught on an open road by a strafing Nazi plane.

rolling mountains in the region of Euphemia, the rusticity of peasant houses, the crudeness of an outdoor family feast to celebrate a wedding anniversary were all indisputably realistic. The fraud of cinematic illusion was totally removed. And so, too, was any misgiving that the actors were not native to the scene. Even though Sophia Loren, who had in the past few years appeared in a run of Hollywood movies, was unglamorously cast in the role of the peasant-born mother, prey to wild anxieties and fears, she was overwhelmingly authentic, without the slightest taint of "Hollywood." Her aloof endurance of testy tirades against Mussolini by passengers on the train taking her and her daughter to the country, her contempt for the rural police who were more interested in her voluptuous body than in nabbing a couple of deserters at a farm, her happy and lusty relaxation at the outdoor family feast were played with a fine edge of sarcasm and humor that bespoke her gritty femininity. And later her cautious intimations of a gnawing hunger for food and sex, especially food for her daughter, whose welfare was uppermost in her mind, were conveyed with intensity and taste.

But Miss Loren's finest acting—and that which made her playing of this role what I, at least, consider the high-water mark of her career—came in the later phases of the picture when the drama was brought down to the singular confrontation of this woman with the forces of irony and fate. The war was presumably over—for these people, at least—and they were stirred to euphoric excitement by American troops and tanks coming along the road. Then suddenly all was confusion as an enemy plane swept overhead and bombed the convoy, ominously warning that all wasn't over yet. In the ensuing mood of uncertainty, the mother and daughter retreated to a bomb-damaged church, thinking it a suitable sanctuary, and prepared to settle down for the night. Their minds were still shaken by the concussion of that bombing attack and the later sight of a passing Jeep-load of Moroccan soldiers howling and gesturing at them.

In the church the child prayed at the shattered altar before settling down to sleep and the mother took up a silent vigil to rest and watch over her. Then out of the gathering darkness, shadows appeared along the floor, moving soundlessly from

147

Eleanora, Cesira and a shy, socialistic intellectual, Michele (Jean-Paul Belmondo), stand by a distraught relative as they witness damage done by retreating Nazis.

Having sought sanctuary in a bombed-out church, Cesira and Eleanora are suddenly set upon by a squad of rape-bent Moroccan "liberators."

Ravished and left in shock by their attackers, Cesira and her daughter start back to join a world turned upside down.

behind the mother, closing in on her. Suddenly, with yells and lecherous laughter, the Moroccans swept into the church and went after the mother and the daughter bent upon ravishing them. There was a momentary scene of frantic struggle. Both were thrown upon the floor and the mother, screaming and fighting, had her legs roughly pulled apart by a half-dozen hands in hideous close-up as a rapist began the act.

The scene held for only a second before being sharply cut. For a long pause emptiness and silence prevailed on the screen. Then the image reappeared and the camera, from a distance, moved in on the mother, disheveled and unconscious, on the floor with the child nearby. Silently and sadly, the camera held on the awful scene. Slowly the mother regained consciousness. Looking about her, she saw the child, whom she tenderly caressed. With a tatter of torn garment, she swabbed her daughter's blood-stained thighs, giving a heart-tearing image of a mother's anguish over the rape of her child. But, of course, in the language of symbolization, which is the eloquence of art, it was more than the rape of two individuals that we were pondering. It was the tragic violation of Italy.

De Sica's conclusion of the picture also said more than it spoke, more than the devastation of the mother and the blank confusion of the child. Stumbling away from the church and toward a small town, the two were picked up by a cheerful fellow in a truck who, unaware of their benumbing experience, began singing and making jokes. Slowly, to the mother's silent misery, the child began to respond, coming out of her empty-eyed stupor and feebly attempting to join the song. Later, after the mother and daughter had found lodgings and gone to bed, the mother awoke and, astonished, saw that the youngster wasn't there. Trembling with apprehension, she ran outside calling for her, racing around the empty barnyard, not knowing what to expect. After a spell of terrible waiting, she saw the truck and the young driver pull up, and out of the cab hopped the daughter. She had been to a dance with the lad.

At first, the mother, seized with fury, abused and chastised the girl. But as her anger subsided, she plainly realized that this was the way things would be, that the girl had become a young woman. She was no longer the pure and innocent child the mother had tried so hard to protect, any more than Italy, ravished by war and alien armies, would be the Italy of old. The last scene was of the mother cradling the girl in her arms and lovingly murmuring, "Sleep, sleep," an ancient invitation to escape, while through the window was seen a simple farm cart, its tongue tilted skyward, which had the profile of a field-artillery piece.

In this picture De Sica used a mother and daughter to symbolize the solidarity of the smallest family unit against the cruelty of an indifferent world just as he used a father and son for the same purpose in *The Bicycle Thief.*

In addition to Miss Loren's fine performance, Eleanora Brown was lovely as the child, Raf Valone was strong as a Roman neighbor, Jean-Paul Belmondo was surprisingly sensitive as the meek, philosophical student, and many others were authentic as peasants, Fascisti, refugees, and an assortment of Nazi stragglers.

This was the last creation of De Sica in a neo-realist style. After it? Well, I prefer to remember him for his three fine achievements in that style.

The novice nun, Viridiana (Silvia Pinal), come to pay a last visit to her uncle before taking her final vows, meditates on her disturbing situation in his house.

VIRIDIANA

1961

Luis Buñuel's *Viridiana* was the best of the dark and cynical films turned out over a period of four decades by this Spanish aristocrat. An exile from his native land, he made most of his films in Mexico. Yet, oddly enough, *Viridiana* was made by him in Spain at the height of the Franco era—a total paradox insofar as accommodation between art and politics was concerned, because this was by far the sharpest comment on social hypocrisy and the moral contradictions of the Roman Catholic Church of the several on the subject turned out by Buñuel in his stormy career. One might have thought *it*, of all his pictures, would have been the one most surely banned.

Why the censors who, first of all, read the script (and even suggested a few changes which pointed up its ironies, I have heard) acquiesced to its production and let it be shown as the official Spanish entry in the 1961 Cannes film festival, where it shared the top prize with Henri Colpi's *Une Aussi Longue Absence*, is a mystery still concealed in the recesses of somebody's bureaucratic mind. A less difficult mystery is the subsequent banning of the film in Spain. (The government official who had approved it originally was later fired.) All of which only supports it as one of the most fascinating productions of its time and one that, as social criticism, comes very close to being unique.

For the statement of *Viridiana* was candid and undisguised, much stronger, I would say, than had ever been dared in a film on a similar theme. The moral standards of society and the Church were ridiculously antediluvian and contrary to the benefit of mankind, the film subtly suggested. The code of honor and proper behavior that was supposedly observed by gentlemen was as silly and hypocritical as the notion that Christian charity was desirable and appreciated by those it was aimed to aid. A society burdened with the tenets of these antique institutions was doomed to disorder and disillusion, this picture mercilessly proclaimed.

Yet it wasn't a grim and totally barren exposition—on the surface, at least. Buñuel was a master of "black humor," and there was plenty of that in his film. There were also some tempting suggestions of the perversities of sex and a beautiful young actress in Silvia Pinal to display the ironies in handsome style.

She appeared at the outset as a young and painfully innocent novice nun dispatched by her Mother Superior to pay a presumably comforting visit to a widowed uncle. He had asked to see her before she was to be secluded in the convent by her final vows. Shy and apparently ignorant of the crudities of nature and of men, the naive young woman was shocked and revolted by the aspects of life on her uncle's farm—the nuzzling of the pigs at one another, the bulging udders of the cows, the immodesty of the horses in openly relieving themselves. And especially was she terrified and outraged when her uncle, proclaiming her to be a duplicate of his wife, tried to seduce her and then to rape her after plying her with wine. This horrifying experience sent her rushing back to the convent in shame.

Then came word that her uncle, mortified by his violation of the code of gentlemen, had hung himself with a jump rope and had made her an heir to the farm. So, full of archaic notions about atonement and charity, she decided to give up holy orders and return to the farm which, in memory of her uncle, she would turn into a refuge for the poor and the maimed. Thither, too, came her cousin, her uncle's illegitimate son, who turned out to be a greedy, lustful, and openly cynical young man, quite a different breed of cat from his father who, at least, tried to *act* a gentleman.

The denouement came when the riffraff who had been assembled to be the beneficiaries of Viridiana's charity chose a time when she and her cousin were away on a visit to town to break into the wine cellar and have themselves a titanic carouse. In indulging themselves thusly they mocked their benefactress, the pompous manners of Spanish grandees, and the sanctity of God. In the classic scene from the pictures, Buñuel sat these drunken ingrates down at a long refectory table in an irreverent parody of Da Vinci's painting "The Last Supper," shouting and spewing their hate to a thundering sound-track accompaniment of Handel's "Hallelujah Chorus."

When Viridiana returned and saw the dissolute spectacle, she threw the riffraff out. The end had the sadly disillusioned and disgusted young woman settling down to life on the farm with her cousin and the maid he took as his mistress, listening

Conversely, the uncle, Don Jaime (Fernando Rey), is moved to erotic memories and thoughts of his dead wife by the young woman's presence.

Viridiana, conscience-smitten by the suicide of her uncle, abandons her career as a nun and returns to the farm to run it as a religious hostel.

to rock-and-roll music on the radio and playing cards.

Thematically the picture was divided into two parts. The first was a semi-humorous mockery of the embarrassment between the uncle and the girl as he made his pseudo-chivalrous efforts to get her into bed. The second was the darkly devastating disclosure of the way intended charity may be scorned by its purported beneficiaries. In both instances, the reflection was upon the grossness of the natures of humankind who do not conform to the patterns that society and the Church have set for them.

Though played in deadpan fashion, it was downright amusing to watch the formality of the uncle as he tried to entice the inhibited girl, whether urging her to take the nipples of the cow's udder in her hands and "squeeze hard," or playing upon the phallic symbolism of the handles of the innocent jump rope, or running his

hands tentatively along her body when begging her to don his dead wife's wedding clothes. It was both amusing and pathetic to see him taking the wife's garments from a trunk, wrapping a tiny corset around his middle, and fondling her shoes with a fetishist's lust. Latent in this exhibition was a crude sexual abnormality, a suggestion of transvestitism, which Buñuel did not pursue. His aberrant sexuality was oddly balanced by a sequence in which the sleep-walking girl emptied a wastebasket into a fireplace then shoveled the ashes into her uncle's bed, which, intended or not as symbolism, was a funny and naughty practical joke. Throughout this first part of the picture, it appeared that Mr. Buñuel was having a romp.

But the tone of the second part was different. It was crafty, vicious, and macabre as the rabble of derelicts descended, virtually possessing the farm, cheating and abusing one another, brutalizing and ostracizing a poor beggar who had a foul

One of the derelict simpletons she takes in garbs himself in the aunt's bridal clothes and mocks the manners of the better born.

A climax of disillusion for Viridiana is reached when her "guests," taking advantage of her absence, have an orgy and mimic the solemnity of Da Vinci's famous painting of "The Last Supper."

disease, and finally plunging into that wild carouse which overwhelmed with its gross rascality the lingering impulse of the girl toward brotherly love. The power Mr. Buñuel concentrated in that cataclysmic episode fired the film to a peak of terrible passion from which it could only decline into dull despair. The face of Miss Pinal at the fade-out was that of a poor, trusting girl who *had* been raped.

Her performance throughout was otherwordly, Goody Two-Shoes on a lust-drenched Spanish farm, yet never so overly pious as to be saccharine and ludicrous. She was able to make one sense precisely the sad delusions of a brainwashed girl. And Fernando Rey made the uncle a stiffly ponderous and pathetic dolt, a man who was hiding earthly passions and perversities behind a saintly façade. Indeed, the juxtaposition of his corruption against the almost cliché purity of the girl seemed to carry the implication that, in the warped world of Spain, at least, it was the male who played the serpent and committed the original sin on Eve.

If that moral seemed somewhat old-fashioned, it was not the only trace of *déjà vu.* Mr. Buñuel was given to a certain antique, almost silent-movie style, as well as a tendency to borrow or repeat images from his previous films. The hints at tranvestitism were very much like a candid display of a similar tendency in the title character of his *Adventures of Robinson Crusoe* (which, considering the substance of the original story, may surprise those unfamiliar with that film). Foot fetishism had also popped up in his previous works. And the parody of "The Last Supper" was surprisingly similar to a scene in his 1930 film, *L'Age d'Or,* wherein he frankly showed Christ as a participant in an orgy organized by the Marquis de Sade.

Even so, this intense *Viridiana* was a powerful dramatic film, as free with its scorn for human frailty as it was with its blistering ironies.

The Tyrone family start the "long day" of their "journey" on the lawn of their New London summer home. Here are younger son, Edmund (Dean Stockwell), the mother Mary (Katharine Hepburn) and the father James (Ralph Richardson).

LONG DAY'S JOURNEY INTO NIGHT

1962

The anguish and downright horror that were packed into Sidney Lumet's film of Eugene O'Neill's most masterful stage play, *Long Day's Journey Into Night*, may not have come through on first viewing as readily as they do today, now that audiences have become more accustomed to long-running movies which emphasize dialogue over action. The almost three-hour-long progression of this conspicuously isolated film which trapped four characters in one location and flagellated them through one day and night was a frankly audacious departure from the usual format of commercial cinema. As a consequence it somewhat taxed the tolerance of many of its initial viewers.

And to a certain degree it *was* fatiguing in its long, drawn-out conversational bouts among the four antagonists in its focal family. There was redundancy in their pounding away at one another with brutal and relentless verbal blows, ever mounting to higher decibel levels. The emotional thumb-screws were ground tighter and tighter until audiences were often past the threshold of enduring further pain. Some critics were of the opinion that it was too agonizing to bear.

But those initial negative reactions were usually flash responses to a kind of drama that was intellectually violent without a single physical blow being struck. They betrayed a not uncommon resistance of the impatient to more recondite works of art. And perhaps they were even valuable conditioning for some of the same of the heavier kinds of mental strain we have been exposed to by certain more recent films.

Clouds of family discord and quarreling begin to form as the same three gather later around a table in the living-room.

Sure, there is ground on which to base a critical challenge to this meticulously faithful screen rendering of *Long Day's Journey Into Night*. It was too faithfully a photographed facsimile of the original play. That old complaint was easily countered by the inherent power that came forth. Too many motion picture renderings of O'Neill's plays have lost strength and thrust because their makers did indeed try to "open them up"—they endeavored to move and disturb them out of their original sets in which the integrity of their substance was appropriately contained. That is what Mr. Lumet and his producer, Ely Landau, distinctly eschewed to do with this capstone achievement of O'Neill's work.

Recognizing the intense concentration of this introverted play about an American theatrical family—a father, mother, and two sons—passing a summer vacation in their seashore house around 1921, he even avoided the convention of having a screenplay prepared. He proceeded to make the picture directly from the original O'Neill text. The intensity of the drama flowed from the characters and the corridors of their minds. The energy and violence of their actions were in their moods and attitudes.

Some critics seemed to think it was "old-fashioned"—that it projected a style that was out of theatrical vogue and was reminiscent of some of the chest-heaving dramas of silent films. That objection, to the extent that it is arguable on purely aesthetic grounds, was easily rebutted by the simple observation that it conveyed the aesthetic of

another age. By its lighting and camera movement, under Boris Kaufman's superior command, it was as modern in style as any movie about the period in which it was set.

There were also some gripes about the casting. Since the leading male character was supposed to be a famous American matinee idol in the three or four decades before and after the century's turn—indeed, he was tacitly acknowledged as the playwright's own father, James O'Neill, and the play, as a consequence, as about his own family—it was protested that the role should have gone to an American. Fredric March, who was so cast in the original stage production, seemed at the time more appropriate than the brilliant English actor Ralph Richardson. Again a matter of aesthetics. Mr. Richardson's performance was superb, catching all the celebrated vanity, cruelty, and meanness of the man. Furthermore, the casting was consistent. James O'Neill was of Irish birth and he had acquired his skill as an actor with English companies in the United States.

The choice of Katharine Hepburn to play Mary, the mother around whom the tension revolved, was a piece of expedient casting. Miss Hepburn was not ideal physically for this role of a middle-aged woman who had lost her way, was cracking up under strong emotional pressures, and had secretly taken to drugs. She performed with too much vitality, she was limber and carried herself with grace, tears welled in her eyes too familiarly, and her face still lit up and sparkled when she smiled. I suppose Mr. Lumet and

Mr. Landau picked her because of the erratic, bravura performance she had given as a demented eccentric in *Suddenly Last Summer,* just a couple of years before. Even so, Miss Hepburn did manage to stand her ground in the free-for-all, and she came through with heartbreaking pathos in the long nightmare scene at the end.

Jason Robards was absolutely brilliant as the older son, Jamie, as he had been in the original American stage production. Dean Stockwell worked hard to be assertive and fight back as Edmund, the younger son. This role was acknowledged to be reflective of the young Eugene O'Neill, which was the name that the playwright had his actors mention from time to time as a prematurely deceased son of the Tyrones.

The film opened on a foggy summer morning. James and Mary were having after-breakfast coffee on the front porch of their New London, Conn., home, looking out toward Long Island Sound. He was grumbling about the foghorn blowing all night and she about his snoring—annoyances they said kept them awake. They remarked they had been thirty-five years married. Inability to sleep, the longevity of their bond, and some concern about their sons—typical husband-wife anxieties—seemed to be all that was bothering them.

But as they moved on to their day's activities, a buildup of bickering and quarreling began. James rebuked Edmund for wasting his life as an occasional reporter for the local newspaper, after a stint at sea. The older brother showed anxiety about the young man's health and indicated the fear that his sibling had "consumption," an illness the doctor was to diagnose that day.

Thus, like a drab continuation of family quarreling that had been going on all summer or since anyone could remember, they proceeded into a round of gripes and self-revelations. James magniloquently complained that Edmund was a sluggard; Edmund charged his father with being cheap; Mary complained that she was lonely; son Jamie, when he came downstairs, revealed that he distrusted his father as much as Edmund did. A whole range of dark recriminations, as noxious and threatening in their way as the possible infection of Edmund and the tacit addiction of Mary to morphine, were spilled out and endlessly wrangled. To Mary, the place had never been a home. "For me it's always been as lonely as a dirty room in a one-night-stand hotel," she cried out at one angry juncture. James heatedly charged his sons with a grave error in "denying" the Roman Catholic Church. Mary likewise blamed her unhappiness on having married an actor and gone

Edmund and his older brother, Jamie (Jason Robards), discuss their own problems, the autocratic ways of their actor-father and the secret addictions of their mother.

157

Mary throws herself on the floor in a dramatic gesture as her husband and two sons regard her skeptically but anxiously.

away with him, abandoning the serenity she had known in the convent where she had set her heart on being either a concert pianist or a nun.

"That's what makes it so hard for all of us: We can't forget," she moaned.

Notable in their conversations were the varying theatrical styles in which they addressed one another or resorted to rhetorical asides. "Ingratitude, the vilest weed that grows," James expostulated to Edmund. "All right, Papa," Edmund wearily replied, "I could see that line coming."

And all through the day this bickering, this verbal flagellation, continued and mounted: Mary, the family charged, was brutal to them for not trying to kick the drugs; James was stingy (it was his stinginess that kept him from getting a decent doctor to attend Mary when Edmund arrived, thus forcing her to go to morphine to kill the pain); James blamed his success (and misfortune) on his having got himself bogged down in "that play" (*The Count of Monte Cristo*) which prevented him from fulfilling his great promise as an actor. Everyone had some gripe against the others and some excuse for his or her inadequacies. The whole web of private resentments became a net in which they all were entwined.

From the fairly mild quarreling at the outset, the anger and heat accumulated, the crescendo of noise and recrimination rose, until the whole family was locked in a dark knot of sado-masochistic abuse. A containable round of family quarreling became more and more a deadly war, emotional violence run riot carried the combat into the realms of nightmare horror. Demons seemed to populate the dark rooms, rushing and ranting in the night. Some hideous act of vengeance seemed poised balefully to plunge. What began as a drama of family discord was a horror story toward the end. Menace seemed to fill the Tyrones' residence like the pending doom of *King Lear*.

It was this powerful buildup of violence, not in physical action but in words, and this increasing of the pressure of menace, of foreboding tragedy, that made the film hold the perceptive. What was more, the characters, for all their brutality, elicited deep sympathy. Their sudden transitions from thrashing to explosions of love and need, clasping one another with frank affection almost in the midst of wild abuse, evoked a piercing realization that, for all their self-pitying abuse, they hung with the death grips of drowning persons upon the feeble support of themselves.

The terrifying climax of this battle came in the final scene, with the two drunken sons confronted by their outraged father in the living room late at night—ranting until one might have reckoned they would soon be clawing at throats. Then they were joined by the mother, a veritable image of the sleep-walking Lady Macbeth, far gone in her drug intoxication but not so far as to be unable to recall in a soliloquy of girlhood reminiscence her happy convent life in France. "Then I came home," she concluded, in a tone of quiet ecstasy, which Miss Hepburn managed superbly, "and fell in love with James Tyrone." She was as breathless as a schoolgirl, with the finite summation, "And I was happy . . . for a time."

With that heartbreaking whisper of nostalgia and despair, the gloomy light in the living room faded and the picture came to an end. Mercifully, the shroud was brought together upon the mournful bier of the Tyrones. And with that was artfully concluded one of the few great American family films. There is strong illumination and wisdom to be found in *Long Day's Journey Into Night.*

In the harrowing climactic phase of the film, Mary descends the stairs to the living-room to face the violent charges and tenders of affection of her family.

The lustful Sicilian baron, Ferdinando (Marcello Mastroianni) and his youthful inamorata, Angela (Stefania Sandrelli), are disturbed during a steamy tryst while on a family picnic at the beach.

DIVORCE, ITALIAN STYLE

1962

The best and most memorable in a long list of Italian screen comedies, was in my opinion, Pietro Germi's delicious, devastating *Divorce, Italian Style*, in which Marcello Mastroianni played the role of a languid but lustful Sicilian baron who plotted to trick his unendurable wife into a compromising situation with an old lover so he could honorably do away with her and thus be free to marry his cousin, a tantalizing nymphet. More than an exceptional comedy of manners, a type of film Italians loved, it was a surprisingly powerful polemic against the antique Italian law which forbade divorce under any circumstances but graciously allowed a husband (or a wife) to defend personal and family honor by slaying a wayward spouse. The penalty for such an avengement was a brief token term in jail.

At the time the film was released in Italy, this strange law was solemnly respected, especially in Sicily where, as Luigi Barzini put it, "the people have a subtle appreciation of such problems." Indeed, explained Signore Barzini, "they know that to kill in defense of one's honor is a man's supreme duty, higher than any other, more binding than mere man-made laws." Such a device for marital sunderance was wryly known as "divorce, Italian style."

Although recourse to this solution had become infrequent through the years, it was still found a shocking incongruity when Germi's film brought it to mind. Pro-divorce advocates were emboldened to step up their challenge to the Catholic Church, which had been the intractable supporter of the civil law against divorce, and within eight years their agitation brought about legislated change. A liberalized law was voted and endorsed by the Italian majority. Thus a truly revolutionary outcome was greatly influenced by a film.

There is no doubt that the Italians loved *Divorce, Italian Style* primarily because they could recognize so clearly themselves and their natures in it. They could see their rich natural foibles, common to all but, of course, pronounced in the Sicilians, their lush pomposities, their inveterate propensities to intrigue, their velvet exercises of conceit, their nimble devices of deception in its skillfully enacted caricatures. Or, if they couldn't recognize their own shortcomings, they could certainly see those of their friends! The handsome and dandified baron with his bland air of *noblesse oblige*, slopping about the shabby palace of his family in a real Sicilian town or strolling with a kind of regal ennui through the redolent streets, was the model of the splendid *maccherone*, which every male Italian secretly felt himself to be. His pretty but hopelessly bourgeois and sexually monotonous wife, running to fat in prominent places and with the shadow of a moustache across her lips, was the dutiful spouse of every husband who was getting a little ahead and had the old itch for something different as he accumulated years. Likewise, the baron's old father, slyly pinching the fanny of the maid and holing up in the palace's single bathroom to peek at the nymphet across the way; the women of the house in their dark dresses and with their rituals of patiently serving their childlike men; the swaggering lawyer with his bold, bombastic rhetoric—all were charmingly consistent with the intimate, annoying, engaging characteristics of—well, at least, the Sicilians.

The funniest aspect of the baron was his concentration upon himself, his way of scanning all around him as the oyster to gratify his tastes. In church, with his wife and mother flanking him proprietorially as the priest thundered probity at them, interlaced with local politics, the baron's eyes drifted slowly in the direction of his sixteen-year-old cousin along the pew to consume her with a look of adoration and unmistakable lust. In bed with his wife, his thoughts were only of the so-near, yet-so-far nymphet despite the beseeching advances of his seriously sex-starved spouse. A blissful union with his cousin was the baron's sole aim in life.

To achieve this aim, he realized (with the inducement of a deftly written script and the mischievous direction of Mr. Germi) he had to get rid of his wife; and since divorce was out of the question, he had to find some other way. In his fertile imagination, he saw himself covertly pushing her into a boiling cauldron containing the family wash or abandoning her to sink in quicksand while on an outing at the beach. His thoughts were as devilishly inventive as those of Chaplin's

Ferdinando parades his seductively garbed wife, Rosalia (Daniella Rocca) through the streets, hoping to attract a possible lover for her so he may have cause to do away with her in defense of his honor.

Verdoux. Then the ideal way came to him while attending the local trial of a pitifully unattractive woman accused of murdering her alleged fiancé, whom she claimed to have caught in an unfaithful act. Her lawyer magnificently proposed that she had a right to defend her honor under Section 585 of the Penal Code and that she should be punished with nothing more than a light jail sentence. The judge and the populace unanimously agreed.

To give some revealing insights into the Italian mind, Mr. Germi and his writers had the baron imagine a couple of ruses by which to lure a likely lover into an involvement with his wife. They had him buy her a new dress which effectively showed off her shapely hips and parade her ostentatiously before the all-male audience outside the town's main café. All this did was serve as an indulgence of the onlookers' slumberous fantasies. Next they had him consider the possibility of a fervent tenor whom he and his wife admired at a concert one evening, but that thought was nipped in the bud when his wife gigglingly whispered a shocking rumor about the tenor in his ear.

Then a surprising thing happened after the bar-

Suspecting Rosalia has found a lover, Ferdinando slides back into their previously vacated bed to test her present desire for him.

on discovered his wife mooning over a packet of old love letters in the attic one night. The next day he encountered the author of those letters, who had come to town to restore some paintings in the church. The baron put one and one together, and that night, feigning penitence, crept back into the connubial bed and found his wife significantly unconcerned. Aha! This confirmed his suspicions! He forthwith began to set the trap. Graciously he invited the old suitor to his palace to consider restoring some paintings. Tactfully he managed to leave him alone frequently with his wife. Secretly he hid a tape recorder to overhear whatever they might say, and, while they were playing the piano, he drilled holes in the wall so he could spy on them. Anticipating a showdown, he hid revolvers in likely places where he could get at them in a blaze of obligatory fury when they would be needed, and he even wrote anonymous letters to himself presumably from indignant citizens warning him that horns were being put on his head. But no occasion came for him to

use them. The wife and her old suitor were discreet. One might even have said they were ingenious. All they did was bill and coo, which struck the baron as totally incongruous. The old suitor had a wife and three kids.

In the midst of this campaign of entrapment, Mr. Germi introduced an episode which was somewhat extraneous to the purpose but was wonderfully comical. He had Fellini's *La Dolce Vita* * open in the town and create a wave of anticipation and mass aphrodisia. Though the faces of the audience viewing the picture were ironically deadpan, the effect seemed to be to arouse the townsfolk to a peak of sensitivity to the scandal that they sensed was happening in their own community.

Thereafter the continuity of events was rapid and direct. Indignation rose against the baron when a local physician spread the inflammatory word that despite the fact that he was definitely being made *cornutu* —a cuckold—he remained impassive. At the same time, the minor misfortune of a mix-up of letters sent from the nymphet, who was locked in a convent, to the baron and to her parents revealed to the latter the extent of the romance, and the father became so aroused that, before *he* could defend *his* family honor, he died of a heart attack. That gave Mr. Germi opportunity to stage an eloquent Sicilian funeral. Passions in the community had by this time become hysterical, and the baron might have shot without beholding his wife actually in her lover's arms. The only trouble was that she and the rascal had mysteriously disappeared.

When the baron finally got information as to their whereabouts (from the local Mafia boss), he went after them prepared for slaughter. But what was his dismay and chagrin to find them not *in flagrante delicto* but in a peaceful setting overlooking the sea, the wife posing demurely in a white dress while the old suitor painted her portrait. Foiled and technically discouraged, the baron was about to turn away when a shot rang out and the painter dumbfoundingly dropped dead. The latter's wife appeared from hiding, holding the smoking gun. The baron needed no further prodding. He raced after his frightened wife and shot her dead.

Such was the climax of the story but not the tag line, by any means. For that, Mr. Germi invented a most aptly ironic twist. The trial was held. The lawyer expounded in his most magniloquent style. The baron was duly applauded. He was sentenced to serve three years in jail—which was reduced to eighteen months for good behavior—and he came home to marry his nymphet. But a final flash of them luxuriating aboard a sailboat on their evident honeymoon caught him blandly unaware that while he was holding her in a loving embrace a handsome young sailor was caressing her invitingly stretched out feet!

This film from Mr. Germi, who had heretofore been known for bitingly realistic dramas that were concerned in the main with the social and moral dilemmas of postwar Italy, was without any question the capstone of his long career and, in the genre of satire, one of the finest ever made. The accuracy and flavor of the Sicilian atmosphere matched the uncanny precision of the characters. The pace and momentum were exciting, the music set a tone of parody, and the comic invention was cunning without being forced. One example: the close-up image of the baron's drill breaking through the wall into the room in which the wife and her old suitor were flirting innocently tickled the mind with dual suggestions—first, of the baron's suspicious zeal and, second, a bit more esoteric, of envisioning a hoped-for phallic thrust.

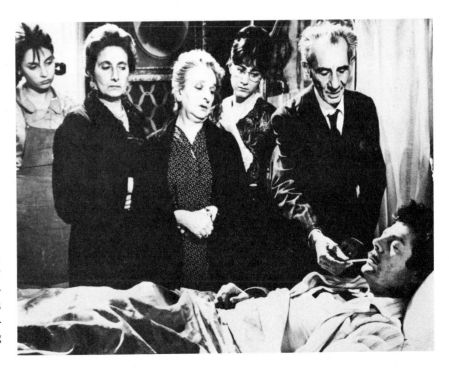

With elaborate histrionic embroidery, Ferdinando feigns illness from anxiety about his wife, while his mother (Bianca Castagnetta), flanked by other ladies of the family, watch him under the ministrations of the doctor with varying emotions.

Although we all knew that Mastroianni was skilled at comedy and farce, having seen him not only in *La Dolce Vita* but also in *Too Bad She's Bad* and *Big Deal on Madonna Street*, it was surprising to find that he could manage such exquisitely fine embroidery in developing the baron from a scoundrel into a counterpart of a naughty boy. As did Chaplin, he turned a willful Bluebeard into a charmingly ingenious sport. In support of him, Daniela Rocca did a subtle, amusing parody as the wife; Leopoldo Trieste was uproarious as the old suitor nimbly walking on eggs; Pietro Tordi was fustian as the lawyer; Odoardo Spadaro made the baron's father a finely modulated burlesque of every old Italian fanny-picher; and Stefania Sandrelli was torrid as the nymphet.

Though one might think this film would be dated by events that have occurred since its release, it stands as such a brilliant piece of satire that it repays seeing again and again.

Free of his wife and embarked at last on a honeymoon with Angela, the happy baron is unaware that, even at that moment, the nymphet's seductive feet are being caressed by a handsome young crewman on the yacht.

Hud (Paul Newman), the arrogant, unscrupulous son of an aging Texas ranchman, shows a happier and more playful side of his nature at a cowtown jamboree.

HUD

1963

Those of us who recall with virtual reverence the profound impression that Martin Ritt's *Hud* made upon our minds and our emotions when it came out in 1963 are likely to find ourselves reacting even more strongly when we see it again today in the light of all that has since happened, especially the shock of Watergate. For here in this finely honed drama of a bitter conflict between a father and his son over the matter of moral scruples and respect for the law was thrashed out the philosophical issue that has racked our people for the past decade and which is probably more crucial to our continuance as a substantial nation than petroleum or the nuclear bomb.

That issue was key to the contention between an aging Texas cattleman, played brilliantly by Melvyn Douglas, and his arrogant, unscrupulous son, played equally well by Paul Newman, over the question of the course of action they should follow when they suspected that their fine herd of cattle was infected with foot-and-mouth disease. The son was all for selling the cattle—"ship the whole herd out"—before the vet could report the

situation to government agents who would probably condemn the entire stock. His attitude was "this whole country's run on epidemics—crooked TV shows, people out to do other people," so why shouldn't they get theirs. "You gonna let them shoot your cattle out from under you because of some schoolbook disease?" howled the disgusted Hud. But the old man was for doing precisely what the law required and abiding by the agency's decision. He wouldn't cheat someone by surreptitiously selling them possibly infected cattle. His reply to his son's expostulation was short and simple. "You're an unprincipled man, Hud."

That wasn't the only testimony to Hud's self-serving nature exposed by Mr. Ritt and Mr. Newman in the fascinating course of the film. Working from a script which Irving Ravetch and Harriet Frank Jr. derived from a novel by Larry McMurty, they showed in many sly and striking ways how Hud himself was a carrier of a virulent modern disease—or perhaps we should say an old one which has become more invidious in our times—that of personal avarice and self-seeking, which is called "looking out for Number One."

Already in the opening sequence, they had shown us Hud's teenage nephew, Lon, going into a nearby tacky cowtown in the cold light of dawn

With his characteristic insolence and brashness, Hud attempts to take liberties with Alma (Patricia Neal), the wised-up housekeeper at the family ranch.

to fetch his carousing uncle back to the ranch to handle the crisis of the sick cow. And, significantly, Lon located him by his pink Cadillac parked outside a house in which Hud had been spending the night with another man's wife. It was a commonplace situation—almost a comical one, indeed, as Lon hustled the disheveled adulterer out of the house two jumps ahead of the returning husband and got him away in the car. But the incident had about it a certain air of ugly insolence that gave the beholder an idea as to the sort of trespasser Hud was.

Later, when he shot a couple of buzzards that were hovering around the sick cow and his father quietly remonstrated, "I don't like you doing that, Hud. The buzzards keep the country clean," his son snapped back in defiance and charged his father with being a fuddy-dud. Again the old man answered him flatly, "It's breaking the law."

That was the succinct summation of the difference between the two men. Hud didn't care if he ran counter to all the laws and the moral rules so long as he got what *he* wanted *and* he didn't get caught. His father believed in abiding by the law and by what he thought was right, adhering to the tradition of simple honesty in which he had been raised. And that was the difference to which the old man was quietly and ruefully resigned. He was heartsick with anxiety as to the influence that Hud might have on Lon. Obviously the boy was impressed by some of the more *honcho* aspects of Hud. He was torn between respect for his grandfather and what he saw were the things for which the older man stood, but he was also inclined to hero-worship the brazen and bashless younger man.

And why not? On many occasions, Hud had virility and charm. Once, when Lon got himself trampled in a chute while they were rounding up the cattle for testing, Hud leaped in and rescued him, rushed him home, and turned him over to Alma, a humane woman who kept house for the three. Again at a typical cowtown Kiwanis Club whoop-de-do, Hud was the most aggressive and amusing in the pig-catching match, to the obvious delight and admiration of the impressionable Lon. And again, when the two went together into town on a Saturday night and Hud konked the protesting boyfriend of a girl to whom Lon had taken a shine, the experience was thrilling for the nephew, especially when Hud said afterwards, with a note of happy reminiscence, "Your daddy and I used to take 'em all on on Saturday nights."

But a much different memory of Lon's father was silently nursed by the old man, and here was another tacit reason for his despising Hud. Evidently, as it finally came out, Hud had been responsible for the death of Lon's father in an automobile accident and the old man had never forgiven him. It was a hurt that deeply rankled. And one night, when Hud let it be known that he had seen a lawyer about taking the ranch away from his father—had mocked him by saying the lawyer's judgment was "when the old folks can't cut the mustard any more, you can take it away from them''—the old man lashed at him in a fury and a terrible verbal battle ensued. In the aftermath, Hud, drunk and disordered, stumbled out to the house where Alma slept and tried to rape her but was stopped by the horrified Lon.

That was the ugly situation in the household when the word came through that the cattle were indeed infected and would have to be destroyed. Hud was still full of the rage he had burst out with earlier: ''We're just gonna roll over an' play dead and let 'em shovel dirt on us!'' He wanted to forget the cattle and start drilling for oil, which was a reasonable enough suggestion, but the old man was set against that, too. ''There'll be no holes punched in this land while I'm here,'' he stubbornly replied.

The sequence of the slaughter which followed was the mortifying highlight of the film because it vividly pictorialized the passing of everything that was important to the old man—everything but his pride, his honor, and his integrity. With the silent and stoic dignity of a noble king who was forced to see his kingdom and authority taken over by an ironic fate, he grimly watched from the saddle of his anachronistic horse the huge bulldozers move onto his ranchland to scoop out a mammoth pit into which the cattle were driven, moving nervously and suspiciously; and there he sat while men in slickers and with rifles lined up around the pit and waited for his order, ''Start shootin','' which he dragged from the depths of his soul. The ensuing fusillade was deafening as the men pumped bullets into the herd and the beasts bleated fearfully on the sound track, which was more torturing than it would have been to see them die. When the shooting was finally ended and the last animal dead, there was a long and painful silence, except for the moaning of the wind. Then the men in slickers brought up disinfectants and began dumping them into the pit. Even though the slaughter was completed, the old man still sat there on his horse. Lon, who had been one of the shooters, alongside the laconic Hud, came up to his grandfather and said gently, ''It didn't take long.'' The old man's reply bespoke his heartbreak: ''It don't take long to kill things, not like it does to grow.''

Afterwards someone noticed that two old longhorn cattle, which the old man kept as mementos

Hud defies and taunts the standards of honor and integrity of his father (Melvyn Douglas) and threatens to have him legally declared incompetent.

of his early years in ranching, had not been destroyed along with the others as they should have been. But when the government official started toward them, the old man waved him away. ''I'll kill them two myself,'' he murmured, ''seeing as how I raised them . . . Lord, I've chased them longhorns for many a mile.''

Some critics at the time the picture came out—including myself, I must say—sought for some deep symbolic meaning in this awesome episode. I sensed it was meant to say something about the old man's acquiescence to the principle of wiping out infection for the common good. Now I feel we all were pushing too hard under the emotional shock of the scene. I think it simply symbolized the torment of the old man having to face the reality of the passing of the ideals and traditions for which he stood. His standard of honest dealing had been challenged by his son; his authority over his cattle had been assumed by the government. The past was dead around him. And though it may have been a mythical past, skillfully compounded of romance and sentiment, it was also compounded of the virtues in which we like to think most people believe. This is what moved the audience. I know now it's what moved me.

The rest of the film was wrap-up. Alma decided to leave, no longer able to abide the humiliating

In this most graphic and dramatic sequence, the infected cattle are herded into a pit and slaughtered by riflemen.

presence of Hud. Not that she found him unattractive. Earlier she might have succumbed to his animal allurement if he had treated her decently. But he didn't, and she saw through him. She had her standards, too. When Lon drove her to the bus station, she hugged him and parted silently. One got the melancholy feeling that she was bidding farewell to *her* dreams. Hers was a warm and generous character, as played perfectly by Patricia Neal, and her departure from the Bannon household left it only more loveless and forlorn.

Then a few nights later, Hud and Lon were driving home from town when they saw the old man lying alone in the road. When they reached him, he tried to tell them, "I wanted to take a look around the place and fell off my horse." Then he conceded he was dying: "I feel like throwing in the sponge." And that was it. After the funeral, Hud asked Lon to stay on with him, but the youngster was sad and disgusted, and to Hud's insensitive boast, "I guess you can say I helped him about as much as he helped me," Lon shot back the grief-charged rejoinder: "How'd

you help him, Hud—by taking the heart out of him?" The last scene was of Lon carrying his suitcase, walking away from the old house down the road and Hud driving alongside in his Cadillac, trying to discourage him. When he finally saw he couldn't, he shouted angrily, "You know something, Fantan, this world is so full of crap a man's gonna get into it sooner or later, whether he wants to or not!" And with that he swung away from his nephew, drove back to the house, and slammed the door behind him. To that extent, the old man had won.

Quite as much as a clash of philosophies between two strong-willed men, this film drew vivid pictures of the characters themselves. Amid the rough and raw surroundings of an old-fashioned cattle spread, standing alone and strangely barren in close proximity to a cheap Texas town, with its jukebox joints and burger lunchrooms, the old man was the picture of age, as remote from such alien accretions as he was from the vulgarity of his son. Only once did we see him bend slightly to the culture shock of the modern day. At a Saturday night movie with Lon, he was coaxed into lustily joining a sing-along chorus of "My Darling Clementine." To be sure, he was like an old pine wardrobe in which too-painful memories were locked away, but he had something of the kind of poetry in him that is in a piece of plain old furniture.

As for Hud, he was a compound of baffling complexities which we could only deduce and unravel from the glints of them that were shown. His cruel attitude toward women, for instance, yet his obvious voracity for them suggested that there had been some trauma that had scarred his psyche in his youth. And his evident ambivalence toward his father, for whom he seemed at moments to have a deep, overwhelming affection, was apparent when he recalled the old man handing him a five-cent candy bar and saying uncomfortably, "character's the only thing I can give you" when he went away to World War II. From that one could reconstruct an image of a lifetime of tensions between the two that might well have led to the warping and cynicism of Hud. And the fact that the two were striving to be surrogate fathers to Lon, who was guilelessly played by Brandon De Wilde as though he were the grown-up youngster out of *Shane*,* told us a lot about their secret, pathetic, unrecognized desires to give some extension to their egos. Yes, there were depths to these two men.

Other achievements that should be mentioned were the fine camerawork of James Wong Howe, which gave the whole scene and the characters a stark monochromatic reality; the musical score of Elmer Bernstein, which ran to poignant strains on the guitar; and the cold, disciplinary precision of Whit Bissell as the government agency man.

There have been some mocking put-downs of this picture, notably by Critics Dwight Macdonald and Pauline Kael, who found it conventionally moralistic and misleadingly mythical. Miss Kael's particular objection was that it came down too hard on Hud, whom she found "just about like everybody around here," which was an early defense for him put up by Lon. That was the tragic thing, precisely. Everybody was getting to be like Hud. Nixon's White House was full of characters infected with his disease. But that didn't make it acceptable or—shall we say?—pardonable.

Hud's young nephew, Lon (Brandon De Wilde), leaves the ranch, turning a deaf ear to the urging of his uncle to stay, after the death of his grandfather and the departure of Alma.

The highly imaginative and neurotic film director, Guido Anselmi (Marcello Mastroianni), fantasizes himself genuflecting humbly before his producer (Guido Alberti) and the latter's haughty girl friend (Annie Gorassini).

8½

1963

The ultimate self-indulgence that a filmmaker can enjoy is to create a motion picture entirely about himself. That is the peak of narcissism to which only the boldest or the brashest dare aspire. But fortunately Federico Fellini had the *hutzpah*, the story to tell, *and* the financial underpinning to support such a frank extravagance when he settled down after his classic *La Dolce Vita** had magnified his fame and made a film about—Federico Fellini. It was his equally classic *8½*.

To be sure, the focal figure in this surmise about a successful filmmaker who was experiencing a terrible time, deciding on a sequel, after directing a world-famous movie. He was pseudo-nonymously called Guido Anselmi. But so much about him betrayed the personality and problems of the model upon whom he was based that no one who knew Fellini—and their number was legion—had any doubt as to who Guido was.

In the first place, this fictitious fellow reflected precisely the strains that were known to have troubled Fellini after the huge success of *La Dolce Vita*. He was harassed by hordes of admirers and suffocating sychophants. He was wrestling with nervous anxiety as to what more he had to say in films. He was haunted by painful intimations that old age was creeping up on him, and he was torn in his dichotomous relations with women, especially his mistress and his wife. Deep down, he had gnawing guilt complexes involving his parents and the Roman Catholic Church. And he was constantly worrying about the producer who was putting up the money for his films. Finally, in one key scene, Fellini was so frank in proclaiming his identity that he had Guido wear a black fedora, Fellini's traditional headpiece when directing on his sets. No wonder, then, that all the people who held Fellini in great affection and esteem and had been tantalized by his refusal to reveal what his new film was about until it was ready for release were astonished and delighted by what they finally saw on the screen.

But this wasn't just a private diversion for Fellini's friends and acquaintances—a smashingly truthful confessional of an artist's problems in finding himself and making a film. Nor did one have to know the artist or anything about him to be absorbed, fascinated, amused, and even troubled by what he put on the screen. For *8½* was, above all, a unique psychoanalytical film which revealed the mind and the emotions of a vastly complicated egotist—a person full of self-doubts, confusions, and indecisions about future projects, not unlike those of millions of lesser people who slog and worry their way through a troubling world. The added excitement, in this instance, was the luster and glow of the ambiance—the

Guido sees himself enclosed amid a swarm of rich and dull bourgeoise in the steam-room of a health spa to which he has gone to prepare his next film.

glamorous realm of filmmaking, and the kinds of people within the industry. It was, after all, Fellini's domain; thus he was afforded the opportunity of being, by turns, witty, satiric, cruel, and often iconoclastic in depicting the cinematic world, of which he had full and first-hand knowledge.

Most inventive and audacious was the narrative and pictorial style that the director and his writers developed—the sharp departure from the straight, conventional ways that stories are generally told in movies. Fellini entirely eschewed the direct and naturalistic placing of narrative brick on brick to build up the structure of a story. He chose to convey the tensions and suspense of a drama that was happening in a man's mind, not in realistic confrontations with others but through inner controversies. He shifted back and forth from his experiences in the literal world to parallel remembrances, nightmares, and symbolistic imaginings that his problems and tensions provoked. It was a style reminiscent of that which Ingmar Bergman used in his likewise introspective *Wild Strawberries*. But there was a significant difference: in *his* film Fellini spent more time in the corridors of the mind of his director than in the depiction of the actual experiences he was having with other characters.

And yet the shifts and transitions from actuality to imaginings, or to fanciful stream-of-consciousness conceptions that complemented Guido's literal affairs, were so smooth that there was no hesitation in the pictorial flow. His mind drifted easily from the present to the past and on to lurid imaginings, as so often happens with people who have similarly troubled and fertile minds. It was a wonderfully fluid and expressive way to turn Guido inside out—to give us intense and startling insights into his whole psychic personality and the drama that was seething within him. It put the viewer inside his skin. But it was such a novel and unfamiliar method that it mystified many early viewers and challenged their own intellects.

The ambiguity surfaced at the outset. In the opening scene a man sat in a car in the middle of a paralyzing traffic jam, looking helplessly around at zombielike people in other stalled vehicles, bewildered and terror-stricken by claustrophobic immobility. What had we here—a stylized rendering of an actual urban traffic jam, a troubled

In another elaborate fantasy, Guido sees himself (in a Fellini hat) cracking a whip and ordering about all the women who have been involved in his life. Here he is domineering a massive prostitute, La Saraghina (Edra Gale), who was the center of an awesome boyhood experience.

concept of modern man's frustrations, a surreal symbol of dead souls crossing the River Styx? Any or all could have been considered, just as many meanings were derived from the opening scene of *La Dolce Vita* in which a helicopter flying over Rome conveyed a huge dangling statue of Christ with arms outstretched.

But Fellini didn't spare time for reflections. Suddenly his man, Guido, flew aloft into the sky and floated serenely for a moment above a beach, suspended from a kite, which was as abruptly pulled down by its manipulator, a man in a curious astronaut costume. And, in a gauzy dissolve, he was found reclining, somewhat bewildered, in a bed in a sterile room. It was soon revealed to be part of a fashionable health spa, where Guido was being attended by a studious physician and a pretty nurse. Thus did Fellini bring Guido out of an evident modernistic dream into the realm of consciousness. And thus did he tip the audience that peculiar transitions were ahead.

In a series of casual conversations it was conveyed that this autistic man was a famous film director, that he was here at this immaculate health resort recovering from a nervous breakdown induced by overwork on his last film. That he was played by Marcello Mastroianni, who had been to a certain degree the alter ego of Fellini in *La Dolce Vita*, was a significant coincidence.

Some cautious critics protested, upon its release that *8½* proceeded in a mélange of random episodes that had no particular pattern. Furthermore, its detractors claimed, the film had constructed no thematic synthesis. It was said that the emotional climax, wherein the director went virtually berserk at a huge press party on the towering rocket-launcher that was to be the climactic set of his next film, was preceded by no buildup. The objections were glib and unperceptive. For in ways distinctly subtle and incisive, Fellini assembled his picture to present the several main hangups of Guido in a pattern that identified them, established their significance and implications before going on to the next, then picked them up in contrapuntal arrangements which built a powerful pressure of suspense before exploding the whole disquietude of Guido in that wild catharsis of surrender at the end.

172

The first anxiety placed in focus (after that hint of claustrophobia at the start) was a violent and oppressively recurring dread of growing old, of reaching obsolescence. The images of the aged at the spa, the doddering old people, ugly and deformed, creeping about and taking the waters at a rococo marble fount presided over by a beautiful young woman (Claudia Cardinale) who was clearly Guido's fancy of nubile youth, revealed his dread. This image of aging, repeated in later episodes, especially one of Guido taking a steam bath among a group of hideous old men which included a Roman Catholic cardinal, was a haunting specter of the transience of life.

Next, in a mix of actuality, fancy, and grotesquely distorted memories, Guido equated his mistress, a busty, brainless bourgeois matron who came to the spa to join him, with his mother and subsequently his wife. From a sexual exercise with his mistress, during which he persuaded her to approach him like a whore, he fell into a sleep in which he visioned the funeral of his father, stretched out on his bier, then his mother taking Guido in her arms and kissing him passionately on his lips. Whereupon his mother quickly metamorphosed into his wife embracing him. This grew into the image of all the women who wanted to possess him—a fixation from which he could not escape.

The third anxiety of Guido was his problem with the Catholic Church and his guilt-ridden agitation in breaking away from it. Laced through his dreams and nightmare fantasies were successive indications of this: his strange recollections, in surreal visions, of a visit as a boy to a mammoth prostitute, his excitement and fear and that of his companions as they explored this daring quest for forbidden fruit; the horror of little Guido as he was chased by and hauled before the priests, with his mother silently watching, to be rebuked severely for trafficking with the Devil. Not that he was deterred from another visit to the prostitute.

But the source of his greatest anxiety was the pressure to prepare a script. Manifestations of this dread were the rebukes from his weazened scriptwriter, who abused and criticized him in his dreams; his grave apprehensions about confronting his impatient and demanding producer, symbolized by Guido salaaming in front of this arriv-

ing vulgarian and his expensive tart; his inability to select actors to fill roles in his upcoming film after numerous screen tests.

Then came the famous harem scene in which Guido visualized himself as a whip-lashing lion-tamer, driving all the women he had known to do his bidding, grandly subjugating them, and forcing one aging Parisian singer to go upstairs, screaming at her, "House rule! Old ones upstairs!" This was an amusing intimation of rebellion (in his mind) against his lifelong domination by women and his bent to get revenge for all the times that he as a child had been punished by being banished to "upstairs."

The climax came when the producer, impatient with Guido's foot-dragging, threw a big press party. It was on the set of the great outdoor rocket-launcher in celebration of the start of shooting. Guido, without even a finished script, was afflicted with a fearful hallucination in which, unprepared to meet the press, he crawled under a table, resolved to commit suicide, and in general did all that he could to flee this heavy and pressing responsibility. Meanwhile, his scriptwriter droned to the gathering how he respected Guido for not trying to fool anyone, for wishing to stick to his principles (without knowing precisely what those

In this final, fanciful muster of the people who have invaded Guido's life are his mistress, Carla (Sandra Milo), his father (Annibale Ninchi), a Cardinal (Tito Masini), an actress (Madeleine Lebeau) and an aging Paris music-hall dancer (Jacqueline Bonbon),

Guido makes a last wishful reconciliation with his often betrayed wife, Luisa (Anouk Aimee).

principles were!), for refusing to go commercial, for being an honest man.

Whereupon Guido, in a burst of riddance, assembled his associates, his wife, his mistress, and his actors on the set, all dressed in white. With himself, outfitted in a sort of ringmaster's uniform, he led the procession as they marched down the long flight of stairs to the accompaniment of a band. This was Guido's—and conversely Fellini's—way of confessing he had nothing to say, save that life was too snarled and complicated for him to try to tell people anything, and that the charge of an entertainment is simply to dazzle and entertain. And then, as the crowd of marchers thinned out and quietly disappeared, all that remained were a few old clowns tootling resolutely on their piccolos, led by the little boy Guido, dressed in a schoolboy's uniform. Then even the clowns evaporated and only the little boy was left, walking away from the camera in a contracting spotlight that dimmed and died.

There are those who think this ending was a cop-out, that it showed Fellini himself walking away from the artistic responsibility of solving the puzzle presented by his theme. But that's not what he did. He acknowledged that the minds of Guido and himself were too clouded by contradictions and confusions to allow them to break into the clear. He topped off the image constructed throughout the film of a mind so trapped by "recollections" that all it was able to do was seek escape. And that in itself was a valid estimation of the human dilemma—the completion on Fellini's part of a complicated theme.

More important, the creative mind was abundantly apparent in the immense imagination, the humor, the visual patterns that evolved through the film. And the acting was superlative—by Cardinale, who played two roles; by Mastroianni; Sandra Milo as the mistress; Anouk Aimée as the wife, etc. And the music of Nino Rota, which followed the trend set by him in his score for *La Dolce Vita*, was a major element in the film.

Finally, the acknowledgment by Fellini that he qualified mainly to entertain—to make beautiful and fascinating movies that captured the fancy but didn't really say too much—has been borne out by his subsequent films: *Juliet of the Spirits*, *Satyricon*, *Roma*, *Casanova*—all have been pictorially dazzling but substantially superficial. Only *Amarcord* got beneath the surface with its penetrating probes of the filmmaker's sentimental memories of his provincial youth.

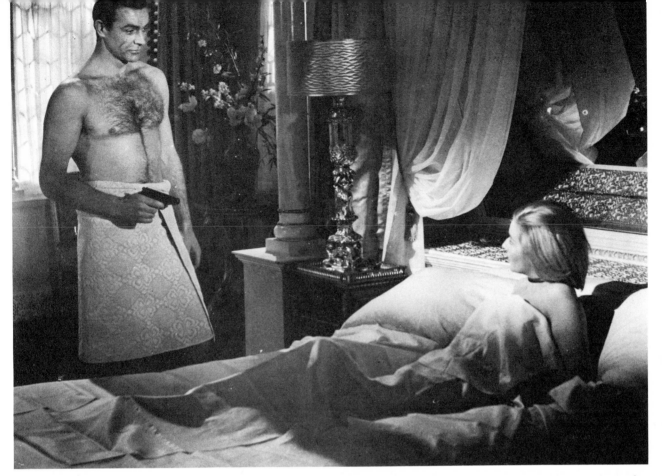

The intrepid James Bond (Sean Connery), on a mission to steal Lektor, a piece of invaluable electronic equipment, from the Russian Embassy in Istanbul, finds Taliana (Daniela Bianchi), an agent for his rivals, planted purposefully in his hotel bed.

FROM RUSSIA WITH LOVE

1964

There seems to be a nasty disposition on the part of a few critical cads to reflect nowadays with scorn and mockery upon the image and activities of James Bond. We refer of course, to the spectacular and indestructible British secret service chap who emerged from a string of Ian Fleming novels into visible life on the screen in a succession of derivative thrillers. The character was played most aptly by Sean Connery.

Too violent, said one revolted critic after seeing a postdiluvial Bond film, not remembering that she and most of her colleagues had wallowed luxuriously in the gore of *Bonnie and Clyde.* "The ultimate kitsch hero," said another. "The phallic fantasy of the middle-aged man." "The

overkill of comic book virility that offered hate as a high morality."

Well, no matter how much revisionists may now scorn the lusty Bond as a symbol of male chauvinism and of killing for political ends, the fact remains that this durable champion, a superfigure in 1960s films, has been one of the screen's most popular heroes and a social phenomenon, to whom I am pleased to pay tribute by including a film about him in this book.

He made his first screen appearance in 1962 in *Dr. No.* Sent on a mission to discover the mastermind behind the operation of a secret installation on Jamaica that in some mysterious way interfered with the launching of American rockets from (then) Cape Canaveral, Bond leaped into uncontested prominence as a fantastic supersleuth, as capable at handling delicate machinery as he was at handling indelicate females. No one could possibly accomplish the destruction of this

175

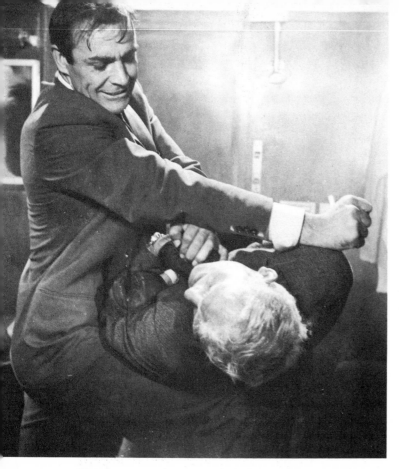

Bond engages in one of his characteristic violent battles with an enemy, in this case Red Grani (Robert Shaw), the top assassin for SPECTRE, a mysterious international network, also out to grab Lektor.

versatile chap, even though his life was put in desperate danger at least ten times per film.

The character and pattern of Bond films were well set in *Dr. No*; the secrecy, élan, and efficiency of British Intelligence (M1), whose most extraordinary agent was indisputably Bond; his cool, self-confident manner, which Mr. Connery most artfully conveyed; his deft performance with females, of which there was an endless parade; his knowledge of all things exotic, from automobiles to wines; his skill at physical encounter with firearms, karate, and knives and, of course, with deadly gadgets that M1 devised for him; and, finally, the axiomatic detail that the enemies that Bond smoked out were always agents of a communist country or some vast supranational conspiracy intent on world conquest.

Bond was, indeed, the quintessence of the heroic prototype. He bridged several genres of movies—from spy films to wild adventure larks; from way-out science fiction to muscular costume romance. His lurid encounters with villains and his miraculous conquests or escapes were traceable to the serial adventures of Pearl White in *The Perils of Pauline*. His secret agent involvements recalled those of Bulldog Drummond and the Scarlet Pimpernel. And he was infinitely smoother with women than was the brutal Mike Hammer of Mickey Spillane, and much more of a gentleman and scholar than was Bogart's historic Sam Spade.

It is known that just before the opening of the inaugural *Dr. No*, those involved with the film's production had no idea what a blockbuster they had wrought. Adapted by Richard Maibaum and two others from the Fleming novel of the same name, it was produced in England by Harry Saltzman and Albert (Cubby) Broccoli and directed by the Britisher Terence Young. The hope—indeed, the expectation—was that it would be just a good spy film. The uncommon bursts of laughter and seemingly painful groans that arose from the first sneak preview audience led them to believe their property was a first-prize dud. Only after they discovered from the deluge of rhapsodic preview cards that these unfamiliar reactions were caused by delight and surprise did they realize they had unwittingly turned out a real entertainment phenomenon.

The succession of Bond films thereafter came at the rate of about one a year—*From Russia with Love, Goldfinger, Thunderball, You Only Live Twice*, and *Diamonds Are Forever*. Those were the gilt-edged Bonds. Subsequently, the quality of the series has variably declined or changed, mainly because of the absence of Mr. Connery, who was exhausted and probably bored with the role.

It is something of a challenge to pick *the* representative vintage film from the series. Each had its certain distinctions and every Bond fan had a personal favorite. But for purposes of illustration and because I did think it was, all-round, the best, I have chosen to include in this volume *From Russia with Love*. The story was conspicuous for its prototypical extravagances; Mr. Connery, now fitted to the character, was at the top of his form, and Mr. Young, who departed the series after *Thunderball*, had perfected the style and the tempo that gave the Bond films their unique cachet.

Here Bond was given an assignment to go to Istanbul and join with the local MI agent, played by Pedro Armendariz. Their mission was to steal an electronic decoder, known as Lektor, from the Russian Embassy. (Why such a supermechanism should be left sitting out on a table in an embassy in Istanbul was a minor but interesting question left unanswered. Suffice it to say that Istanbul was a very colorful and appropriately exotic locale.) From the rather grisly prologue, one learned that a rival group, the secret and deadly organization known by the acronym SPECTRE, was also out to seize Lektor. Anticipating the intrusion of Bond, SPECTRE had been drilling its ace assassin in stalking and killing a rubber-masked replica of him. It had also recruited, through blackmail from the Russian secret organization SMERSH, a luscious young blonde called Titania (Daniela Bianchi) to assist in snaring Bond. Thus the stage was set for action when he dropped off the plane in Istanbul. He very quickly discovered he had rivals upon finding his hotel room bugged and, later, the voluptuous young lady curled up cozily waiting for him in his bed.

Let us not dwell too intently upon the subsequent twists of the plot—on how Bond got the young lady (rather obviously) to fall in with him; how the two laid hands on the plans of the Russian building, sneaked in through an underground way, and made off with Lektor, their escape facilitated by the tossing of a diversionary bomb by a confederate. All this transpired, I should add, a few days after Bond and his associate (Armendariz) had visited a gypsy camp on the edge of the city. Expecting to meet a supposedly collaborating agent, they were instead almost trapped and killed by SPECTRE raiders who arrived in force.

With Lektor safely snuggled in his baggage, Bond, the young lady, and Armendariz boarded the Orient Express (of course!), hoping to escape to Italy. Unknown to the trio, a fellow passenger was the SPECTRE killer (Robert Shaw) posing as another British agent. His instructions were to kill them when he got the machine. So the journey was not without its quota of accumulating deadly incidents, including the mysterious murder (by Shaw) of Armendariz, a couple of bruising hand-to-hand struggles between the finally enlightened Bond and Shaw, and an ingenious escape from the train in Yugoslavia by Bond, carrying Lektor, and the girl.

A helicopter, which menaced Bond until he gunned it down with a sniper's rifle signaled that they were not yet in the clear. Free of that deadly harasser, the two hijacked a speedboat and confidently made for Venice across the Adriatic only to be beset by a swarm of speedy SPECTRE craft. Bond ingeniously dumped some gasoline drums in the path of the determined pursuers, who were blown to smithereens. Finally, apparently safely harbored in a luxurious Venice hotel, the couple met their ultimate challenge. The mastermind SPECTRE agent (played in wonderfully evil fashion by Lotte Lenya) entered their room disguised as a hotel maid. She almost dispatched Bond by kicking at him with a poisoned stiletto protruding from the toe of her shoe, but he and his girl overpowered her. ''She got her kicks,'' was his laconic last word.

Let us not be supercilious about the substance and significance of Bond. He was a fascinating token of the taste and impiety of the moviegoing audience in the 1960s, the years when he was regnant on the screen, and the essence of him that is transmitted in those old films has stood the test of

Bond, suspecting treachery by the seemingly defecting Taliana, tries a little pressure on her.

time. Bond was not written or acted to be taken seriously; he was, in every essential, a titanic parody. He was a patently irreverent, good-humored, and deadpan burlesque of the then popular advertising slogan "the man who has everything." And the areas in which he operated and the activities in which he engaged were parodies of social, mechanical, and political realities.

Were there ever such high-powered, super-gadgeted motor vehicles as those that 007 or his enemies used in their chases and pursuits? Was there ever a craft as fantastic as the hydrofoil yacht in *Thunderball*, which could shed its outer skin like a lizard and extrude a superspeedboat? And were not the elusive SMERSH and SPECTRE extravagant caricatures of the darkly feared "cold war" opposition or of our own country's sinister CIA? Yes, one might argue, the latter has been exposed in recent years to have engaged in deadly activities almost as wild as those imagined in Bond films. But the very fact that such were subject to risible parody might have helped subsequently to alert the public to the political extremes of CIA.

And the notion of Bond as a sexist was quite inaccurate and unfair. Sure, he had an eye for

Bond, armed with his special rifle and carrying Lektor, is pursued across a hilltop in Yugoslavia by a SPEC-TRE helicopter.

The final obstruction faced by Bond is Rosa Klebb (Lotta Lenya), top agent for SPECTRE, posing as a chambermaid in a Venetian hotel.

beautiful women, and some of the remarks he made might have given his audiences the impression that coition was always on his mind—e.g., his dry rejoinder to the beautiful Titania in *From Russia with Love*. Expressing the fear that he might be disappointed with the size of her mouth he replied, "I will tell you, in the morning." *Honi soit qui mal y pense*. Actually Bond was quite casual, often indifferent, and sometimes brutal with the opposite sex, especially those who tried to hustle him more deceitfully than he hustled them. The impression he gave of being consistently lecherous was part of an oft-practiced technique, to mislead those who thought to bait him by putting beautiful women in his way. The overemphasis on this activity was an obvious spoof of sex.

To be sure, the multiplication and repetition of the clichés of Bond films did lead to their homogenization, and that we can only regret, as we do the spinoffs of some successful movies into deplorable series on TV. But in their pristine exposures the Bond films were brilliant parodies, not only of international intrigue but of the vainness of our overgadgeted age. And they *were* deliciously entertaining. Epic, indeed! Long live James Bond!

The Beatles—Paul McCartney, John Lennon, George Harrison and Ringo Starr—face the press on their arrival in London to do recordings.

A HARD DAY'S NIGHT

1964

If anyone had told me early in 1964 that I would some day be looking back fondly on the Beatles' first film, *A Hard Day's Night*, as one of the outstanding movies of the sound era, I would have thought it a preposterous proposition—that is, *before* I saw the film. Now, more than ever, with hindsight, I regard it as a true phenomenon.

For to my complete amazement and that of practically everyone else who saw it (excepting the several million youthful idolaters of the famous rock singing group who were already sold at the start), this simulated account of a couple of days in the hectic career of the most famous of the 1960s bands turned out to be a superbly energetic and witty farce comedy. And, indeed, if one had the predilection to so regard it, it was a sly, salubrious satire on the cult of Beatles worship itself.

Such satire was commendable. "Beatlemania" or the catatonic craze of otherwise healthy young people for the four British lads with the shaggy hair—George Harrison, John Lennon, Paul McCartney, and Ringo Starr—had reached epidemic proportions in England and the United States. The swelling cult was threatening to turn a generation—of teenage girls, at least—into screeching, screaming fiends. The youngsters were going crazy as they never had before for any of their pop-singing idols—Frank Sinatra, Elvis Presley, Vic Damone—in the years when having fits over singers was being cheerfully encouraged and engineered. And the time had come for somebody to make fun of the whole ridiculous thing.

Here was a movie that did so, with bland sophistication and nimble wit, but also with a feeling of affection for the musicians and their free and easy ways. It did not make fun of them as people or diminish their reputation in the least. Indeed, it rather profiled the quartet of lively

179

The four fellows, escaping briefly the throngs of fans, race happily through a London alleyway.

young men. Their lightning success had led to neither conceit nor pomposity. Indeed, they seemed rather stunned and bewildered by the fanfare and simply took it all in breakneck stride. The fun was poked at the ambiance of confusion in the lives of a highly popular group: the frenzies of their rapid transportation; eluding crowds of clamoring fans; the inanities of jammed press parties, with silly questions from free-loaders; the madness of rehearsing for TV programs; the endless prodding by anxious managers in hotel rooms; and always—always—the menace of intrusion by those frantic, faceless fans.

Credit the singularity of this picture to a remarkably light and fluid script, written by Alun Owen to allow for free improvisation throughout, and to the cunning direction of Richard Lester. Lester, who had only one previous feature film to his credit (*Mouse on the Moon*) showed here a saucy bent for satire that took everyone off guard. Imagine a Hollywood producer or talent manager allowing a film as clever and sly as this one to be made about the difficulties of their clients with their adoring fans!

The story was insubstantial, a loosely strung account of how the Beatles took Paul's wacky old grandfather under wing while en route to London to do a big TV show and their endurance and indulgence of the old boy while they were busy rehearsing and playing games. Nevertheless, it uncovered a subtle paradox in the flagrant behavior of the grandfather and the Beatles' own quest for privacy.

" 'e's a nice old man, isn't 'e?'' remarked John when they first encountered him waiting on the train which was to take them up to London after a gig in Liverpool. And George replied with courteous unction, which parodied the cliché remark generally made about the Beatles themselves, " 'e's very clean.''

But, of course, Grandad, whom Wilfrid Brambell played with an owl-eyed air of stealth and cunning, wasn't so "clean" after all. He was something of an old Irish rascal whose favorite reading was the pictures in the "girlie" magazines and whose preferred pastime was pinching fannies whenever the chance was presented. In mercenary fashion, he would sneak out into the streets with piles of autographed photos of the fellows to hawk up and down the lines of fans. He roundly abused his benefactors—for instance, he bluntly labeled Ringo's protuberant nose a "hideous grey hooter''; he persistently got in the way during run-throughs in rehearsal, and, toward the end, he ran afoul of the law for his unlicensed peddling of the photos and had to be skillfully sprung. The legal maneuver was like a tangle with Keystone cops.

Indeed, Mr. Lester freely borrowed from antique comic styles, including that of the beloved Marx Brothers (another mad foursome). He kept his fellows moving at a continuous head-over-tea-kettle pace, racing to and fro, tossing off throwaway lines (such as this comment upon a piece of freak art: "You don't see many of those these days"), and blithely setting up sight gags that they handled with absolute deadpan technique.

The turbulence of the press party was typical, with the boys vainly trying to get their hands onto passing trays of sandwiches and answering such nitwit questions as "What do you call that haircut?" ("Arthur") and "How do you like your girl friend to dress?" (responded to with a glance of shocked remonstrance and a suddenly explosive "Hah!").

At one point in a tiring rehearsal, the boys suddenly beat it off the stage, tumbled one after the other down several flights of an outside fire escape, and romped into a nearby playground, as

Ringo, having played hookey from the group and wandered alone in London, is picked up by the police and questioned at a stationhouse.

though driven by some juvenile exuberance or perhaps a freakish impulse to break free. In a jumble of shots of this activity, Mr. Lester cut in a few from high above which caught the racing figures in surreal patterns and gave a slashing sense of exuberant escape.

And in another, longer sequence, he had Ringo slip away to wander through London, cloaking himself in anonymity with a pulled down cap and a long gray duster which he picked up in Portobello Road. Ambling along the river, he threw taunts at rambunctious kids and (to a plaintive musical background) suggested a tinge of loneliness. Ringo, in fact, was the most subtle and winning of the lads, the most poignant captive of their fortune. He was the Harpo to the on-beats in the group.

Of course, there was an abundance of music throughout the film—songs twanged out happily and loudly by the fellows wherever they might be and whenever Mr. Lester took the notion that the Beatle fans were itching to groove. And his filming and editing of the numbers—"Money Can't Buy Me Love," "And I Love Her," "I

At a recording session, with their director (Victor Spinetti).

Should Have Known Better,'' and fully a half dozen more—was done with a rapid fire of close-ups, fast cuts, and punctuating thumps of visual shock that matched the excitement and infectious rhythm of the songs. Even to a non-rock fan, the music did have ear-splitting charm.

Every Beatles film endeavor after this picture seemed to be anticlimactic, self-conscious, and attitudinized. Indeed, this was characteristic of the trend of their group career, which finally dissolved in a shambles of ego-tripping and internecine strife. But they, at their peak and at their happiest, were well positioned and immortalized in *A Hard Day's Night*—and so was the spirit of their era, which soon was drowned in drugs, despair, and cold, hard rock.

Paul's wacky grandfather (Wilfrid Brambell) earns a little change for himself by hawking photos of the boys along a line of fans.

One of the first victims picked up by the Nazi-controlled police in the Slovakian town is Mr. Kruchar (Martin Holly), accused of being a "white Jew."

THE SHOP ON MAIN STREET

1965

One of the great surprises that enlivened the cinema world during the busy 1960s was the burgeoning of a group of mostly youthful, progressive filmmakers in Czechoslovakia. Up to that time, the movie output of that small country following World War II, while financially helped by the postwar nationalization of its film industry, had been considerably hampered and restricted by rigid controls imposed by a socialist government. Czech moviegoers had been offered mostly little more than ingenuous diversions, such as Jiri Trinka's *The Emperor's Nightingale*, a delightful cartoon-puppet picture shown in this country in 1951, and Karel Zeman's ten-years-later trick puppet film *The Fabulous World of Jules Verne*.

But apparently the sturdy stimulation of an excellent cinema school in Prague and a lessening of restraints in the 1950s following the death of Stalin and the World Congress in Moscow in 1956 gave encouragement and boldness to a group of artists who had patiently learned their craft, and happily a wave of astonishing pictures flowed from them during the next decade.

At first, recognition was limited to the approval of their own countrymen and, to a lesser degree, to the attention they received in foreign festivals, and of course, from occasional bookings in the smaller European theaters. But nothing outside the examples of their cartoon films mentioned above penetrated the commercial theaters of the United States until 1965, when there was offered at the New York Film Festival, without much

183

With their rabbi standing among them, the rounded-up Jewish citizens await deportation.

advance tub-thumping, an intensely dramatic and compassionate little picture from the Barrandov studios in Prague. Titled *The Shop on Main Street*, it was made by the veteran co-directing team of Elmar Klos and Jan Kadar.

The critical response was excellent and the festival audience foretold with visibly emotional enthusiasm the film's subsequent success in theaters. Suddenly commercial eyes turned toward Czechoslovakia, perceiving the possibility of a duplication of the sensation of the French "new wave," and in the next few years some ten or a dozen exceptional films were imported from Prague. Among them were works of Jiri Menzel, Milos Forman, Ivan Passer, and Evald Schorm, all graduates, significantly, of the influential cinema school. Awards of Academy "Oscars" to *The Shop on Main Street* and to Menzel's *Closely Watched Trains* as best foreign-language entries of 1965 and 1967, respectively, further attracted wide attention and the future seemed bright for the Czechs. But as suddenly as they had jumped into the limelight they were knocked out of it by the blow of the Soviet Union's invasion of their country in 1968. Promising productions were cancelled, a few finished pictures were shelved, and

some of their top directors were either banished or found it prudent to leave, among them Kadar and Forman, who emigrated to the United States. The brilliant but brief Czech "renascence" was disastrously ditched and doomed.

While it flourished, however, the contributions it made to the quality of cinema, and particularly to the extension of the familiar European neo-realist style, were such as to render its output inspiring and memorable. The main achievement was the adornment of everyday, solid characters with deftly applied and piquant dressings of humor and wit. No body of films in this period displayed quite the blend of seriousness with a leaven of dry and homely humor as did that of the Czechs. It seemed that a very special aptness for discovering in ordinary folks deep reservoirs of spirit and drollery in spite of tragedies and woes was pronounced in the films of these directors. Along with more traditional works they succeeded in turning out masterpieces full of serio-comic poignancy.

Such a film was *The Shop on Main Street*. While its theme was profound and grim, embracing the shameful betrayal of the Jews in Europe by their Christian fellow men, the depiction was developed in the simplest, most human and humble terms, and the tone throughout the first part was disarmingly wry and droll.

The story concerned the testing of an average little man named Tono, a day-laboring carpenter in a Nazi-held Slovakian town when he was appointed as the "Aryan" controller of a pitiful little button shop owned by an elderly Jewish widow early along in World War II. There was nothing malicious about Tono. He was just a caustic, good-natured *schnook* who followed the rule of live-and-let-live, endured the badgering of his harridan wife, hated his brother-in-law who, as the newly appointed "gauleiter" in the town, had given him his job, and looked with frank suspicion upon the Nazis and their local sycophants. He was even resigned and good-natured when he discovered that the sales at the little shop were so poor that he would not be getting any of the rake-off from it that he had been led to expect, and that the nice little old Jewish lady, rather than defer obediently to him, treated him as a helper who had been got for her by her friends.

Out of this humorous situation might well have been derived nothing more than a sweet *gemütlich* little domestic comedy. Tono, the *schnook*, had been duped by the greedy insistence of his wife and the apparent stupidity or roguishness of his big-mouthed brother-in-law. He was a prime example of the eternally befuddled little man. And humor, indeed, was made of it as Tono was joshed at first by Mr. Kuchar, a mutual friend of his and the lady, who told him he had been given "a bone to chew." Then he was rendered helpless by the little lady's quaint, possessive attitude. She stubbornly put her foot down on his opening the shop on a Jewish holiday, then revealed her naive gratitude toward him by giving him some of her late husband's old clothes. "I look like Charlie Chaplin," Tono wryly remarked as he amusedly showed himself to her in the antique suit and derby hat. A solid foundation was established for mutual affection and trust, and the audience was warmly embraced in this atmosphere of friendliness.

Then the ominous note was sounded. Suddenly Mr. Kuchar and a few others were brutally arrested by the local Guardists and hauled away. What was their offense? They were "white Jews," meaning friendly with the Jewish community. That was all we were told about them. We did not see them again. Later, at the beer hall-billiard parlor, Tono heard some Guardists boast of "killing Jews," and that night a tall wooden "tower of liberty" was burned in the town square outside the little shop. The old lady, Mrs. Lautmann, was deeply troubled. She didn't understand. She made up a bed for Tono and insisted that he sleep that night in the shop.

At this point, the directors and their writer slipped in a fanciful little scene representing a dream of Tono in which he and Mrs. Lautmann, she decked out in fashionable prewar finery and he in the husband's old clothes, skipped arm in arm into the town square while a band played old Viennese airs. It was a frankly sentimental

Mrs. Lautmann, mystified and frightened, seeks comfort in prayer.

Tono (Josef Kroner) attempts to persuade the bewildered Mrs. Lautmann (Ida Kaminska) to hide in the back of her little shop while the Jews are being loaded into trucks.

digression, which was repeated at the end of the film, excusable for no other reason than as a bit of nostalgia to recall the happy times when all good people, gentiles and Jews, were friends.

But that mood was shattered in the next scene, with Tono awakening to hear the blast of a strident loudspeaker in the square calling out the Jews. Immediately he got the message. The threats he had heard were being fulfilled. And the sight he saw when he peered out of a crowd of silent people gathered around a tall and dignified rabbi, calmly waiting, confirmed his fears. Although it was the Jewish sabbath, he quickly

opened the shop and forced Mrs. Lautmann into a back room where he hoped she would not be seen. Then he started drinking. That was his fateful Rubicon.

What followed after this moment comprised, in my opinion and in those of countless other viewers, one of the most compact, explanatory, plausible, and intense communications of a moral dilemma ever played on the screen. Suddenly the mind of Tono was struck by the paralyzing thought that at this crucial crossroads it was either Mrs. Lautmann or him. To continue to try to protect her could well mean the forfeit of his life, yet in all good conscience and friendship he couldn't turn her in. In mounting indecision and hysteria, he became more drunk and disturbed. At moments he was brutal to the lady, at others he was gentle and contrite. Once, when he pushed her roughly back into her room as she glimpsed the dismal gathering of the rounded-up people outside, a look of dumbfounded comprehension and terror came into her eyes and she gasped in horror, "Pogrom!" All her shock and despair were in that word.

Some time later, as Tono was watching the captives being loaded into trucks, an inner voice forbode, "Woe to him who shelters a Jew." His brother-in-law, the gauleiter, stopped at the window, peered in for a few breathless moments, then passed on. Relief and hope swept over Tono. He went to the old lady's room, calling

In a supplemental fantasy included in the middle and at the end of the film, Tono leads a happy Mrs. Lautmann in a dance through the erstwhile peaceful streets.

joyfully, "You can come out now," and found her dead on the floor. She had evidently suffered a heart attack.

Credit the film's directors. They did not stretch and magnify this scene into an outraged and superfluous reminder of the atrocity committed upon the Jews. They simply had Tono look about him at mementos of better days—old photos of Mrs. Lautmann and her husband when they were young, simple souvenirs of holiday outings, small and inconsequential memorabilia but all so fragrant of a kind of old-world living and happiness that were forever gone. Then they had him very quietly and methodically fetch a rope and fashion a noose, put his dog out and lock the door, close the shutters, loop the rope over a beam, stand on a chair beneath it, and, with the noose around his neck, kick out the chair. That was his final atonement for the hideous crime in which he had become involved and, symbolically, it was the film's summation of the spiritual guilt of all mankind.

Onto this solemn conclusion, Klos and Kadar attached the epilogue I have already mentioned—a repeat of the fanciful scene of the old lady and Tono dressed in old-world fashion, dancing into the street, carefree and joyful together, while the band played the Viennese waltz. This coda, so frankly sentimental, was here and there criticized for putting what was a "happy ending" on a film that concluded otherwise. But Kadar later explained it as an effort to suggest that "little people" are fundamentally kind and friendly, that their natures are corrupted and betrayed only by vicious leaders, and that *all* are victims as a consequence.

Obviously the character of Tono, who was most revealingly and brilliantly played by the splended Czech actor Josef Kroner, was the focal figure in the film, the one whose challenges and reactions were most expressive of the theme. But because the little Jewish lady was such an object of sympathy, with her abundantly warm, grandmotherly image, and she, too, was beautifully played by the fine Polish actress Ida Kaminsky, her character tended to take command and become the more conspicuous and affecting, especially with audiences in the United States. Frantisek Zvarik as the gauleiter, Hana Slivkova as Tono's wife, and Martin Holly as Mr. Kuchar were also excellent in their roles.

I daresay the thrust of this picture as a shattering reminder of the effect of Nazi power upon Europe will fade as we draw further away from the memory of that experience. But the impact of it simply as a tale of one man's response to a moral challenge will remain as long as we appreciate strong screen art.

Leonie (Vanessa Redgrave), the estranged wife of Morgan, is horrified to find a sample of his odd sense of humor in her bed.

MORGAN!

1966

Karel Reisz's *Saturday Night and Sunday Morning* was a superior example of the spate of "angry young men" films turned out by British directors in the early 1960s. So it was surprising but also startling to see the extraordinary change in attitude toward social matters that Mr. Reisz took in 1966. Following the trail blazed six years earlier by the Boulting brothers with their *I'm All Right, Jack*** and pursued in a way by Richard Lester's Beatles film, *A Hard Day's Night*, Mr. Reisz chose the route of antic satire to spotlight and ruefully withdraw from the dismaying paradoxes of the class conflict in his *Morgan, A Suitable Case for Treatment*, shortened to *Morgan!* in the United States.

Here his principal character was not a troubled factory worker, as in *Saturday Night and Sunday Morning*, nor a broodingly angry young man. Rather, he was a bizarre backsliding Marxist and way-out painter who was being divorced by his incongruous upper-class wife and on the verge of eviction from the apartment which he thought he had happily shared with her. Unable to compre-

hend why she should choose to leave him for the foppish West End art dealer who handled his gaudy daubs—"She married me to secure insecurity," he warned the fellow, "and you're trying to take it away from her!"—Morgan continually tried to regain her with wildly grotesque blandishments which betrayed a schizophrenic simian complex that caused him at times to fantasize himself as an ape.

At first his quixotic predilection to adorn the apartment with posters of apes and to smear his wife's dressing-table mirror with hammer-and-sickle hieroglyphs seemed eerie but refreshingly original in a day when chaps were doing nutty things to display themselves as nonconformists and rebels against the Establishment. Even such pranks as hiding a skeleton in his wife's bed or placing an explosive beneath it timed to go off when his wife and her boyfriend got in seemed little more on the surface than slightly perilous practical jokes, the sort of things that an overimaginative youngster might be inclined to pull.

But then as we were shown more of Morgan as an offshoot of the working class (similar to Alec Guinness' Gully Jimson in Ronald Neame's underrated *The Horse's Mouth*), the son of East End parents who were Marxists of the old traditional stripe, it began to appear that he might also be intended to satirize dedicated Communists with the hint that persons of that persuasion proved the Darwinian theory in reverse. Although this might seem an odd departure for a socially conscious filmmaker to take (and I am not altogether certain that Mr. Reisz meant it that way), it happily contributed to the humor and the lively abnormality of the film.

Certainly a charming episode in which Morgan, dejected and confused, went to stay for a bit with his Cockney mother in her East London slum, during which they paid a dutiful visit to the grave of Karl Marx in London's Highgate Cemetery, invited the vagrant impression that Mr. Reisz and David Mercer, who wrote the script from his own highly popular TV drama, were pulling more than a wry political spoof. As Morgan stood looking quizzically at the bearded, beetle-browed bust of the father of Communism, the head appeared to Morgan to turn into that of an ape. Softly he growled and gestured at it, to his mother's unhappy surprise. "You've grown into a peculiar sort of fellow, Morgan," she disapprovingly said as her son turned away and told her, "The Revolution, it'll all come tumbling down." And later, she sadly told him, "You're a class traitor, Morgan, that's what you are." She had hoped it would be "lads like Morgan who would take over the world."

As the story moved on, however, to more positive and violent events, it was evident that this was not simply a comic blast at the Establishment or a mischievous political spoof. Mr. Reisz and Mr. Mercer were saying more about the disordered state of society and the human condition than might have been found comfortable. When Morgan finally realized that Leone, his wife, had abandoned him (although she did respond rather agreeably to a bold invasion of her apartment and a semi-rape) he recruited a Marxist friend of his parents, a professional wrestler who went by the name of Wally the Gorilla, to assist him in kidnapping her. With an old van in which the stalking Morgan had taken up residence outside her home, they grabbed the wife out of London and took her to a lakeside in Wales where Morgan had beautiful visions of their living a primitive life. And true to her own quixotic nature, which was almost as childish as his, Leone submitted to his embraces in evident pristine bliss and allowed him to enjoy the fantasy of himself as Tarzan and her as Jane. But, of course, cruel reality soon intruded upon this idyllic state. The new boyfriend arrived in his Rolls-Royce, with policemen to nab Tarzan and snatch Jane away. Wally, with simian resignation, drove the van back alone.

The upshot of that misadventure was to land poor Morgan in jail, which was a reasonable retribution for society to take but a cruel and inhuman injustice so far as Morgan was concerned. It clearly exposed the weakness that Wally had complained of earlier: "That's what's missing in the law, Morgan, the human element." Or, to justify the kidnapping, he had quoted Morgan's dad (deceased), who went by the anarchistic dictum:

Momentarily reconciled, Morgan (David Warner) happily watches his wife take a bath.

Disturbed and frustrated by the capriciousness of his upper-class wife, Morgan seeks solace from his Communist Party mother (Irene Handl) in her London slum apartment.

"Crime puts the human element back."

That period in jail (which was not pictured) was the nadir of Morgan's defeat, but he had one more shot left in his locker to accomplish his dream of simian superiority. At the elegant wedding reception of Leone and her new playmate, while the guests were expensively socializing on the penthouse roof of the London Playboy Club, there came the terrifying apparition of a gorilla suddenly swinging down from the awnings and attempting to snatch Leone out of their midst. It was, of course, a desperate Morgan in his cherished gorilla suit trying, in his elemental concept, to take what he rightfully felt was his. The ensuing melée was brief but furious and it ended with Morgan repulsed, his suit set afire, his disguise riddled, and himself forced to flee. In ignominious panic, with the seat of his costume belching smoke, he was seen on a motorcycle racing toward the Thames. Thus the incongruous spectacle of a gorilla-suited man racing on fire through the streets of London was the climax of Morgan's fantasies.

Mr. Reisz and Mr. Mercer arranged a delightfully roguish, poignant, and enigmatic epilogue. Put away in a mental institution, where he could live a life of comfortable ease, Morgan was visited by Leone, who told him that she was with child. A happy gleam came into the eye of Morgan, recollecting that idyll by the lake, and it was obvious that both he and Leone were pretty sure who was the father of the child. That was sufficient to assure us that Morgan had not lived in vain. And, as the camera craned up from the two-shot of their sitting together in the asylum's garden, we saw that somebody had planted a flower plot in the familiar hammer-and-sickle shape.

Some critics felt that the screenplay was too random and diffuse, that Mr. Mercer tried too hard to develop it beyond the concept embraced in his TV play, which was simply the funny as well as the poignant aspects of a schizophrenic character, and had got tangled up in a confusion of political and class differences. I disagree. I think that the capricious and elusive nature of the film was what gave it character and importance beyond the fascination of farce. In its eccentricities and confusions it reflected a mad society. It made you wonder, indeed, who *were* the crazies. Like Morgan, it kept you on your toes.

Much credit was due to David Warner, who played the title role with such an air of aggressive independence and irrepressible buoyancy that he left the viewer groggy and bewildered, as he did the other characters. Decked out in his habitual bargeman's cap, dark glasses, and fisherman's sweater that hung almost to his knees, he strode through the film on his long legs as though he

Morgan, seeking to recruit his old wrestler friend, Wally (Arthur Mullard), is conveniently ready to help when he is thrown from the ring in a match.

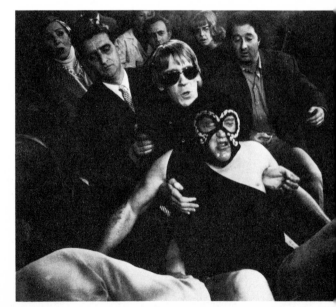

were indeed some sort of animal—or, rather, an overgrown, precocious youngster with a nimble wit and an abnormal appetite for sex. But behind what appeared sheer egoism and unshakable self-confidence there showed at times a hint of frenzy and finally of pathetic fear. Being schizoid wasn't fun for Morgan but it was for those who saw the film.

As Leone, Vanessa Redgrave was deliciously kooky, too—but in a soft, voluptuous, self-indulgent, unpredictable way. She made it appear that Morgan, while he vexed and disturbed her very much, had at times an elemental tidal attraction, like in certain phases of the moon. She, too, might have had a disposition to let herself go as Tarzan's Jane, if she hadn't suffered the constraints of her class upbringing and her stagnant West End friends. Robert Stephens as the prissy art dealer was the perfect stereotype of that breed, and Nan Munro as Leone's mother was a proper upper-class snob. But for pure muddle-headed social dimness, she couldn't hold a candle to Morgan's ma, who was played by Irene Handl to the Cockney manner born. And Arthur Mullard made Wally the Gorilla a cheerful credit to wrestlers and apes.

Since *Morgan!* we've seen a succession of films about the mentally deranged, some of them serious and heavy, such as *Equus*, but most of them grotesque and comical, presenting the notion that being kooky was not as ugly or cruel as being sane. A striking example of that sort was *One Flew Over the Cuckoo's Nest*, which gave Jack Nicholson his best role of the many he has played as a wised-up nut. But in my estimation *Morgan!* was the best that has come along so far. Although set in England, its relevance was to the whole mad western world.

Morgan, dressed in his gorilla suit, attempts to throw confusion into Leonie's wedding reception and kidnap her from its midst.

This small Spanish hunting party which includes Enrique (Emilio Polack), Paco (Alfred Mayo), José (Ismael Merlo) and Luis (José Maria Prada) is out for a day of seemingly innocent rabbit shooting in the region of a notorious Civil War battlefield.

THE HUNT

1966

The Spanish director Carlos Saura is perhaps best known to moviegoers in the United States for his 1977 film, *Cria,* and for his well-publicized attachment to the actress Geraldine Chaplin, who appeared in *Cria* and is the mother of his child. But my favorite film of this director was his powerful allegory *The Hunt,* which focused on the corrosion of three middle-aged Spaniards who had fought on the side of Franco in the Spanish Civil War and tacitly implied they were symbolic of the decay of their generation of Spanish men.

At the time of this film's production in 1966, Mr. Saura's reputation did not extend beyond his native land, where he was one of several talented directors whose work was notoriously confined by politically imposed regulations to subtly satiric

themes, at best. He had made one grim neo-realist drama, *Los Golfos,* about juvenile delinquents in Madrid, which revealed him as an earnest disciple of his countryman Luis Buñuel, and a less interesting adventure drama, *Lament for a Bandit,* which was in the traditional western vein. But officially neither he nor others could touch the delicate subject of the Civil War, unless the aim was to glorify the triumphs of Franco's fascist party, the Falange.

However, through a misunderstanding of the script by the censors, which was comparable to the "mistake" by which Buñuel was allowed to make *Viridiana,* Mr. Saura was given clearance to make *The Hunt.* The consequence, while not a repetition, was ironically much the same. Finished but not booked for distribution, it was shown to me while I was on a visit to Madrid in the spring of 1966. On the strength of what I then wrote about it, which was endorsed by a couple of scouts, it was invited to the New York Film Festival in the fall of that year. Its critical reception was approving, to the surprise (we learned) of people back in Spain; and although it was not exactly a blockbuster in its subsequent theatrical engagements in the United States, that festival showing (and an award the film won for best direction at the Berlin Film Festival that same year) did bring it and Mr. Saura to the respectful attention of the cinema world.

Why it was not as appealing as *Cria*, let us say, was obviously due to its relentless morbidity and the obscurity of its political theme. Where *Cria* was intensely sympathetic to the psychological torments of a child, disturbed by the disharmony of her parents, *The Hunt* was a hard, concentrated contemplation of the viciousness of men who have been warped by the barbarity of their experiences and the cruel divisiveness of the times in which they lived. It was lean, compact, isolated, not emotional in a familiar movie way but highly charged with passions that literally exploded at the end.

One might have been forgiven for not perceiving in its first phase the direction in which it was headed. Four men, gathered at a bar outside Madrid, were about to set out for a day of presumably normal rabbit shooting in the barren countryside. The three older men were established as old companions from the days of the Civil War, when they fought together on the side of Franco. This was not necessarily a significant point, since most Spaniards who were middle-aged in the 1960s had fought on one or the other side. There was Paco, a lean, hard, and forceful business-executive type, played by Alfredo Mayo. He was clearly the most firmly disciplined and successful of the three. Next was José (Ismael Merlo), who was comparably tough but appeared to lack the confidence and drive, the dogmatic resolution and assertiveness of Paco. The third was bald-headed Luis (Jose Maria Prada), a seemingly gentle and amiable type who was described as a business partner of Paco, but not very effective in recent years. He was regarded with mild concern by his companions because he had recently separated from his wife and taken a mistress, which they thought foolish and dangerous. The fourth member of the party was a much younger man, a nephew of Paco, who appeared to have been included mainly to tote the guns and gear.

Once the men had reached their destination—a treeless, desiccated plain—and set up camp in a minor declivity from which they could spread out for the hunt, meaningful innuendos and references began to creep in. Their conveyance was a military vehicle, similar to the small troop carriers used in the Civil War, and the three older men were conspicuously knowledgeable about and skillful with guns. One of them, displaying a pistol with which he was particularly adept, identified it as a German Luger of the sort that "frequently exploded" in the rebel soldiers' hands, thereby inviting the remembrance that the Nazis were on the Franco side in that bitter struggle between Spanish liberals and the fascist rebels. And the fact that the area in which they were hunting had been a much-fought-over battleground came out when one explained to the youngest that a series of small caves in a low escarpment had been hiding places of the Loyalist soldiers. "We shot them as they came out," he casually said.

A moment later, the context of that image was vividly visualized by a savage and deafening sequence in which the hunters began blasting away

Enrique, Paco and José examine an infamous type of German pistol.

at a colony of rabbits flushed out of the scrubby bushes by the hunting dog and scrambling in pitiful frenzy for the sanctuary of the caves. Suddenly the concrete brutality of Spaniard killing Spaniard in the war was visible in the ferocity with which the older men shot the animals. And the hideous slaughter was climaxed with the dog chasing and catching one of the beasts and, mocking the men's passion for killing, shaking it to death. No words were spoken in this sequence. The sound track was simply overwhelmed with the deafening blasts of the rifles, the martial thumping of drums, and the terrified squealing of the rabbit as it was killed. Fast-cutting through the sequence enhanced the sense of frenzy and speed. The whole effect was like that of watching a documentary of a fierce encounter on a battlefield.

To this guarded but unmistakable metaphor, Mr. Saura added indications of the natures of his men and what they had become in the three decades since Franco had come to power. Paco was frankly autocratic. He believed in killing the weak, an allusion to the rabbits, and those presumably diseased. He hated the sight of cripples. He was obviously selfish and cruel. José was shifty and devious. Though he appeared the most rugged of the lot, he was suspiciously unreliable and fundamentally weak. Luis, the one with the mistress and the most knowledgeable about guns, was apparently the least interested in hunting. He chose to bury his nose in a science fiction book.

Thus, within the classical dimensions of this one-day hunting trip, Mr. Saura laid out his principal characters and the kind of society in which they were involved. As they lay dozing under the shelter of a canvas tent, exhausted by the morning of slaughter and the withering heat of the midday sun, he hinted, through voice-over mutterings of the thoughts running through their minds, the shape of their troubles with women and their anxieties over business affairs. Drifting innuendos of their varying lack of sexual potency complemented the evidence of their obsession with guns. Sadism poked its head meanly through social and sexual apathy. One might sense, if one had the wits to do so, the effects of Franco's long repressive rule.

Against the profiles of his elders, the young man played by Emilio Polack, was innocent and

Luis comforts himself with a familiar consolation.

dull. He was less interested in the barren, decaying mementos of the Civil War than in the vagrant fun of hunting and in the clumsy coquetries of a peasant girl who came to the camp with her aging uncle to bring a meal of rabbit stew. This girl and her naive fascination with the jazz music that came from a radio reflected, along with the young man, the indifference of two levels of Spanish youth.

The approach to a climax of the drama came when the old man brought a pair of ferrets to enliven the hunting by chasing the rabbits out of their holes. Already the ferrets had been mentioned as being similar to women in the sense that they had gentle faces and sleek bodies but quick and ferocious ways. This led to another round of slaughter as the rabbits came fleeing from the caves and then a sudden, deliberate shooting of one of the ferrets by Paco. The point was clear enough. In the angry confusion that followed, adumbrated by the plaints of the old man, who couldn't understand why his pet had been slaughtered, Luis and the nephew went off to hunt alone, leaving José and Paco to smolder under the tent. There, seething with anger and resentment because Paco had earlier refused him a large loan that would have saved him from financial disaster, and inflamed by the noise of the nearby hunt, José went into a frenzy and killed Paco with a blast from a shotgun. And when Luis, hearing the shots, came racing toward him in the truck, José turned the gun upon him and let go with another blast. Badly wounded, Luis kept bearing down in the truck as José turned and tried frantically to claw his way up the embankment and into a hole. But Luis would not show mercy. He unlimbered his gun and shot him dead. Then, with blood streaming profusely from the wounds in his face, he collapsed and died. The nephew, coming up, was dumbfounded. The hunt was at an end.

Even on its most superficial level, with no thought of its allegorical depths, *The Hunt* was an astringent melodrama, as stinging as salt on an open wound. Reaction in Spain was significant. General audiences, brainwashed as they were to believe that all was rosy in that best of all possible worlds, could not comprehend the grim dissension and bitterness among the older men. They felt incredulous and uncomfortable in the face of this ugly exposé. But the intellectuals grasped its meaning, and the liberals among them were moved. Today Saura is sometimes referred to as the Goya of latter-day Spanish cinema.

Old Juan (Fernando Polak), caretaker of the barren area, spits saliva into the mouth of a pet ferret as a token of affection before turning the animal loose to chase rabbits out of their burrows.

Luis lies dead after being mortally wounded by José.

Train Dispatcher Hubieka (Josef Somr) casts a casually critical eye upon the performance of the railway station trainee, Milos (Vaclav Neckar)

CLOSELY WATCHED TRAINS

1967

In discussing *The Shop on Main Street*, I spoke of the characteristic style of many of the Czechoslovakian films of the 1960s during the brilliant but brief renascence they enjoyed. This style was especially evident in the works of the younger men, directors such as Jiri Menzel, Milos Forman, Ivan Passer, and Evald Schorm. It was marked by an essentially easy, completely naturalistic approach to deceptively mundane material which was seemingly treated casually with the individuality and humor of its characters predominant.

Conspicuous examples of it were in Milos Forman's *Loves of a Blonde*, in Ivan Passer's *Intimate Lighting* and in Jiri Menzel's *Closely Watched Trains*. In the first, a poignant theme of

frustration emerged touchingly from behind the human and humorous manoeuvers of a little shoe-factory-worker to snag a mate. In the second, dark shadows of envy and resignation to fate lurked within an amiable story of the reunion of two old musician friends. And in the third, which I judged the most surprising and penetrating film from the younger Czechs, it was a theme of fortuitous heroism that suddenly came to the fore out of the gropings of a young railway trainee to prove himself nothing more than a sexually competent man.

The first three-quarters of it was simply a facile comedy, even routine in the eyes of some critics, with only occasional hints of something more serious pending than the unfulfilled sex dreams of the lad. Now and then, random emissaries from the world outside the little Bavarian railway station, where the hero was starting his career as an apprentice train dispatcher, bore news that a war was going on. Once an officious inspector came riding down the tracks in a comical little gasoline buggy to remind the station personnel that they were all "fighting for a common victory"—Nazi victory—and that it was their duty "to lure the enemy into our trap." Naturally the inspector was indignant when the young trainee innocently—even stupidly—asked, "Why?"

Again, a squad of Nazi soldiers straggled along the tracks, looking for all the world like a handful of work-camp escapees, and listlessly responded to the invitation of a clutch of nurses in a hospital train that was lying on a siding at the station, thus moving in ahead of the hesitant hero, who was trying to get up the nerve to climb aboard. And then there were a couple of angry outbursts from the old station janitor who claimed he had heard of the Nazis brutally blinding cattle, but no one paid attention to him.

For the most part, interest was directed to Milos, the solemn trainee, as he devoted himself to learning his duties and keeping his hat on straight. Here, in the limited circumference of the railway station, with its mystical array of signal levers that had to be pulled and telegraph instruments that had to be tended by expert acolytes, was a world in itself whose sole connection to a world outside appeared in those huge and fearsome trains that occasionally whooshed by in great clouds of steam bearing freight, which, unknown to Milos, was munitions bound for the east. The critical cargo was the reason the trains had to be closely watched.

The principal focus of Milos' attention was his immediate superior, the dispatcher Hubieka, who blandly performed his tasks, giving the trains the wave-through with magnificent poise and nonchalance, pulling the proper levers and keeping his fingernails trimmed. His protégé watched with spellbound envy the casual competence of this matchless paragon as he coolly addressed himself to females with amazing charismatic confidence.

Ever so deftly, Menzel made his modest railway station appear as teeming with sexual activity as a pasha's seraglio. There was the visit one day of the buxom countess in her old-style jaunting cart, teasing Hubieka with sly suggestions which aroused him voluptuously. There was the time when Hubieka locked himself in the station master's office with one of the female personnel

An enamored Milos runs alongside a departing train waving farewell to a little conductress he has just met.

and vastly angered the station master when he later found that the couple had ripped the sofa with their heels. "Why can't you use the waiting room?" the outraged official screamed. And then there was the girl conductor off one of the local trains who blatantly signaled to Milos that she was ready whenever he was. But when finally he did get up the courage to meet her for an off-duty date on a couch in the backroom of a nearby photographer's studio, poor Milos was so tense and anxious that he was unable to perform. The aftermath of the sexual fiasco was a black depression which led to a suicide attempt.

This sudden transition to a rueful and serio-comic episode, in which the lad slashed his wrists in the bathtub of a sleazy assignation hotel and was saved only by a passing workman and speedy care in a hospital, was characteristic of the blending of emotional contrasts in the Czech folk films, and was what led some critics to tag them "black humor," which was not precisely fair. For the switching to this grim occurrence after that funny-poignant failure in bed, which itself came af-

197

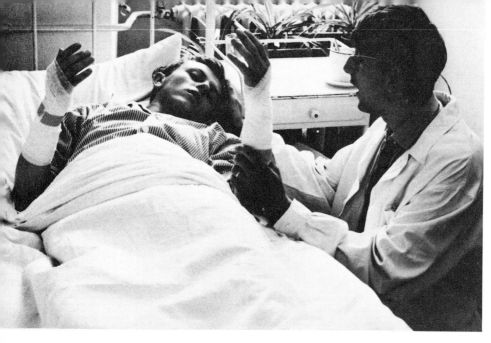

In hospital with slashed wrists from an attempted suicide because he feared he was impotent, Milos receives some sage advice from Dr. Brabee (Jiri Menzel).

ter a hilarious bit of comic picture taking in the studio, was a vicious and honest recognition of the way things do occur, and it sounded a note of premonition as to the hero's destiny.

While the comedy was just as nimble following Milos' return to his job after being advised by a doctor to relax in his intense approach to sex, a perceptible shadow of sadness and fatalism did fall. (At least, one can surely sense it on seeing the film a second time.) The feeble attempts of Milos to find *someone* to help him overcome his disposition to "premature ejaculation" (the term used by the doctor in diagnosing his problem) were awfully funny but pathetic in a peculiarly pitiful way. His clumsy and childish inquiries of the station master's middle-aged wife (who was caught as she graphically fingered gobs of food down the long neck of a goose); his whispered request to the inspector, who was pop-eyed with amazement and alarm; his maladroit question to Hubeika as to whether he had a sister who might oblige—all were importantly reflective of the naïveté of the lad.

Finally, without prearrangement in the earlier plotting, an opportunity came from a quarter that was quite unexpected. Almost casually the word was passed by an engineer on a locomotive that a big munitions train was coming through and that an underground agent would precede it and give the password "Victoria Falls." This agent would bring explosives with which the station personnel would blow up the train. And, surprisingly, Hu-

The underground agent, "Victoria Falls" (Nada Urbankova), suddenly arrives at the provincial station with an innocent-looking package containing a bomb.

beika and a couple of others were prepared to accept the job.

The plans were made. Milos was assigned to climb a signal tower and drop the bomb on the train as it passed under. "Victoria Falls" arrived and turned out to be a woman, and Hubeika quietly persuaded her first to relieve Milos of his virginity, which she did, on the station master's sofa. Thereafter, Milos climbed the tower and was shot by guards on the train as it passed beneath. But in falling, he carried the bomb along with him. Such was the tautly melodramatic, ironic, and poignant climax of the film.

Obviously there were several meanings that could be taken from this strange comedy, beyond the major one of assumption of a crucial responsibility. There was the veiled criticism of the Czech people during the early years of the war, when they were historically apathetic and inclined to think mainly of themselves. There was the bitter suggestion that Czech youth had been grossly ill-informed of the issues at the outset by a sadly divided populace and then had been casually exploited by demands for self-sacrifice. And there were many possible permutations of the ambiguous importance of sex in ego building *and* in entertainment, which was certainly the use to which it was put here!

It is significant that Menzel and the others who were conspicuous in the Czech "renascence" were mostly of the postwar generation, young people who had not known first-hand the hardships and dislocations of mind and spirit that were caused by the war. Their major preoccupations were the strictures imposed by a socialist state. Therefore the issue of self-identity and fulfillment was really foremost in their minds and was most perceptible in *Closely Watched Trains*.

Another notable aspect was the splendid conjoining of theatrical and cinematic skills that went into its crisp production, manifesting the great attention paid to the arts of film and the theater in Czechoslovakia. Vaclav Neckar was superb as Milos, making this doltish young man an object of common recognition and abiding sympathy. Josef Somr played Hubieka with a wonderfully dry conceit, and Jitka Bendova was winning as the conductress, as were all the others in the cast.

It is nothing short of tragic—to the cause of cinema, at least—that the talents of an artist such as Menzel, who himself has chosen to remain in Czechoslovakia, earning his living at minor theatrical jobs, have been suppressed or politely diverted by his country's tough political regime. In such "disappearance" is symbolized the tragedy of the whole abasement of the Czech "renascence."

As a reward for his forthcoming mission of planting the bomb, "Victoria Falls" generously accommodates Milos in losing his virginity.

199

At their first casual meeting, Clyde Barrow (Warren Beatty) proudly displays his firearm to a greatly impressed Bonnie Parker (Faye Dunaway).

BONNIE AND CLYDE

1967

Those readers who may remember the strong position I took in my original *New York Times* evaluations of Arthur Penn's *Bonnie and Clyde* may be surprised that I now venture to include it in this book, for I was one of the few professional critics who took it severely to task. My principal criticism was that it perniciously romanticized and lamented the careers of the bank-robbing team of Clyde Barrow and Bonnie Parker—notorious in the 1930s in the Southwest for their sadistically brutal and unnecessary murders committed in the act of armed robbery. For Mr. Penn to make his simulations of the actual Bonnie and Clyde, who were mean, ugly, sexually maladjusted roughnecks, a pair of free-wheeling, fun-loving kids, as handsome and artificially charming as Warren Beatty and Faye Dunaway could make them be, friends of the poor and scourges of the occasionally encountered Depression rich, seemed to me a dangerous distortion not only of the facts but of plausibility.

Furthermore, I was aesthetically offended and morally disturbed that Mr. Penn should have loaded his picture with such excesses of visible violence. All of his scenes of shootings and blazing gun battles were intense, offering prolonged and detailed close-ups of shattered faces and blood-streaming wounds, to the point where such latherings of violence became narcotizing and perverse. This seemed to me deliberate pandering to an increasingly voracious public taste for blood and killing in movies, as evidenced in such previous films as Robert Aldrich's *The Dirty Dozen* and Mr. Penn's own *The Left-Handed Gun.*

So those were my major criticisms of *Bonnie and Clyde* when it was released, and I still hold that they were valid in the broader context of a moral point of view. But the great surge of critical approbation and overwhelming popular response that the film received when it opened, plus the stature it has achieved as a cinematic trailblazer as the years have passed, have caused me to reappraise it in comparison to films that have followed it and to perceive that its arrant amorality and its candid looseness with violence and death did indeed manifest a passover into a new style and thrust in social films.

I concede now that Mr. Penn's employment of pictorial incongruities was deliberately designed to establish conspicuous contrasts for his profiles of Bonnie and Clyde. Against strongly realistic backgrounds of the barren southwest in the Depression years, he vividly showed the depredations of his jolly bank-robbing team. Everything looked scruffy and dismal—the dusty streets of the rural towns; empty roads strung through treeless country, lined monotonously with telephone poles; ugly, bare wooden houses and knots of bereft farm workers come across like characters out of Pare Lorentz's classic dust-bowl documentary *The Plow That Broke the Plains*. These provided a contrapuntal pathos to the rollicking spirits of Bonnie and Clyde and tacitly justified the notion that survival could best be achieved by a cheeky ex-convict and an ex-waitress in this environment through robbing banks and country stores.

The utter sang-froid of the two characters was pointed at the start. Right after an opening and affecting montage of faded photographs of poor and seedy country people looking lonely and forlorn as the soundtrack blared an old, nostalgic gramophone rendition of the 1930s popular song "Blue Skies," Mr. Penn lightly introduced his hero and his remarkably good-looking heroine by having her catch him in the act of trying to steal her mother's automobile. "Hey, boy, whatcha

Clyde and Bonnie make an unnoticed getaway from one of their early bank holdups.

doin' with my mama's car?" she yelled at him from an upstairs window of a frame house. It was not an angry challenge; she was amused and obviously a little more than interested in this good-looking, arrogant kid. And he was shamelessly boastful. "I was in the state prison," he volunteered. "It was armed robbery." And to confirm his boast, he stepped across the street and nonchalantly stuck up a poor grocery store. The deed electrified Bonnie. She rushed out, jumped into the car, and away the two drove together, with her remembering only then to ask, "Hey, what's your name?"—a moldy funny, but childishly apt, in this case.

Soon after, Mr. Penn and his scriptwriters, David Newman and Robert Benton, introduced a psychological detail that was crucial and quite a surprise. "I'm not much of a lover boy," Clyde sheepishly explained the first time he and his companion had a fruitless tussle of an amorous nature on the back seat of the car. "Ain't nothing wrong with me," he added and assured her, "I don't like boys." He simply couldn't manage an erection. And that, along with a later shot of him lying in bed with his pistol significantly close to his crotch after another unsuccessful attempt to satisfy Bonnie, was an open signal to everyone that his pistol was his unconscious substitute for masculine power. (It is hard to believe, but that shot of the pistol was cut in some theaters.)

Indeed, as the picture continued, it was evident that Mr. Penn intended the impotence of his hero not only as an explanation for his reckless, irrational aggressions but as a teaser to agitate the viewers with a kind of subliminal eroticism that derived from his fruitless exertions of lust. This meld of Clyde's sexual frustration and Bonnie's growing impatience with him actually infused the picture with a whiff of pornography—a departure which soon began to creep in to more and more subsequent films, until violence and sexual abnormality or perversity are now commonly equated on the screen.

Further, the impotence of the hero gave Mr. Penn and his writers a convenient peg on which to hang the high point and ultimate catharsis of the film. After the couple had been through a series of crimes, disasters, and realizations of the miscarriage of their careers and were teetering on the brink of apprehension, Bonnie wrote a piece

201

of childish doggerel which she called "The Story of Bonnie and Clyde" and which she read to her lounging companion while they were sitting alone in a car in the rain. "Hot damn!" whooped Clyde in joyous approval of this far from poetic gem which Bonnie said she was going to send to the newspapers (the real Bonnie actually did such a thing). "You made me somebody they're going to remember!" And with this ego-nourishing nudge he climbed aboard his companion and achieved what both agreed was a satisfactory sexual embrace. Almost laughable in its absurdity, this was still an oddly touching episode.

Most importantly, it climaxed the exposure of the criminals as a couple of pathetically immature hicks, romping and rollicking through the picture with a giggling nitwit named C. W. Moss, whom they impulsively snatched from his job as a grease monkey at a filling station to string along as the mechanic for their stolen cars. Later, they also enlisted Clyde's footloose brother, Buck, and his silly wife, Blanche, to be members of their mobile entourage as they continued to race across the country, their notoriety ever increasing.

But all was not fun and cheap publicity, of which they were foolishly proud, as the drama moved beyond a succession of robberies and fast get-aways to the lively and accelerating accompaniment of a banjo and fiddle country-music score. Slowly the antisocial couple realized not so much the error of their ways as the isolation enforced by their existence and the peril of being caught. A funny but pathetic encounter with a young undertaker and his wife whom they kidnapped and lightly badgered until they learned his morbid profession and saw how terrified the couple were suddenly seemed to sober the two fugitives and increased Bonnie's feeling of despair. She begged to go home to see her mother, to which Clyde agreed. But the visit caused only more depression. Clyde's diminishing boasts and his half-hearted effort to convince the family at a prosaic picnic party that "this here's the way we know best to make money" were countered by the old mother's terse reply: "You best keep runnin', Clyde Barrow, and you know it." The farewell was sentimental and grim.

In a blazing shoot-out with a sheriff's posse attempting to catch them at a grubby tourist camp,

Clyde engaged in his chosen occupation of "robbing banks."

Buck was mortally wounded and Blanche had an eye shot away. The next morning, after spending a bleak night in a field, they were ambushed again and now both Bonnie and Clyde were slightly wounded in the ensuing fusillade. Buck died with Blanche screaming in anguish, as the others again got away in another stolen car and beat a grim path through a dismal Oakie camp to C. W.'s distant home. But there was still no hiding place for them. Blanche, in a hospital, spilled the beans to a questioning Texas Ranger, and their actual whereabouts was revealed by C. W.'s frightened father, after Bonnie and Clyde alone had moved on to that pitiful, fleeting achievement of sex at last in an open field. But their joy and following talk of getting married were inevitably nipped in the bud as the ruthless and relentless Rangers, on the old man's secret tip, surrounded them. In what is now a historic sequence, they were suddenly opened fire upon and, unable to fire back, were viciously slaughtered—torn to ribbons—by a hail of bullets that became at its climax a veritable slow-motion nightmare of spasmodic death. If one chose, one could take this conclusion as the final metaphor for orgasm. Or perhaps as the fate into which some hapless young people in the 1960s were being plunged.

As anyone who knew the circumstances could readily perceive, or even one who could recognize the devices of manipulating fiction on the screen, this film assumed no responsibility as authentic biography or social history. It was a clever and effective distortion of a legend in the annals of American crime that was aimed to generate entertainment, compassion, and the appearance of tragedy. And that it did, skillfully and swiftly, each step studied and programmed, so that the buildup to final realization and resolution was through stages of diminishing buoyancy, which made the ultimate deflation and atonement the more shattering and sad.

There was no more resemblance between the characters in this picture and the real-life Bonnie and Clyde than there was between the later movie parodies and the real-life figures of Butch Cassidy and the Sundance Kid. These were fabrications of romanticized, independent youths to gratify the preconceptions and illusions of young

Here is the Barrow Gang posed for one of their boasted newspaper photos. From left to right: Clyde's brother Buck (Gene Hackman), the latter's wife Blanche (Estelle Parsons), Clyde, Bonnie and C.W. Moss (Michael J. Pollard).

people who had come of age with the Beatles and Bob Dylan, the philosophy of doing-your-thing and the notion that defying the Establishment was beautiful and brave. And who could have been more consistent as images of bold, rebellious youth than the handsome, aggressive Mr. Beatty and the beautiful Miss Dunaway? They were apt and, to their credit, it had to be said that they played their roles of fated lovers with interesting and affecting emotional range. Likewise Michael J. Pollard as the tag-along C. W. Moss; Gene Hackman as Buck, the loyal sidekick; and Estelle Parsons as his pitifully jangled wife contributed much to the dimension and distinction of the film.

But the major, most memorable distinction of this still nettling *Bonnie and Clyde* was the daring it showed in departing from the familiar criminal types and formulae, the anarchy with which it nose-thumbed the strictures of the old Production Code. At no point were its proponents exhibited as evil or corrupt, as were the sinister characters in the old familiar gangster films, and their eventual apprehension and destruction were not designed to show that crime does not pay. These were just pathetic young people looking out for themselves and whose misfortune it was to be so naive that they barely realized they were bucking society.

No film turned out in the 1960s was more clever in registering the amoral restlessness of youth in those years. This is why it became so popular and is a landmark film today.

Ambushed by Texas Rangers, Bonnie and Clyde are shot down during a running battle in an open field.

Elvira Madigan (Pia Dagermark), who has abandoned her career as a circus performer to elope with her lover, privately practices her tightrope-walking on a clothesline at a country inn.

ELVIRA MADIGAN

1967

When most of us had about decided that the age of the romantic film had passed—in Europe, at least, where Ingmar Bergman had pretty well set the pace through the late 1950s and 1960s with his great run of solemn Swedish films—there came from that same northern nation a film of such warm romantic glow, such intense and compassionate feeling for the agonies of young people meshed in hopeless love, that it captured the hearts of all us skeptics and renewed our faith in the lyric capacities of motion pictures. It was Bo Widerberg's exquisite *Elvira Madigan*—and "exquisite" was the one word that encompassed all its visual, idealistic, and poetic qualities.

Its color was absolutely gorgeous—as gorgeous as any color photography I have ever seen—and beautifully used to capture the atmosphere of its theme. Its countryside scenes in Denmark, its shots of faces and furnishings in old-world farms, its fine compositions of food and flora were recollective of Renoir—not only the great painter, Auguste, but his cinema-artist son, Jean.

The aural effects were also splendid: the use of music—particularly Mozart's *Piano Concerto 21*, which was so appropriately used to embrace the romance that it is now popularly referred to as the Elvira Madigan Theme; the eloquent use of country noises, the hum of bees, the song of birds, the cackle of chickens, the rustle of leaves and grasses; and the use of silences, so expressive of the tenderest moments and embraces.

The story was that of a runaway couple, an aristocratic young Swedish cavalry officer and a tightrope performer from the circus. Both had fled their responsibilities—he from his regiment, his wife, and children (as we were later informed) and she from her troupe and an adoring public— to escape social condemnation and be free to enjoy their boundless love. Set in the 1880s, the story was said to have been based on a true and celebrated incident that became a legend in Scandinavia.

Discovered at first in the clean seclusion of a distant countryside and modest inn, where they frolicked in childlike rapture and made love passionately in summer fields and on soft beds, these two seemed answerable only to themselves. And the aim of Mr. Widerberg's idyll seemed no more than to show the ecstasy of love.

But this realm of pure sensual pleasure was subtly intruded on by him with quiet, insistent awareness of the ties of the world from which the lovers came and the fragile limits of their resources, both in money and in self-supporting skills. Actually, they were soon discovered to be pathetically immature—nineteenth-century counterparts of the "flower children" we have known in our own age.

This mounting sense of frustration of the free enjoyment of isolation and love underlay the beauty and sadness of this insinuating film. Successively, the securities of the couple were loosened and cut away. When their identities, which they had tried carefully to disguise (he by cutting off his beard and the buttons from his military jacket and she by reassuming her real name of Hedvig instead of her *nom de theatre*), were discovered at the inn, they were forced to move on. But they were exposed again by a friend of Sixten, the officer, who hoped to shame him into giving up the liaison and returning to his regiment and his wife.

The increasing looks of anxiety in Hedvig's eyes and her quiet moods on occasions had struck a note of apprehension. Disconcertingly, she would draw into herself or secretly toy with an improvised tightrope stretched between two trees. Now, with a full comprehension of the crisis their love affair had caused, she fled from a luncheon with their visitor and alarmingly disappeared. When Sixten after a frantic search found her in a hayloft and took her back to their bedroom to surrender again to love, it was clear that she had foreseen disaster and prepared herself for their fate.

Then followed a pitiful succession of random and vain attempts by the couple to scrounge for bits of money and provide for themselves. Sad little incidents marked their degradation and despair: her lonely attendance at a concert in the

Elvira's lover, Sixten (Thommy Berggren), who has deserted his post as a cavalry officer, and she scan the newspapers to read reports of their disappearance.

village featuring a traveling string quartet she had known in other days; her quiet disposal for a pittance of a drawing of her that had been made by "a dwarf in Paris" (who we later learned was Toulouse-Lautrec); Sixten's prideful encounter with the champion of the village in a hand-wrestling match; Hedvig's one-night job dancing in a village festivity, and his shame and anger when she was forced to show her legs.

In the aftermath of a bitter quarrel triggered by the last incident, they sat apart beside a stream, each clearly shattered and desolate, sundered forever, it seemed. Then he floated a one-word note down to her. "Sorry," it read. She slowly got up, walked to him and clasped him pathetically in a silent embrace. To me that was the most romantic, heartbreaking moment in the film, a simple, eloquent affirmation of the total commitment of their love.

Thereafter hopelessness closed in. Hunger drove them to extremes. Alone in the woods, she scrounged for berries and mushrooms, which, when she ate them, caused her to throw up, dropping a hint that perhaps she was pregnant. In the village, he filched bread, wine, and eggs, a humiliating reduction for an aristocrat and cavalry officer.

We sensed the ultimate desperation, that they

Elvira, frightened and apprehensive, seeks work in a small provincial town.

were finally resigned to taking their lives, when he covertly slipped a pistol into a picnic basket containing the eggs and wine he had filched. Then off they went for their last outing in their beloved fields and woods. Two occurrences poignantly suggested their solitary, irreversible state. Passing an old wood gatherer, whom Sixten had previously talked with by a pond, he paused to say to him, "By the way, I never knew your name." And when the old man remained silent, the younger one said softly, "Mine's Sixten." How pitiful it was that he wanted to establish this last remembrance of his identity!

Proceeding through a field in which children were gleefully playing blindman's-buff, Hedvig fell to the ground in a dead faint and Sixten tenderly lifted her up, caressed her back to consciousness, and led her to a spot beneath a tree where he slowly spread out the meager picnic and poured two glasses of wine. The quiet adoration in his caresses, the lingering slowness with which he made every move, were heartbreaking indications of his desire to prolong their lives.

Then, embracing her tightly with his right arm

and pressing his cheek against hers, he slipped the pistol from the basket and placed the muzzle against her head. (All of this was shown in painful close-up, engaging the viewer in its harrowing intimacy.) But after an agonizing pause and tension, Sixten could not do the intended deed. He dropped the pistol and cried out in protest. She looked with love and sadness into his eyes. Then she got up and walked away casually into a nearby field where, in a medium-close shot, we saw her take a butterfly gently in her hands. It was a beautiful, childlike gesture. Suddenly a shot rang out, and the image of innocent beauty was frozen in the frame. A pause, then a second shot rang out. There was silence, then with the image still held, there came the sweet sound of children singing off-screen. The ending was a quick, expunging cut.

There was not a false note in this picture, not a trace of superfluous sentiment. Mr. Widerberg carefully saw to it that every scene was low-key and underplayed. The tempo was equally restricted. Some scenes were in slow motion, indeed, enhancing a sense of rhythmic movement and of extracting the full flavor from experience. Even the exquisite music of Mozart was not too frequently

Sixten runs through a summer field towards his melancholy destiny.

or insistently used. It was discreetly slid onto the sound track for tonal emphasis at times and that was all.

And the two young actors who played the lovers were perfect—that's all one can say! Thommy Berggren, an experienced professional, with a softly sensitive face and a graceful way of moving, reflected all the emotional changes in the thoughts and resolutions of the essentially weak young man. And Pia Dagermark, a rosebud blond beauty whom Mr. Widerberg discovered in a nonprofessional environment, conveyed through quiet restraint and calm expressions the dignity and intensity of the girl.

Other performers in the picture were mainly for atmosphere, since Mr. Widerberg, who also wrote the screenplay, kept the action almost entirely centered on the lovers. Sixten's wife and children, the circus background of the girl, how they met—all of that was incidental, never visualized and dismissed as memory. The crux and essence of the romance were in its isolation and personal purity.

And this, I think, was the secret of the popular appeal of this film. It concentrated concern on romantic adoration without any thought of time or place. It made inseparable devotion between two people an absorbing entity, immune from social ties and customs. That was awesome and to be cherished in our day and age.

Sixten and Elvira embrace for the last time before going to their deaths.

The timid and inexperienced Ben (Dustin Hoffman) ushers Mrs. Robinson (Anne Bancroft) into a hotel room for their first assignation.

THE GRADUATE

1967

The sadness and cynicism contained in what Mike Nichols's *The Graduate* had to say about the immaturity and vulgarity of the affluent American middle class tended to be lost at the outset in the cascade of smooth satiric farce that gushed from this seemingly innocent and raunchy romantic comedy. None of the crude, corrosive characters of a Los Angeles suburban set that comprised its intrinsic social background were merely dull, monotonous clunks nor the farcical nitwits you might have expected such homogenized creatures of patio society to be. All, quite as much as the principals, showed signs of pathetic poverty.

Ben, the Eastern college graduate around whom the drama turned, —and was, incidentally the glittering apple of his silver-spoon-feeding parents' eyes,—was not in the least the smooth collegian, as predictable as *Playboy* magazine, that you might have expected a product of an Ivy League college to be. He was a shy, indecisive, unobtrusive, and blankly immature lad who laboriously withdrew from social contacts and was a virgin in the realm of sex. And Mrs. Robinson, the middle-aged matron, one of his parents' best friends who methodically set out to seduce him upon his return home from school, was far from the obvious lustful matron you sometimes saw working around the edges of the Production Code in earlier pseudo-collegian films. She was as bold and aggressive about her lechery as Ben was shy and embarrassed about his. And she, in her way, was quite as barren of constructive education as he.

Likewise, the secondary characters in this mischievously stinging film, which was scripted by Calder Willingham and Buck Henry from a novel by Charles Webb, were starkly pathetic, neo-Babbitt types, saved from being totally distressing by the screenplay and Mr. Nichols's gift for gags.

Some critics cautiously protested at first that Mr. Nichols had indulged his famous talent for flip humor and the quick sight gag to the extent that it undermined the substance and credibility of his basic idea. They feared that his shaping of his characters ran a little too much to caricature, and that the purport of the latent commentary was lost in the flow of well-honed farce.

That was possibly so at the outset, when the diffident Ben arrived home and his idolizing parents threw a party on their luxurious patio terrace to show him off. "Hey, there's the award-winning scholar!" screamed his father as the brooding, expressionless Ben came forth from the womb of his upstairs bedroom to face the chattering mob of family friends, nipping away at their martinis and chomping on their barbecue. The guarded reserve of the youngster toward those vulgarians was laughingly bizarre, and his dismay was revealed when one Babbitt ponderously drew him aside and volunteered to advise him on business.

"Ben," the old coot commanded. A long pause.

"Mr. McGuire," finally prompted the politely attentive Ben.

Another long pause, then the gentleman pontifically proclaimed, "I want to say one word to you, just one word. Are you listening?" Ben continued waiting, as did the audience, for the magic word from this fount of wisdom. Then it came. "Plastics!" A pause. "There's a great future in plastics." That was the pregnant word.

And the mountingly funny progression by which Ben was maneuvered into bed, as timid and fearful as a rabbit, by the outrageous Mrs. Robinson became the composition of superbly sophisticated farce, laced through with coy eroticism and parody of the rituals of sex. There was nothing in the film more amusing than the paralyzed confusion of Ben when he amazedly grasped the intention of the oncoming Mrs. Robinson as she coolly put the proposition to him after ordering him like a child to drive her home from the party.

"Oh, my God, Mrs. Robinson, you don't think I'd do something like that!" he gasped as she moved him into position in the shadowy depths of the family-room bar. Then, "Mrs. Robinson, you are trying to seduce me—aren't you?" he moaned when she lured him up to her bedroom and began to disrobe. "Oh, God!" came a wail of mortal terror as she stepped from her bathroom nude. In frenzy he tore open the door and dashed down the stairs, with her throaty invitation, "Call me any time. I'm available to you," ringing in his ears.

That and the interlude which followed, after Ben had screwed up his courage to ask her to meet him at a hotel and one gaucherie after another displayed his naivete in the ways of sex, established what I consider the high-water mark of making fun of the whole mannered ritual of seduction and of the confusions of the inexperienced male.

"Isn't there something you want to tell me?" Mrs. Robinson wearily inquired when Ben had finally completed the transaction of registering and was reporting to her on a house phone.

Ben, misunderstanding, made a solemn stab at gallantry: "I want you to know how much I appreciate this."

Her indifference was withering. "The number, the room number?" That was all she was interested in.

Ben's preparation for romance included brushing his teeth and kissing Mrs. Robinson rather clumsily; at the conclusion of the old-fashioned gesture she emitted a surprised puff of smoke. He was trying so hard to be blasé, to disguise his terror, to handle the situation like a man of the world. When she asked him, with just a note of incredulity, "Is this your first time?" he could only answer flatly, "That's a laugh, Mrs. Robinson."

Of course, the soothing unguent for this farcical rehashing of the old Fata Morgana situation—the older woman seducing the younger man—was

Ben makes a fruitless attempt to engage Mrs. Robinson in a meaningful conversation.

Ashamed of his earlier rudeness to Elaine Robinson (Katherine Ross) while on an enforced date with her, Ben tries to console and reassure her.

the perfect pacing of it by Mr. Nichols and the performances of Anne Bancroft and Dustin Hoffman in the roles. Miss Bancroft, cool and remote toward her bashful lover, was the picture of affected hauteur, permitting—or commanding—sexual contact as a dispensation of *noblesse oblige*. And Mr. Hoffman, a surprising newcomer making his screen debut, played the goof with all the seeming lack of humor of a bookish young intellectual.

"Mrs. Robinson, do you think we could say a few words to each other for a change?" he pathetically asked after it was evident they had been having these hotel trysts for a while. "Would you like to tell me about some of your college experiences?" she obligingly replied, while casually buffing her fingernails. "Oh, my God" was Ben's reply to that.

And, in a wonderfully garbled conversation, betwixt her admitting that she had been compelled to get married because she became pregnant and his wanting to know what her major in college was, she let slip that the crucial encounter

with her future husband was in the back seat of a car.

"What kind of a car was it?" Ben asked obliquely. And when she answered a Ford, he hooted with delight, "So old Elaine Robinson got started in a Ford!" We knew already Ben had an Alfa Romeo, which his parents had given him as a graduation gift.

But, despite the farcical fooling with these elements of travesty, an undercurrent of pathos subtly flowed into the film. Mrs. Robinson slowly became apparent as a woman of frustration and loneliness, bored with her husband, a flabby, middle-aged lush whom Murray Hamilton finely revealed as an affluent nothing just as empty and lonely as she. She was an admitted alcoholic. And her insatiable hunger for sex, even with a kid as incongruous and incompatible as Ben, was an unmistakable symptom of a bleak psychotic state.

Likewise, Ben, in his clumsy efforts to achieve some sort of rapport with this spiritually empty woman, this hollow mockery of a *femme fatale*, was a pitifully limp and lonely fellow, reaching for—what? Maturity?

"Ben, what are you doing?" his father called to him as he lay on a raft in the family swimming pool, letting luscious, erotic fantasies of Mrs. Robinson float through his head.

"Just drifting," he answered wearily. And this aspect of him, a college graduate, going nowhere, was the sad and cynical theme in this early part. The sadness was complemented and pointed up most effectively by the excellent music that Mr. Nichols and the producer, Lawrence Turman, selected for the film. It was a classic score, we now acknowledge, composed by Paul Simon and sung as background by him and Art Garfunkel, topped by the haunting "Sounds of Silence" for Ben's intimate and lonesome moods—a composition of musical comment that served as an appropriate theme for all the footloose young people of an unsettled age. Then "April Come She Will" for the moods of hopefulness (and the passage of time in the Mrs. Robinson trysts) and the rather bittersweet folksong, "Scarborough Fair" for the happier and more active scenes.

But, of course, the tune we best remember and associate with this film was the taunting, rollicking "Mrs. Robinson," which was used to coun-

Love-wracked and frantic, Ben snatches Elaine from her incipient wedding to Carl.

With the church doors latched behind them by a large crucifix, Elaine and Ben race away happily to—what?

terpoint with light sarcasm the seductive rendezvous.

The issue was fully joined when Ben, succumbing to the urgings of his parents and her father, took Elaine Robinson on a date, against the furious protests of her mother. He found, after being deliberately rude to this initially colorless girl who became as needful of compassion as Ben was (in the performance of Katherine Ross), that he really was taken with her and wanted to continue the dates. So when Mrs. Robinson, frantic with jealousy, threatened to tell Elaine of her own affair with Ben, he dashed to the Robinson house with the intention of telling Elaine himself. However, the appearance of the mother's anguished face behind Ben as he started to confess was sufficient to reveal all to Elaine. In the next scene, her silent parents were packing the anguished girl off to college and Ben was watching from afar, full of woe.

But he was intrepid and determinedly followed Elaine to the University of California at Berkeley, where he diligently laid siege to her, urging her to go out with him, begging her to marry him. She finally relented to the point of saying she couldn't marry him until she spoke to Carl. Who was Carl? Another suitor. Why did she have to speak to him? "Well," Elaine blandly admitted, "I said I might marry *him*." And that was, indeed, the arrangement her parents had made for her.

Thereafter the film rushed to a frenzied climax. Ben, having lost touch with Elaine, finally discovered that she and Carl were to be married the next day. After an all-night drive and a veritable riot of Keystone delays—car running out of gas, phone calls—poor Ben arrived at the church the next morning just as the marriage vows were being spoken. "Elaine," he screamed from the back of the church. Abandoning the ceremony, she ran in her wedding gown toward him. Wrapping an arm around her, he grabbed up a large wooden crucifix and used it to ward off the pursuers, then jammed the cross into the door to lock the attendants in while he rushed to a bus with Elaine and plunked into a back seat. As the film came to a close the two were riding off, in a common public conveyance, emotionally exhausted and confused. Sudden rebels toward the world they'd been brought up in, they were plainly unprepared for the one ahead.

Obviously, Mr. Nichols was not interested in tidying up loose ends, any more than he was with his first picture, *Who's Afraid of Virginia Woolf?* His aim was to contemplate the landscape of a drifting society, unwittingly cruel to its young people and destructive eventually to itself. He meant to make us laugh at human folly. And that he managed most admirably.

The futuristic lobby of a way station orbiting in space.

2001: A SPACE ODYSSEY

1968

In light of the phenomenal popularity of George Lukas' 1977 *Star Wars*, which seems to have done for science fiction movies what Mickey Mouse did for screen cartoons, it may seem a bit acrimonious for a veteran critic to persist in the belief that Stanley Kubrick's earlier probe of the empyrean, *2001: a Space Odyssey*, remains the most exciting and intelligent motion picture in the science fiction genre. It may even be the best film ever to try to suggest in pictorial terms the mystery of creation and the awesome nature of the universe.

2001 captured the mind at the start with a promise of exciting exploration and the unfolding of an age-old mystery. What, it implicitly inquired in a preface entitled "The Dawn of Man," with a gaggle of apelike creatures gathered in wonder and awe around a shiny black monolithic object set in a barren plain, was the touchstone of creation, the animator of *everything?* Was this extraordinary object, which the ape creatures ogled and tapped with much the same air of mystification as a group of space scientists later betrayed in contemplating a similar object discovered below the surface of the moon, a key to the great ki-netic forces that have conglomerated the universe and have somehow held it together through the eons of endless time?

That was the challenging question that *2001* boldly put as the singular "grab" and motivator for its quest into outer space. No fancy stuff here about warfare between galactic enemies who looked like comic book creatures and shot it out like their terrestrial counterparts in Western films. No glamorized speculation on the menace of those pesky UFOs. The excitement which Mr. Kubrick and his collaborator, Arthur C. Clarke, chose to rouse in the minds of their viewers was on the more intellectual plane of conquest. What *is* the secret of the system that unifies all matter, time, and space? Is there an extraterrestrial magnetic "missing link"?

Smartly, they chose to pitch their fancy in the twenty-first century so that the pictorial elements in their assumptions would have a fresh, futuristic look. The spaceship in which their team of scientists was transported to the moon to study that slab of screaming matter isolated in a subsurface pit was a super-deluxe cruise liner with ultramodern furnishings, hostesses in trim, sex-muted costumes, and a menu of concentrated foods. The spotless and shiny quarters in which they were lodged on the moon was a glorified Howard Johnson motel with dial telephone connections to Earth and individual television monitors permit-

A group of mystified space scientists contemplate the monolith found beneath the surface on the moon.

ting one to see as well as talk to the wife and kiddies back home. All was as neat and antiseptic as a hospital operating room, and the characters were as casual and unemotional as executives at a sales convention in Omaha. Thus did Mr. Kubrick establish a recognizable but slightly wry atmosphere from which to launch his speculation into the nature of what lies beyond.

In this subsequent section two scientists, played by Gary Lockwood and Keir Dullea, were rocketed onward to the distant regions of Jupiter. Their mission was, hopefully, to discover what was out there with which that moon-slab seemed in some weird circuitry. The science fiction gadgets were assembled and the major melodrama occurred, as well as a subtle buildup of the film's fundamental poetry. Yes, poetry, for the stirring of emotion through magnificent, awesome images and sounds, and through visions of strange man-made machinery moving onward through the void of trackless space, all assisted by the careful stimulation of a brilliant musical score, accomplished the major disturbance of this uncommonly disturbing film.

Significantly, the usual clash of human personalities was absent in it. The two spacemen, Poole and Bowman, were the sole occupants (except for three frozen bodies of scientists "in hibernation" that were being carried as future spares) of the great, cagelike spaceship, *Discovery*. As it moved along silently, they neither quarreled nor raised their voices. The only contention aboard was with HAL, a phenomenal computer which seemed to be the auto-pilot of the ship. At first, HAL, embodied in a glowing yellow bull's-eye of light fluctuating in a circumference of ruby-red and silver rings at the center of the instrument panel, was cheerful and chummy with the men. It talked with them in a throaty, soundbox voice, and they reciprocated with condescending and relaxed camaraderie.

For some perverse reason which was not sufficiently explained but may have been a mere whim of boredom or pique, HAL suddenly made the flat announcement that an antenna outside the ship was malfunctioning. Thus did the trouble begin. When Poole went out in a spacesuit to service it, HAL, acting unilaterally, shorted his magnetic attachment and cut him loose. The situation was nasty, and when Bowman took off in a pod (a

The twenty-first-century space ship, *Discovery*, embarked on its long voyage to Jupiter.

kind of satellite trouble wagon) to try to rescue him, HAL locked the entry door of the *Discovery* with the evident purpose of abandoning both men to their fates.

This was an obvious symbolization of the ultimate Revolt of the Machine, which has been a favorite theme in science fiction since the vivid literature of H. G. Wells. But Bowman rose to the occasion. Realizing that Poole could not be saved—that his life-support system had been exhausted and he had to be left to float away (a vastly chilling image, incidentally)—Bowman tried to reenter the ship. When HAL refused to admit him, he blasted his way through an emergency port. Once inside, and in natural desperation, he undertook the dismantling of HAL, performing on it what was described as a "mechanical lobotomy." In perhaps the most ingenious and (as it turned out) poignant single scene, HAL, terrified and pleading for mercy, slowly lost strength and expired, finally gasping out a brief obituary of itself and then pathetically singing the old song "Daisy, Daisy, give me your promise true . . ." as its voice became weaker and slower, like an old gramophone running down. What a remark-

able association of mechanical imperturbability and human sentiment was made in HAL.

Thereafter, Bowman, isolated, took over manual control and reached the region of Jupiter where, sure enough, floating among the planet's cluster of moons, he spied another shining slab of extraterrestrial matter identical to those we had previously seen. Here was indeed awesome evidence of some mysterious universal force—or just an abstract symbolization of the linkage of everything. But beyond that Mr. Kubrick and Mr. Clarke were too smart to venture. They wouldn't be trapped into attempting to present a cogent scientific theme. Instead they arranged to have the turbulence in the area become so great and the eerie screaming and howling of energy forces so deafening that the pattern and thrust of the project were abruptly changed. Suddenly the battered *Discovery* was whirled away out of control, and the astonished eye of the beholder was almost blindingly suffused by a stupendous giant-screen montage of abstract color images, great swirls of varicolored gases and racing nebulae, displays of Aurora Borealis, streams of white-hot molten matter that appeared like filtered photo-

The two active scientists aboard the *Discovery*, Poole (Gary Lockwood) and Bowman (Keir Dullea), have a consultation with the ship's highly sophisticated computer, HAL.

graphs of overwhelming volcanic lava flows, and a host of visual sensations accompanied by indescribable electronic sound. The effect was to shatter the senses beyond any previous assault and leave the viewer emotionally exhausted and intellectually disarranged. This was the major experience afforded by *2001*—this brazen attack upon the senses that inevitably tended to project the imagination into areas suggesting the phenomena of light, time, and space.

With that supreme explosion of a visual metaphor, which lasted for all of ten minutes, the bombardment was suddenly stopped and the viewer was abruptly projected into a strange, handsome, silent room, meticulously decorated in a French-English eighteenth-century style, where the battered, spacesuited Bowman incongruously appeared. No logical explanation was forthcoming for a spaceman's entrance here, no sequential tie-in with what had gone before. This was simply the setting for Mr. Kubrick's (and Mr. Clarke's) last metaphor, which became in itself an enigma that left the viewer to conclude what he would. For here, in a series of silent tableaux that dissolved from one to the next at a

rhythmic pace, the viewer was allowed to watch Bowman settle down to old age, wither, and die. But at the moment before his expiration, he beheld on the floor at the foot of his bed a gleaming miniature replication of that mysterious slab. Was this, then, a symbolization of his final glimpse of the scientists' Holy Grail, a tantalizing suggestion of the futility of the quest? Or was it a subtle implication of Man's never completed pursuit of all-inclusive knowledge in the endless continuum of time? I choose to conclude it was the latter, since the final image was a dissolve to a close-up shot of a fetus enclosed in a transparent sac, and the bug-eyed face of the fetus strangely resembled that of Bowman—or Keir Dullea!

Enough cannot be said for Mr. Kubrick's superlative use of sound and his exotic selection of music to support his pictorial poetry. Richard Strauss' *Thus Spoke Zarathustra* was the solemn and exalting theme, and its effect was so powerful and impressive that it has become in the marts of trade and in TV commercials a popular science fiction signature. Selections from Gyorgy Ligeti were also suggestively placed, and the use of Johann Strauss' beloved *Blue Danube* to auralize the thrilling images of the *Discovery* moving majestically in space was a reminder (to those who could remember) of the soaring musical theme, "Beyond the Blue Horizon," that filled the star-studded dome of the huge globe at the theme center of the 1939 New York World's Fair.

Indeed, all accessible facilities of modern advanced cinema were employed by Mr. Kubrick—the giant Cinerama screen, stereophonic sound (in larger theaters), the finest color photography and special effects—to charge the minds of average viewers with speculations about the universe in ways that no amount of simplification of scientific literature could match. So here was the ultimate achievement in science fiction upon the screen—at least, in our generation and probably for several to come. I only wonder how audiences will view it—if it is still available to be viewed—in 2001!

One of the scientists aboard the *Discovery* walks along the passageway connecting the two main pods.

On their exaggerated customized "bikes," Wyatt (Peter Fonda), and his pal Billy (Dennis Hopper), give a hitchhiker a lift in a southwestern town.

EASY RIDER

1969

Dennis Hopper and Peter Fonda's *Easy Rider* caused a good deal of disagreement upon its release, as to just what this seemingly aimless movie about two motorcycle riders was really trying to say. Some thoughtful and well-respected critics took it as a devastating blast at the kind of hostility and intransigence felt toward contemporary free-wheeling youth by a bigoted middle-class society. Others, less sympathetic, found it rambling and without specific point, distinguished only by the brief intrusion of Jack Nicholson in a secondary role.

Despite a mixed bag of criticism, this disarmingly casual little film, which many motion picture professionals initially labeled just another "bike film"—meaning another in the already long list of cheap pictures about motorcycle gangs—became a phenomenally popular attraction for a wide range of moviegoers, especially the young, which indicated there was something in it that older critics did not fully understand.

The film signaled, in my opinion, a surge of genuine sympathy toward the new generation of restless youngsters that the 1960s spawned—the hippies, the passive resisters, the pot smokers, the seekers of a cultural alternative to a dull, materialistic social order. They included the kids who formed the communes, the religious weirdos, the pathological freaks, the "flower children" who banded themselves into grotesque theatrical troupes and weird art colonies in which they could separately "do their things." The vocabulary of these youngsters was virtually limited to the plaintive guitar and the piteous lyrics of endless folksongs that expressed the basic melancholy of the "group." Long hair and freakish clothing were the badge of their separateness.

Actually, the essence of these rebels—or dropouts, as they were termed, to designate them as deserters from the rigid Establishment—was a subtly pervasive commonality of pathetic helplessness, a sad inability to carry off the ways of living they had commenced. They had fantasies and dreams but no real order, intentions but no consistent aims. And this is what *Easy Rider* implicitly and wistfully conveyed.

The story was of two hippie bike riders who provided themselves with a bundle by transporting a haul of hard drugs from Mexico to a Southern California "drop." Thereafter, they started across the great Southwest on a random trip to the New Orleans Mardi Gras. The film casually

219

Locked up overnight in a country jail, Billy and Wyatt meet a delightful kindred spirit in an alcoholic lawyer, George (Jack Nicholson).

scanned in easy stages various aspects of the alienated groups and the reactions to them by bourgeois elements. They visited with underprivileged people—a blacksmith, a white farmer trying to scratch a living from the land with his Indian wife and kids, a hippie commune where swarms of children tugged at their scruffy parents' trousers and skirts and all seemed to live for the mere purpose of doing weird theatrics and folk dances in an adobe ruin.

They were arrested in a southwestern town and thrown in jail, allegedly for joining a parade without a permit. The real reason for their incarceration was that the residents resented them. While behind bars they met another prisoner, a young lawyer. The son of one of the town's leading citizens, he was often collared for public drunkenness. With this most charming, loquacious companion hanging on the back seat of one of the bikes, they continued on to another cowtown where they were harassed again by redneck punks. Indeed, the resentment was so bitter that that night, while the three were camped outside town, they were set upon by a swarm of the local bullies. The two bikers were badly beaten, but their happy-go-lucky friend had met a more gruesome fate. He'd been axed to death.

Continuing on to New Orleans, they went directly to the House of Blue Lights, a plush brothel, and fell in with a couple of whores. The inarticulate foursome went into a cemetery and swallowed tabs of LSD. It was a bad trip, a horrible garble of wild hallucinations and nauseous spells, which left the two riders despondent and ready to get out of town. Obviously their dream of El Dorado, of a happy haven at their rainbow's end, was shattered. They saw no more of Mardi Gras than the mottled faces of two sad whores. On their way west again, they were accosted on a country road by a couple of hicks in a truck who blasted at them with a shotgun, causing one of the riders to pile up in a blazing wreck. While the other raced his bike to seek aid for his companion, the bullies turned about and pursued, and gunned *him* down in cold blood. The end was a symbolic high shot of the burning motorcycles in a field, the shattered bodies of the riders lying near them and a column of black smoke rising lazily in the air.

Clearly there was protest in this picture—protest of the hippies toward the world of materialism from which they were trying to escape, and

Off again with George as a companion, Billy and Wyatt continue their journey east to the Mardi Gras in New Orleans.

especially toward the bigots and the reactionaries who showed their hostility in such deadly violent ways. The beating up of the young fellows and the shooting of them at the end were shockingly vivid and recollective of the sort of intolerance and harassment that young Freedom Fighters for racial equality were encountering in the South at about that time. It was a quality of protest too obvious and intense for any logical response. The shame of such reaction toward the aliens was beyond any rationality.

But beneath all the protest in this picture and all the agreeable empathy for these rootless young men who were symbolic of a significant subcultural class there ran an even deeper strain of sadness and irrevocable despair for the wastage and the futility of their alienated lives. Obviously withdrawn from the conventional for reasons too complex to describe—political, psychological, emotional, or perhaps just inability to cope—these nomads of the road were revealed as fundamentally vulnerable, without the means, strength, or vitality to do anything positive for themselves.

The last line of one of the bike riders to the other just before they were accosted and killed, "You know, Billy, we blew it," seemed to sum up the lives of many of their generation. The remaining biker assumed he was alluding to the wash-out in New Orleans. More perceptive minds recognized it as a cryptic comment on the futility of the whole hippie class, the epitaph for a misconceived, misled age.

Easy Rider paralleled extraordinarily the theme, ambiance, and summation of John Ford's great film *The Grapes of Wrath.** The latter, too, was a film about nomads moving across the magnificent face of the great Southwest, encountering both the beauty and the hideousness of certain aspects of the United States, confronted by cruel and bleak resistance to their dreams and search for a better life, and left at the end with disappointment and only a sliver of hope.

Metaphorically the hippies of the 1960s were, in a socialistic way, the descendants of the 1930s Oakies. They were symbolically dispossessed from the land, which would no longer support them, just as the Oakies were. They were seeking

221

With George lost to murderous hoodlums outside a Texas "red-neck" town, Billy and Wyatt seek the company of two prostitutes (Karen Black and Luana Anders) at the House of Blue Lights in New Orleans.

a better place to settle, as Americans have traditionally done since the beginning of our national expansion—and since the settlement of America, indeed. And the implications of their frustration and failure were grim reverberations of the terminus of the flight of the Oakies, which was the Southern California of today!

Indeed, I do think it quite ironic and prophetic that Peter Fonda, who played the role of Wyatt, one of the two lads in *Easy Rider*, is the son of Henry Fonda, who played Tom Joad, the laconic, independent, stubborn hero in *The Grapes of Wrath*. This coincidence struck me forcibly when I first saw the film and the irony of it has magnified on a philosophical level since. Could it be that the lanky, solemn Wyatt of *Easy Rider is* the son of Tom Joad, the grim young man we last saw escaping across a California hillside in a dreary dawn? Could it be that Tom ended up a laborer or an oil-field worker in that shabby, materialistic land and that the fruit of his loins rebelled against it? It is romantically conceivable.

But, of course, this had no relation to the quality of the film, or to the performance of young Mr. Fonda. He was a monolith by himself, a strange, self-contained individual who let himself be known as "Captain America" and wore a brown leather jacket with a huge flag of the United States on his back. What this told us about his

antecedents, his attachments, was anybody's guess, but I took it to be a peculiar piece of private sarcastic wit. This young man, who seemed to guide the expedition and keep his vagrant, continually stoned sidekick in line, considered himself a current version of the kind of American who made this country great. He was a comicstrip hero, a mythic character, in the idolatry of the young.

Likewise, his sidekick was a playout of a juvenile fantasy. Billy, the second "easy rider," whom the film's director, Dennis Hopper, played with a minimal use of vocabulary and in a nondescript costume that seemed to be inspired by the frontier regalia of Wyatt Earp and Buffalo Bill, was an eloquent representation of the kind of "dress-up" affected by kids who had nothing more to distinguish them than the mimicry of their costumes. In a way not too fully appreciated, Billy aptly mirrored the enslaved, the mindless, methodical dependents on the cult of grotesquerie and grass.

In notable contrast to the bikers was the alcoholic lawyer, George, whom they unwittingly conveyed to his doom. George, played with witty, caustic dryness by young Jack Nicholson, a veteran of low-budget pictures, gave a voice and a rhetoric to the film, articulating the revulsion and the urge toward freedom that the other two only felt. It was George's drawling, droll expatiation on everything from the foibles of mankind to his theory of how the "Venutians" from outer-space have already taken over the world that thoroughly captivated viewers and gave a calculated lift to the film by putting the disgruntled feelings of the voiceless into sardonic words. As the first of the nonconformists to be a visible victim of bigotry, he gave a sudden, shocking focus to the whole. His contribution was noted and generously praised by the critics, and Mr. Nicholson became, as a consequence of this performance, the popular personification of the valiant loner-loser in a succession of films.

Contributing to the tone of *Easy Rider* and to the hypnotic effect it had upon so many youthful viewers was its fine background music score, a skillful medley of popular hippie folksongs, Bob Dylan favorites and straight-out rock-and-roll. Likewise the color photography of Laszlo Kovacs was wonderfully apt in absorbing the Western panoramas in the naturalistic *cinéma vérité* style.

For so many coalescing reasons, including the pertinent fact that it was produced on a "shoe-string" by Mr. Fonda, Mr. Hopper, and Burt Schneider (the son of Abe Schneider, the chairman of the board of Columbia Pictures, which ultimately and somewhat reluctantly distributed the film), *Easy Rider* was a clarion inspiration to young people, especially those who were fanatic about films, and a historic register of an era which should be looked at appreciatively for years to come.

Shot off his bike by a couple of passing bigots on a lonely road outside New Orleans, Wyatt finds the end of his dream in death.

The gang of American outlaws known as the Wild Bunch, enter a Mexican border village, with Dutch (Ernest Borgnine), and their leader Pike (William Holden) in advance.

THE WILD BUNCH

1969

When Sam Peckinpah's *The Wild Bunch* exploded upon the screen in a splatter of blood and shattering violence such as never had been seen in a film before (and I do not forget the excesses of the two-years' previous *Bonnie and Clyde*), the understandable reaction of most critics was shock, disgust, dismay, revulsion, regurgitation. Sensitivities were stunned and outraged by the gluttonous concentration on gore and the visceral aspects of killing in what might have been a simple western film. The litany of routine gun battles and standard shoot-outs between the good guys and the bad, familiar in western dramas embracing bandits and the upholders of the law, became explosive confrontations and horrendously murderous massacres in this studied perversion of the ritual western in which there were no perceptible good guys. *All* were bad.

As a consequence, *The Wild Bunch* swiftly blew up into a critical *cause célèbre* that was wrangled over on the basis of its violence alone, as displayed in an obfuscating foreground of hu-

man brutishness and blood. It was, indeed, the disturber of more critical indignation and apprehension than *Bonnie and Clyde.* So generally discouraging and condemnatory were the reviews of *The Wild Bunch* when it appeared that I, then retired from reviewing, decided it was one movie that could wait.

Sometime after its release, however, I did take it in, devoid of any great expectations. To my astonishment, I began to grasp, behind the foreground scrim of violence, the scope and significance of its theme. Then I recognized that *The Wild Bunch* was not about violence per se, as were the run of cheap "spaghetti westerns" or "bounty pictures" that had been coming out of Italy and Spain. Nor was its intention, as one reviewer assumed from talking with Mr. Peckinpah, to achieve some sort of antiviolence therapy by producing "a wave of sickness in the gut." It was a drama about man's deterioration in the face of the erosion and loss of those ideals, beliefs, and traditions which are supposed to support the structure of society and existence among civilized men. It was about the ultimate obliteration of the rule of law by excessive greed, cynicism, betrayal—all the passions that break loose in men when they have lost whatever faith or reliance they may have had in society's codes. Excessive violence was but a symptom of the intensity of its characters' despair. Survival was the only purpose that determined their thinking and their deeds.

It was also a melodrama calculated by Mr. Peckinpah and his associate scriptwriter, Walton Green, to describe the decline and dissolution of the romantic myths of the Old West. Their protagonists were a gang of roving outlaws, bank robbers, and train hijackers who, working along the Mexican border in 1913, were tagged as "the last of a dying breed," relics of the troops of folk heroes made lustrous by such as the Daltons, Butch Cassidy, and Jesse James. And their antagonists were agents of the railroad hired to hunt them down and bring back their bodies for the bounties that would be the coldly mercenary rewards. Both factions were corrupt and venal, far beyond regard for the legendary codes of good-guy and bad-guy behavior that their predecessors had observed. Indeed, the chief bounty-hunter was himself a former highwayman paroled from prison on the condition that he catch the bandits or else be returned to jail. Thus the aim of the pursuers was not to uphold the law, not to serve the noble ends of "justice," but to wipe out those vicious nuisances.

Insofar as both factions were in adversary roles that used to clash in the long-gone ritual westerns and were thus distorted shadows from the past—not the past of the real historical frontier but of the legends of it in western films—

there was a structure of nostalgic sentimentality built into this film. Though the outlaws were cruel and ruthless villains, it was possible to feel sympathy for them. They were traditional folk heroes, fighting with their backs to the wall and doomed to extermination. That was well sensed by Mr. Peckinpah.

Every step in his picture marked their advancement on the road to death. From the moment they rode into a peaceful cowtown disguised in U.S. Army uniforms for the purpose of robbing the railway office and were ambushed by the force of bounty-hunters under the command of their old sidekick recruited for that purpose, the predestined fate of these fellows was to be hounded down. The modern world had caught up with them. Private armies of railroad goons had replaced the stalwart tin-star marshals who accomplished their purposes alone. And although this time the bandits managed to shoot their way out of that trap in a devastating gun battle that foretold even fiercer ones to come, pursuit and eventual destruction were inevitable as they fled into Mexico.

Indeed, the suspense of the picture—and there was plenty—hung tinglingly upon the crucial question of just how long the "wild bunch" could manage to keep alive, caught as they were between the Scylla of the vengeance of the bounty-hunters bearing down and the Charybdis of a band of Mexican rebels with whom they were forced to throw in their lot. And when the pincers were finally closed upon them—when they were

Death and confusion are wrecked upon the troops accompanying an American ammunition train raided by the Wild Bunch.

225

Robert Ryan (right), as the former outlaw Thornton, coerced by railway agents to capture the fugitive train-robbers, is flanked by his vicious, moronic gunman, T.C. (L.Q. Jones), in an attempted ambush.

tumbled into a hurricane of slaughter with the treacherous rebels, after hijacking an ammunition train—the last tatter of suspense was in the question of how many Mexicans they could kill before they themselves were destroyed.

This emphasis on killing, beginning with the opening ambuscade and continuing through the havoc accomplished in the attack on the ammunition train, the wreckage of bridges exploded and clashes in Mexican streets, and climaxing in the hideous carnage of that final holocaust, gave powerful visual symbolization to the passions of the chief participants. Anger, hatred, and frustra-

tion were rendered demoniacal in the images of bodies riddled and faces blown away. Some critics went so far as to label the climax of slaughter a "blood ballet," done as it was in slow motion, as was the climax of *Bonnie and Clyde*, with details minutely inspected and torturingly prolonged. The concept was apt, if one expanded the usual definition of "ballet" to cover a cadenced compilation of charnel-house images, turned by a bit of camera trickery into a moviemaker's version of an awful dream. No wonder the chief bounty-hunter, when he came upon the debris of this scene, looked on it with a revulsion that was

Pike is joined on his way to junction with a Mexican rebel force by Sykes (Edmund O'Brien), a veteran gunslinger.

Pike and one of his vicious confederates, Lyle Gorch (Warren Oates), make a last blazing, bloody stand against the erratic Mexicans.

unbearable even for him and went off with the sole surviving outlaw, an old campaigner, to lose himself in the Mexican hills.

In this role of the chief bounty-hunter, the veteran Robert Ryan was superb, projecting a sense of the repugnance and humiliation of a man who had put himself to a shameful service in order to survive. William Holden, too, was superior as the leader of the outlaw band, looking at the ugly world around him with icy-eyed hostility and contempt. Other familiar actors who were vivid in character roles were Ernest Borgnine as a bulldog sidekick to Mr. Holden, Warren Oates as a gibberingly maniacal outlaw, Edmond O'Brien as the one old bandit who survived, and Emilio Fernandez as the frenzied and deceitful leader of the Mexican rebel force.

The extraordinary popularity of *The Wild Bunch* at the time it was released seemed to baffle and discourage some critics who were especially revolted by it. But to my mind, on retrospection, its success is not hard to understand. Beyond the excitement of its story, the brilliance with which it was performed, and the electrifying intensity of Mr. Peckinpah's precipitate style (for instance, he made five times as many editing cuts in it as are in the average same-length movie) and also the hard-focus quality and clarity of Lucien Ballard's photography, there was always rumbling through it a muted thunder of despair about civilized man. Not only were the outlaws, their pursuers, and the Mexican rebels repulsive types. Supposedly respectable citizens were seen as sadists and hypocrites. Innocent children in the cowtown laughed with delight to see a battle to the death between two scorpions they were studiously tormenting, while a group of their pious elders stood apart, singing revival-meeting hymns as the bandits and bounty-hunters slaughtered one another in their midst. And when the body of one of the outlaws was dragged through a Mexican town, children ran along beside the corpse cheering as adults watched in dull passivity.

One did not have to be a cynic or a hate-spewing student activist to sense in this film a simulation of a world gone mad. At a time when our faith in institutions was being shaken by the Vietnam War, the corruption of politicians, and the spread of racial strife, one could subtly absorb from its depiction a monstrous metaphor, a philosophical intimation of the crack-up of all society. In its way, *The Wild Bunch* was a horrendous and terrifying modern parable, which made it not only fascinating but a permanently educational film.

227

Adolf Hitler

Pierre Mendes-France

Sir Anthony Eden

THE SORROW AND THE PITY

1971

The onrush of documentary movies during and after World War II, when they were widely used for spreading propaganda, education, and slanted news, has been largely diverted into the area of commercial and educational TV, which found a device of great convenience in a variety of factual films. But happily the documentary has not been stripped completely from theatrical screens. Every so often a great one does still come along to remind us how dramatic and effective the nonfictional film can be.

Such a one in recent years was Marcel Ophuls' unbelievably powerful French film *The Sorrow and the Pity*, which I state without reservation was the most ambitious, audacious, and stunning documentary I have seen to date. Exploring in depth and detail the Nazi occupation of France during the years of that nation's darkest period between 1939 and 1945, it provided not only reflection upon the quality of French life in those times but a frank and devastating comprehension of the political polarization of the populace. Without pulling any punches or endeavoring to put a kindlier face upon the treacheries and deceits of many people, from generals and politicians on down, it recalled how the passions and prejudices that had torn the French people for

centuries—deep racial and religious divisions and resentments of economic class—had eroded the "patriotism" of the people and their will to resist, and, indeed, had emboldened many of them to collaborate with the enemy.

More disturbing were strong indications and implications that in the quarter of a century that had passed since the war and the dreadful occupation, France had still not been cured of internal strife. Anti-Semitism, which was rampant before and during the war, continued to be an ugly and darkly divisive force. Pro- and anti-Communist feelings boiled in government and industry. And neo-Nazi organizations were creeping again through the land.

But also contained in the more than four-hour length of *The Sorrow and the Pity* were counterindications of how some French, during the darkest days of the occupation, organized themselves to resist, joined in underground activities to harass the enemy at great peril, and how others, more cautious but no less fervent, managed to keep low profiles and endure. A remarkable cross-section of the French people who had been involved in one or another way, as leaders, resisters, collaborators, or just plain citizens, was assembled and interviewed by Mr. Ophuls and his associate, André Harris, over a period of months, and their recollections and reflections were cast into this monumental mosaic.

Along with these were compiled the reflections

228

rave   Maurice Chevalier   Helmuth Tausend

of a number of outsiders who had been close to France during the occupation. Among them were Sir Anthony Eden, old and worn, who recalled as Britain's wartime Foreign Secretary what he had known of the agonies of the French; Helmuth Tausend, a paunchy German burgher who, as a Nazi Wehrmacht officer, was in command of the SS contingent in the focal city of Clermont-Ferrand; Nazi general Walter Warlimont, who pompously told of his surprise at finding the French nonresistant to the invading Nazi troops and recounted how the French general, Hunsiker, obligingly surrendered himself; and, most surprising among these old observers, an odd little man named Dennis Hake, who revealed his astounding experiences as a British double-agent in France who picked that perilous occupation because he wished to prove that "homosexuals could be brave."

It was, in sum, an overwhelming roster of active participants and witnesses to what was and is the most bewildering exemplification of a nation's travail and shame, at least, in modern history. And it was aptly encased in a matrix of wartime newsreel and propaganda film, both German and French, that hauntingly pinned down and illustrated the testimonies of interviewees and brought back—or imaged for younger viewers—the literal look and atmosphere of those grim days.

Billed in an opening subtitle simply as "the

chronicle of a town during the occupation," that "town" being Clermont-Ferrand, a large industrial city where the resistance movement was said to have begun, the focus widened quickly to envision the confusion of all France—The Collapse, as this dismal phase was titled—in the early part of the war. With newsreel shots of the advancing Nazis, people fleeing Paris in frenzied fear, the French army in complete disorder, the government removing to Bordeaux, the structure of the film began to take form with the introduction of Pierre Mendès-France, an early Resistance fighter and briefly a postwar premier. With the ample advantage of hindsight and mellowness acquired through the years, M. Mendès-France brought into context the shock and turmoil of those first disastrous weeks and established a tone of calm and candor for his frequent appearances throughout the film. Indeed, he was placed by Mr. Ophuls in the position of a quasi-anchorman, ready with vivid recollections and occasional humorous anecdotes—especially one of his escape from an early incarceration by the interim government of Marshal Pétain and his flight to join the Free French in North Africa—which helped to clarify the historical sequence and move the documentary along.

This trick of introducing and talking a bit with his principal subjects, then cutting away from and later back to them for continuing recollections and comment as though they were partici-

229

Marshal Petain

Suzy Velair

A French soldier bids good-bye to wife and son.

pants in a vast symposium, was a key to the film's fascination. Although they were not face to face and, indeed, were often widely separated in the places and times they were interviewed, the effect of this method of assembly was to give the viewer an exciting sense of dramatic confrontations in the exchanges and clashes of points of view. The impact and intellectual seeding was far above that of even the best TV talk-show. And because of the sharp personalities of most of the participants—people who were bathed in the aura of living witnesses, people who *were there*—one was forced to listen to them and watch them intently and be variously but always strongly moved.

The most effective of all the participants, for my taste, was M. Mendès-France because of the scope of his knowledge, the fairness of his point of view, the warmth of his compassion and humor, and the eloquence with which he spoke. But there were literally dozens of others who, in one way or another, struck the eye and gripped the mind with mental pictures of how it must have been.

There was the German burgher, Tausend, who, by shrewd and clever staging, was caught at the wedding reception of his daughter. Oozing affluence and amiability he recalled his days as the Nazi gauleiter in Clermont-Ferrand. While insisting that he knew nothing of the transporting of Resistance fighters, he did complain that by not

wearing uniforms which would have identified them as partisans, they were not playing fair with the Nazis. He, being pointedly cut back to, was a balance to M. Mendès-France. Conspicuous was his growing embarrassment and irritation as he was more closely probed toward the end.

In contrast to him was Emile Couladon, the famous "Colonel Gaspar" of the Resistance in Auvergne, who described the operations of his confederates as casually as he might have described his postwar activities as a salesman of TV sets and radios. He was able to point out with respect but dispassion the group grave of four of his underground fighters, teenage youths, who had been ambushed and shot. To him the ordeal of the occupation was ancient history. So it was, also, to others: to Marcel Verdier, who had been and still was a pharmacist in Clermont-Ferrand, and who admitted, in the presence of his genial wife and family, that his only concern was getting food for them; to Louis Grave, a peasant farmer who had worked with the underground and been betrayed to the Nazis by a neighbor whom he knew but did nothing about ("What good would it do?") when the war was over and he came home from imprisonment in Buchenwald; to Emmanuel D'Astier de la Vigerie, a mellow aristocrat who had helped to organize the whole Resistance which he looked back upon with offhand pride; and to two aging Clermont-Ferrand schoolmasters who feebly explained how they "could do

aff officers planning

French prisoners at the time
of Liberation.

Vehicles abandoned on a road
during the flight from Paris.

nothing'' to help their Jewish students, then confused World War II with World War I!

Impressive for the candor and clarity with which he unapologetically described his service with the French ''Charlemagne Division'' whose members went over to the Nazis and fought for them on the eastern front was the handsome and scholarly aristocrat Christian de la Maziere. He rationalized his decision on the basis of what he had been brought up to believe. Less respectable for a forthright admission was Count René de Chambrun, who attempted in a crafty, lawyerish fashion to justify the position of his father-in-law, Pierre Laval, who was the head of the Vichy puppet government and was tried and executed as a traitor after the war.

And there were so many others—Madame Solange, a prim hairdresser in Clermont-Ferrand, who had been branded for ''consorting'' with a Nazi captain and had her head shaved after the war; Jacques Duclos, chief of the clandestine Communist Party, who blamed the *French* ''gestapo'' for hounding ''patriots''; author-biologist Claude Lévi-Strauss, who gave statistics on the number of Jews, including children, who had been transported to Germany with the approval and cooperation of Laval; Maurice Chevalier, who was accused (and later cleared) of aiding the enemy; Georges Lemirand, an aging firebrand who had organized a fascistic French ''youth corps''; Henri Rochat, the loyal and eloquent

lawyer for Mendès-France; Flight Sergeant Evans of the RAF who told how the French had courageously hidden and helped British flyers downed in France—and more.

The whole film had—and still has—in its timeless frame of *déjà vu* the effect of a sad, profound reflection upon an immense human tragedy. There were the obvious ''good guys'' and ''bad guys'' (and plenty in between), but it was remarkably free of thumping for a partisan attitude. The people who let themselves be questioned tacitly made it clear that they did so out of a sense of duty, or, as ''Colonel Gaspar'' explained, to help set up a barricade against neo-Nazism in France. They were neither nostalgic nor sentimental in casting back in their minds. The impression got from most of them was that they were performing a sort of therapy—an exorcism of witches—with their painful rembrances of things past.

I would say the most profound piece of wisdom one could take away from this film was that it is perilous to praise or blame the motives of people, when they act under the most extreme survival stress. Everyone questioned had his or her burden to bear, his or her set of circumstances and personal decisions to make. Truly, the total resolution was the sorrow and the pity of the tragedy of France. As Sir Anthony Eden compassionately put it, ''If one hasn't been through the horror of occupation, they have no right to judge those who have.''

231

Charles De Gaulle

Captured collaborationists at the war's end.

French people celebrating the Liberation.

I noted at the outset of this critique that the postwar trend of documentary films was toward the voracious TV. Ironically, this one was initially conceived as a project for the French TV network, ORTF, but financial backing for it still had to be obtained in Switzerland and West Germany. When it was completed, ORTF refused it on the grounds that the French bourgeoisie were not yet "mature enough" to accept the notion that most Frenchmen did *not* fight in the Resistance during the war. Eventually it was given a test run in a small movie theater in Paris and was so successful there that it was moved to a large theater on the Champs-Elysées. There it was immensely successful, as it later was in New York and, indeed, in theaters (and finally on TV!) all over the world.

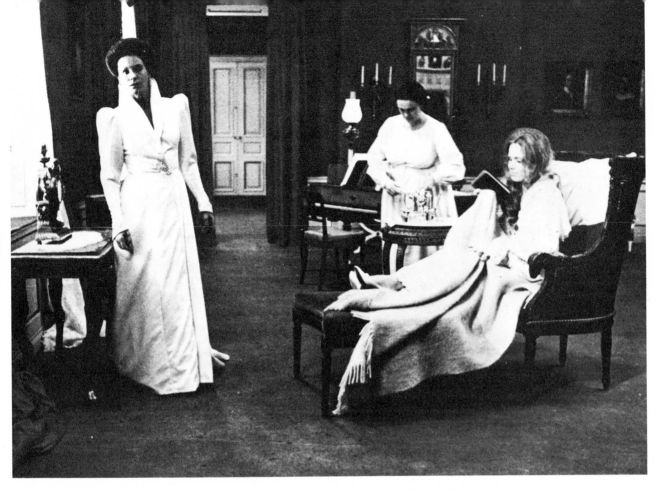

The two sisters, Karin (Ingrid Thulin) and Maria (Liv Ullman), with the family maid, Anna (Kari Sylwan), start another day in their vigil with the sister who is dying of cancer.

CRIES AND WHISPERS

1972

Few motion picture makers have dared to confront audiences with even a fair simulation of the literal occurrence of death. In most of the memorable screen enactments of this most certain and universal event, which is usually matter-of-factly referred to as "the deathbed scene," they have been guarded, cautious, romantic, and theatrical, loathe to involve the viewer in the literal anguish of life coming to an end. From the absolutely gorgeous expiration of Greta Garbo in *Camille* to some of the more melodramatic death throes of victims in gangster films, the efforts have been to make these happenings more emotional building-blocks in the plots, artificialized to suit requirements, not fundamental terminals in themselves.

Such cosmetic circumvention was categorical-ly shunned in Ingmar Bergman's *Cries and Whispers*, perhaps the most devastating drama this director has ever made. With a full and ruthless candor such as we had come to expect of him, Mr. Bergman chose to show the truth of dying with all the hideousness and finality it may have, especially when it happens slowly, accompanied by great agony and dread. And, more than that, he explored the significance that such a fundamental crisis may have upon the lives of loved ones and their responses to the concussion of death.

There were those who said with some misgiving that this picture was like none Mr. Bergman had done before, that it took audiences into areas that neither he nor anyone else had explored. They protested that it departed from the line of doubt and cynicism that prevailed in many of his previous films, such as those of his famous trilogy, *Through a Glass Darkly, Winter Light*, and

233

Maria reverts to a childhood reverie during the tension of waiting.

The Silence, and his massive, philosophical *The Seventh Seal*, to achieve a kind of sadistic impact with an intellectually commonplace theme.

I do not agree. In my opinion, *Cries and Whispers* was a confutation of the moral groping and theological confusions that disturbed Mr. Bergman in previous films. As did *The Virgin Spring*, it brought the issue of man's tormenting antipathies toward life down to a sobering realization that life, with all its doubts and woes, is potentially ennobling and certainly preferable to death. Further, it carried the implication, which some considered a platitude, that the secret of contentment is doing for others, not concern with and indulgence of oneself, and acceptance with gratitude and benevolence of the simple things of life.

Mr. Bergman's focal characters in this film, set at the turn of the century, were three Swedish sisters. Two, handsome, healthy and married, had returned to their family home to pass a prolonged and painful death-watch with their middle sister, a spinster, terminally ill with cancer and tended by a loving nurse, Anna, who had apparently

been a servant with the family for a long time. The home was a gracious old mansion, full of fine furniture, upholstered in a soft red material matching the rich color of the walls, and adorned with antique clocks ticking untiringly and chimed with crystal tinkles through the endless hours, betokening that time was passing as inexorably as was life. There were also occasional sounds of voices, very faint and incoherent, as though generations of previous inhabitants of this old house were whispering reflectively among themselves.

Enclosed in this rural isolation, with its reminders of their past, the sisters endured their ordeal, tried fitfully to render comfort and aid, and experienced painful flashback recollections of episodes that exposed the nature of their lives. The younger sister, Maria, whom Liv Ullman luminously played, recalled a significant encounter she had with the family doctor on one of his visits. She had accosted him in a darkened hallway and had tried to arouse in him an old passion he had once had for her. But he had taken her to a mirror and brutally traced the extending lines in

An old suitor, Dr. Lakaren (Erland Josephson), forces Maria to look in a mirror and recognize the lineaments of age in her face.

her face, reminding her that in the passage of time she had changed, not for the best. Indifference, he had told her, was her weakness, as well as selfishness, which he frankly acknowledged was an equally corrosive character flaw in himself. She also remembered with discomfort how she had confessed that earlier adultery to her husband and how she had fantasized his attempted suicide and her own withdrawal from him when he pitifully cried for help.

The older sister, Karin, whom Ingrid Thulin played with forbidding chilliness and resentment, did not reveal herself in her brutally self-condemning recollections until after the sister Agnes had died and she was brooding alone in somber hatred. Then she shockingly recalled how she had left the dinner table one evening after a dismal, silent meal with her spouse, during which she had willfully knocked over a wineglass and broken it, to her husband's icy reproof; how she had gone to her room, disrobed, and struck the attending Anna for staring at her, had sat on a commode and deliberately slashed her vagina with a shard of the glass. When her husband came apparently to seek her body, she had hide-

ously exposed the wound and then deliberately smeared a swatch of blood from it across her leering mouth. This grisly display of sexual vengeance and, indeed, of hatred for herself, whether fantasized or real, was the most startling symbolization of cankerous guilt in the film. And, to sum up her enmity toward all things, she bitterly mumbled, "Life is nothing but a tissue of lies!"

Likewise, the dying sister, Agnes, was not without her own shard of guilt. She recalled, in the last stages of her illness, how she had clumsily tried to reach out to her mother when she was younger and how she had drawn away when her mother seemed aloof and forbidding, not realizing at the time the extent of her mother's emotional situation and loneliness, which rendered *her* incapable of returning love.

It was against such a morose panorama that the onset of agonizing pain and racking fits of coughing that seized the dying Agnes in her bed were watched with revulsion by her sisters, all of which Mr. Bergman showed without any dissimulation: the bouts of retching, the cries for help, the writhings and the horrible death rattles, and finally the silent passing away of the exhausted woman before her sisters' and her nurse's helpless eyes. No sharper nor more haunting exposition of Agnes' torment can be imagined than that which Harriet Andersson gave.

In the wracking ordeal it was Anna, played magnificently by Kari Sylwan, who was always at the side of the dying woman, tenderly nestling her pain-drenched head against the softness and comfort of her ample bosom, pouring out the love that she had stored for her own illegitimate daughter who had poignantly died as a child. It was Anna, at last, who was the symbol and provider of unselfish love in this stately mansion. And it was she who became the tower of strength in the strangely supernatural and disturbing interlude that Mr. Bergman conceived for the symbolic passing of Agnes' soul.

After the body had been prayed over by a bitter and discouraged clergyman who plaintively called upon the spirit of Agnes to intercede with God for those "left here on this dark, dirty earth," the penultimate phase of the picture had the sisters coming separately to face the corpse of the transitioning Agnes before she passed on into the void. Karin, called first to the bedside,

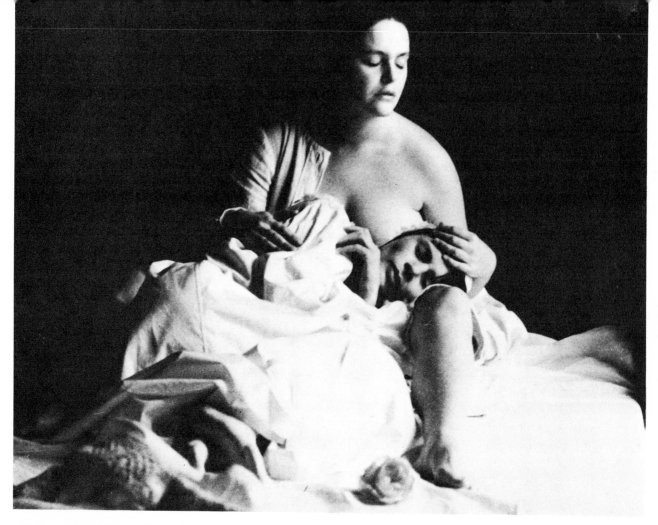

Anna, symbolizing the love and protection of the universal mother, holds the now-dead body of the sister Agnes (Harriet Andersson).

rejected the piteous pleas of the phantom Agnes. "I'm alive and want nothing to do with your death!" Karin cried as she fled from the room in revulsion. "Perhaps if I loved you . . ." Her rejection trailed off into a sullen silence.

Next Maria came to the bedside and, in her sweet, milky way, attempted to console and assure the pleading specter. But when it arose and seized her, trying to plant an avid kiss upon her lips, she too tore away in terror and quickly fled the room. It was Anna who came last with calm assurance, "I will stay with her now," and took the lifeless body and held it softly against her large, bare breasts in a tacit simulation of the pose of Michelangelo's "Pietà."

And it was Anna who, in the final instance, was treated with heartless insensitivity by the selfish sisters and their husbands when they came to set-tle the estate. Deciding among themselves to refrain from making a financial settlement upon her, they offered to let her choose "something of value" from among Agnes' effects. And what she chose simply was Agnes' diary in which she had written, on a day in early fall, of her joy in a final outing on the golden, sun-bathed lawn with her sisters and with Anna, all of them dressed in white, swinging on the swing of their childhood, being happy among themselves. "The people I'm most fond of in the world were with me," the soft voice of Agnes spoke as the scene unfolded. "I closed my eyes tightly trying to cling to the moment and thinking, come what may, this is happiness. . . . And I feel great gratitude to my life, which gives me so much."

Never, as I have said, has there been a movie that has so sharply equated life and death and so clearly pointed the lesson of salvation being achieved through the giving of love. The contrast between the reactions of the embittered and heartless sisters to Agnes' death and that of the warm, compassionate Anna was so evident and intense that the precept of the suffering of Agnes evoked an image of the martyrdom of Christ.

Some critics remarked with disfavor on the fact that *Cries and Whispers* was exclusively concerned with the psychic experiences of women, memories and motives in their minds, and their ultimate varying reactions to the confrontation of death. The four men who appeared briefly were minor, mere statements or intrusions of such peripherally complicating factors in women's lives as male obtuseness, cruelty and inadequacy. I did not find this disconcerting. In the ways of women, Mr. Bergman found the most interesting and elemental aspects of the distortions and vagaries of the human animal. Women to him, in *Cries and Whispers* as in most of his prior films, were the more sensitive, volatile and vulnerable gender, and the more susceptible to the ambiguities of sex. The flash hint of a lesbian impulse in Agnes' sudden lunge to place her avid mouth upon that of the revolted Maria in the fanciful spectral scene was a vivid and solely feminine token of the passing sister's unrequited love.

But that was secondary to the larger and more universal theme of the need of human beings for one another, not only by women but by men.

The last happy memory recorded by Agnes in her diary is of herself with Anna and her two sisters on the sun-dappled lawn of their ancient country home.

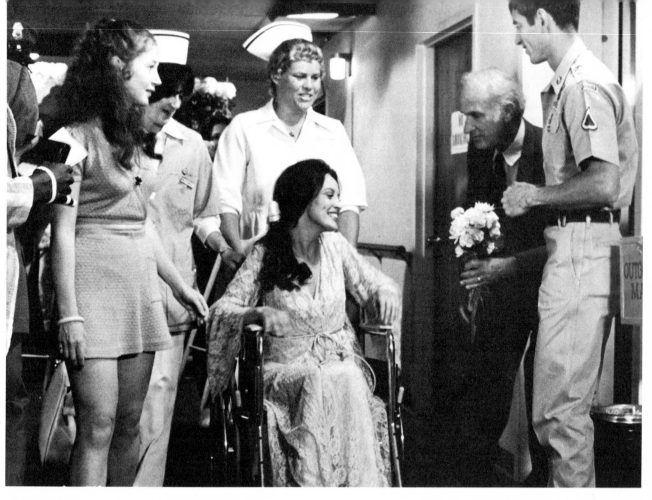

The popular country singer, Barbara Jean (Ronee Blakely), is greeted by two fans, Mr. Green (Keenan Wynn) and Private Kelly (Scott Glenn), as she leaves the hospital.

NASHVILLE

1975

All of us are deeply involved with politics, whether we know it or not . . . That one clear line emerging from the babble of a political campaigner's spiel that blared from a poster-plastered sound-truck as it crawled through the crowded streets of Robert Altman's *Nashville* was the key to the under-running theme of this vividly candid panorama of a great swath of the current American scene. Here was the thread of homely wisdom that pulled together all the lush material in this colorful, tuneful, ugly picture that was one of the best of this decade.

Nashville seemed to bode at the outset to be merely a big, sprawling look at country-and-western music performers and promoters in its so-called American capital. But it began to come in

focus about a quarter of the way through as a grim and sinister diagnosis of the cheap, vicious huckstering that goes on by mass-market salesmen in this country, whether peddlers of fried chicken or soap, automobiles or cosmetics, popular music or politics. And it went on to show the crafty dickering over a marriage of convenience between the music peddlers and the dubious representative of an independent presidential candidate. Its ultimate exposition was of the dangerous susceptibility of the mass of idolatrous, habit-ridden people to what we've come to know as "the con."

This suggestion seeped into the picture as Mr. Altman filled his massive screen with introductions of his large cast of characters and with energetic illustration of the exhibitionism of country-and-western stars. There was a look-in upon a typical music-recording session by one of the elite and powerful male stars, a chubby, self-satisfied fellow by the name of Haven Hamilton, making a virtual Fourth of July oration out of a cheap, jingoistic song ("We must be doing something right to last 200 years!"). There was a long and explosive enactment of an airport welcoming for a popular young singer, Barbara Jean. Arriving home after hospitalization someplace out of state, she was greeted by a massive outpouring of officials, the high school band, accompanied by the usual battalion of high-stepping majorettes, and a horde of euphoric, screaming, police-herded fans—all very neatly programed by the music industry. There was a beautifully staged and funny pile-up of automobiles and trucks as the welcoming throng sped back to the city and two cars collided en route. And there was a splendid illustration of extravagant and mawkish solicitude spent on Barbara Jean when she was hustled to the local hospital after a convenient collapse in front of her fans.

All of this excess ostentation was managed by Mr. Altman in what we used to call semi-documentary (the younger critics now call it *cinéma vérité*) style. His hand-held cameras ranged widely to pick up characteristic action which was woven into a tapestry of palpitating details combining persons and the literal locale.

Then at a Sunday outdoor party at the suburban home of Hamilton—an event which was the epitome of bad taste and supreme self-esteem—careful maneuvers were started by a fancy fast-talker named Triplette to line up the country music people for an appearance at a huge political rally for his sound-truck-advertised candidate,

Hal Phillips Walker, running on the ticket of the Replacement Party.

Conspicuous and ugly in this campaign of bald-faced backstage huckstering was a fund-raising stag party featuring a pretty but pathetically inept aspirant for the "big chance" in Nashville. Conned into doing the act on the promise that it would get her "recognition," she then was forced into performing a striptease when her singing was booed by the boys.

Thus was the essential illustration of a cautious alliance between the music world and the political vote-seekers craftily contrived by Mr. Altman and his clever scriptwriter, Joan Tewkesbury. The ultimate event, the rally, was staged in Nashville's beautiful Centennial Park and on the columned portico of a massive building named the Parthenon. Here, with thousands gathered to enjoy the free concert and give support, not so much, it seemed, to Hal Phillips Walker as to their idolized country-western stars, there occurred first a vicious, violent battle between Barbara Jean's husband and Triplette over the latter's violation of a promise not to display too prominently the name of the candidate. And then, as a fleet of long, black limousines rolled ominously toward the Parthenon, bearing an uncomfortable resemblance to a fascist dictator's entourage, and Barbara Jean and Haven were warming up the crowd with a first-rate country-western number, "One I Love You," shots rang out.

Of course, there was immediate consternation. Who had fired the shots? And at whom? Were

Mrs. Reese (Lily Tomlin), a gospel singer and dutiful housewife, checks on her children during a wayward interlude with Tom Frank (Keith Carradine), a rock star.

Tom is interviewed for BBC by Opal (Geraldine Chaplin), a busy little reporter on the Nashville scene.

they aimed at the candidate, Walker, who had not yet actually appeared? (Mr. Altman wisely never did show him, thus maintaining the political mystique.) A wave of shock and horror followed when it was seen that Barbara Jean had been cut down and Haven, standing beside her, had received a wound in the arm. Hysteria burst like an explosive when the fleeing assassin was identified as a seemingly innocuous young man who had popped up here and there in the picture, apparently a fan of Barbara Jean. The mind reeled with tumbling speculations. Why had this shocking deed been done? Did the gunman bear a grudge against the singer? Did he correlate her with the candidate? Mr. Altman steered clear of explanations. The motivation remained a mystery such as the ones that have so provokingly surrounded the several political assassinations we have known.

But the crowd's next reaction was dumbfounding. After hysterics and confusion had set in, a little singer who had been doggedly trying all through the picture to show her stuff, seized her opportunity. Sidling up to the microphones on the portico she tentatively started to sing, "Oh, it don't worry me, it don't worry me, you may say that I ain't free; it don't worry me!" At first, she went unnoticed in the hubbub. Then a couple of other singers picked up the tune, as did a black choral group in white robes, which had been waiting to go on. Suddenly the song had become infectious, musicians and other singers pitching in, then the crowd, until a thunder of "gospel shouting" rose above the Parthenon. On that startling display of emotionalism—of a crowd too highly charged with the urge to let go and carry on to the next sensation—the film closed, with the music running on.

Of course, the assumption that a gathering under such circumstances would break forth in such a spontaneous show of mania was arbitrary on Mr. Altman's part. He could have concluded the picture with the crowd dissolving in grief. But it was precisely the proneness of the masses to be *led*, to be lured and intoxicated by the stimulation of a "con," whether it came from a howling politician or from the rhythmic singing of a song, that Mr. Altman wanted to show. His aim, as he told Tom Wicker, a political columnist for *the New York Times*, was to give his impression of the culture, not to tout a philosophy. As Mr. Wicker phrased it, he wished to register his impression "by linking country music and politics, two vital threads of a culture desperately clinging to the idea of value while vulgarizing almost every particular value." And that was why his ending for *Nashville* was so grimly characteristic and apt.

Barbara Jean and the veteran country-and-western singer, Haven Hamilton (Henry Gibson), warm up the crowd at the disastrous political rally for Hal Phillip Walker (never seen).

So here was a two-and-a-half-hour movie, crowded with the raw American scene—people at stock car races (where an impromptu singer could not be heard for the deafening roar of the motors), endlessly consuming junk foods, howling with joy at the Grand Ole Opry, listening to their favorites sing the usual hymns in their churches, rutting in motel rooms, impervious to the encroachments of widening highways and deadly fumes, manifested by periodic collisions and junk piles of wrecked and flattened cars. To be sure, this sort of baring of the warts did not originate with *Nashville*; it had been done by documentary filmmakers for forty or fifty years. But it was Mr. Altman's skillful weaving of them into the context of the musical and political scenes that gave *Nashville* its significance and clout.

Noteworthy was Mr. Altman's achievement of the illusion of authenticity through the use of generally unfamiliar actors. When I first saw *Nashville*, for instance, I thought that Haven Hamilton was an actual country-western star, on the order of Roy Acuff or Hank Williams, so credible was

his smug aplomb. He was actually Henry Gibson from TV's *Laugh-In* who had acted in a couple of prior Altman films. The same was true for the Barbara Jean of Ronee Blakeley, whose performance was outstanding because of her skill at conveying the insecurity and instability of a much-too-exalted star. Allen Garfield as her porcine husband; Lily Tomlin as the discontented wife of Del Reese (Ned Beatty), a lawyer and "operator" in both the musical and political realms; Barbara Baxley as a nightspot operator; Michael Murphy as the silken Triplette; Geraldine Chaplin as a nosey reporter sent to view the scene for BBC; and Keenan Wynn as a boarding-house keeper who stood by his dying wife were among the more conspicuous. And there were dozens of singing performers—Keith Carradine, Timothy Brown, Karen Black, Gwen Welles (who did the "striptease"), Barbara Harris (who began the rallying song), the Misty Mountain Boys, and many more. It was pertinent that some wrote their own numbers, which were splendidly arranged and supervised by Richard Baskin, who merited full credit for the effectiveness of the bulging score.

What a viewer took away from *Nashville* depended largely, I would say, upon one's intellectual capacity to sift the deeper implications of what was shown. To the eye and ear of the devoted country-western fan, the reward of a flowing cornucopia of that style of music was immense. As a pure celebration of "C-W," there had been nothing like it before—or since. But to one whose social sensitivities and cultural tastes were sufficiently refined to gauge the expanse of the vulgarities, banalities, and crudities displayed, the effect could only have been saddening and repellent to comfort and hope. For all the mass enthusiasm and energy splashed before the eye, one could see only a cultural wasteland stretching far beyond the boundaries of the screen. And what it said for the conditions and prospects of a working democracy was so cynical and disspiriting that it gave one a sense of shame. What Hal Phillip Walker actually stood for as a presidential candidate did not seem to interest anybody. The singular aim was to "put him across." Even Howard K. Smith, the familiar TV commentator who was cleverly cast by Mr. Altman to do a simulation of a national network profile on the man, simply rattled off a succession of clichés and platitudes which told more about the kind of insight one could expect from the media than about the ambitious candidate. What price political issues? What price victory at the polls? What price the highest rating in the recorded music sales? The trick was to work on the suckers as demagogues have done in the past—the Huey Longs and George Wallaces and Richard Nixons and even Jimmy Carters, perhaps—and as others will probably keep on doing for the *next* two hundred years.

An unknown singer, Albuquerque (Barbara Harris), seizes her opportunity to capture the hysterical crowd, along with a gospel-singing group, after the fatal shooting at the rally.

242

The network executive Max Schumacher (William Holden) and News Commentator Howard Beale (Peter Finch) ruefully contemplate the sudden firing of the latter.

NETWORK

1976

It passeth my understanding why a devastating satire by American moviemakers on the medium that has done so much to obscure and cheaply exploit the kinds of movies I have been recollecting in this book, was not forthcoming until 1976. It was almost as though the better talents engaged in making theatrical films—those that have manifested intelligence, thought, and narrative style—had failed to perceive the deadly damage that television was inflicting on the art industry. Over the years it has grown into a smothering competitor and, worse, has become a menace to our culture and to the fiber of our society.

Occasionally, old-timers did manage a few harmless digs at the grotesqueries of the broadcast media in such films as *The Hucksters* and *A Face in the Crowd.* And they did get off patroniz-

ing parodies of some of the nonsense on the myriad TV shows. But apparently their apprehensions were no more seriously aroused than were those of the powerful president of Loew's-MGM, Nicholas Schenck. When asked early on how the film industry planned to meet the challenge of the broadcast companies, Mr. Schenck responded confidently that they would simply take them over, *if* they ever became big enough to pose a threat!

Of course, it is true there was little theatrical filmmakers could do to stem the tide of competition rolling over them. The diversion of audience interest that the endless TV shows compelled and the crunch of economic pressures that caused the price of theater tickets to rise were not a great deal different from the factors that brought about the inevitable ascendancy of movies over the legitimate theater. And right here it should be remembered that the public that turned to TV with such manifestations of herd behavior was made up of virtually the same kind of people that had

243

Diane Christenson (Faye Dunaway), bucking for power on the executive level, enlists a sensation-making political activist, Laureen Hobbs (Marlene Warfield), spokesman for the Ecumenical Liberation Army.

turned to movies a half-century earlier because they were available and cheap.

Even so, and even though a steady drumfire of criticism and ridicule of television by senior moviemakers might not have done anything to alter the situation, one might have thought the sheer dramatics of the scene would have drawn more reaction from them. After all, they had done rather well in recognizing and exposing the foibles of their own medium in such "inside" films as *The Big Knife, The Bad and the Beautiful,* and *Sunset Boulevard.** But it wasn't until writer Paddy Chayefsky and director Sidney Lumet took a look at the monstrous, overpowering proportions of the shockingly intrusive Trojan horse that the beast was attacked with the sharpest weapons that an able filmmaker has to hand—which is to say pictorial magnification, sarcasm, and devastating wit. *Network* made a full sweep in satirizing not only the character and scope of corporate television and the nature of TV shows but also ripped right into the frailties of the public that soaks up these shows.

Generally unremarked was the fact that the opening episode was a skillful adaptation of a standard TV formula. That is to say, it began with a shock, a sensational demand for audience attention—what is known in the business as a "grab." When Howard Beale, an old-time newscaster in the style of the late Ed Murrow, announced on his evening broadcast that he was being fired be-

cause his ratings had slipped and the big guns at the United Broadcasting System had concluded that he was obsolete, that in itself was no sensation. Popularities on TV waxed and waned, and not only newscasters but other favorites of the air waves had come and gone. But when Beale blandly announced that, on his final show next week, he was going to blow his brains out "right in the middle of the 7 o'clock news," the audience was as startled as listeners had been years before on hearing the famous Orson Welles radio broadcast about an invasion from Mars.

Not only were Beale's TV viewers *and* the people watching this film floored by that crack-brained announcement, which naturally led one to suppose that the poor man had either jumped his trolley or was simply playing for dramatic effect, but it opened a floodgate of discord and dissension in the UBS executive suites. Max Schumacher, graying head of the news department and a long-time friend of Beale, was sure he was having a nervous breakdown and should be eased out right away. But Diane Christensen, a chic, sleek, hard-boiled lady who was bucking her way to the top as head of the program department wasn't so certain. She anticipated the size of the audience that the final Beale show would draw simply to see if he *would* do it—the old morbid curiosity urge. And then, when the ratings came in on a midweek on-camera press conference Beale held at which he loudly and rhetorical-

Diane makes her pitch to an executive conference, with shots of the headquarters of the ELA and its leader, The Great Ahmed Kahn (Arthur Burqhardt), superimposed.

ly proclaimed that the whole world was full of "bullshit" and that he was being fired because he'd run out of same, Diane was convinced they should keep him, not to blow out his brains but to serve as a latter-day prophet for the American people "to articulate their rage." He had been "dumped in their laps," she told Frank Hackett, a tough sharpshooter recently put in command of the whole UBS network when it was taken over by a mammoth conglomerate. Beale was perfect for an "angry man" show. "Let's not blow it," she begged. And Hackett, listening closely for the tinkle of money flowing in, agreed with her over the protests of the outraged, suspicious Max.

Thus, within fifteen minutes of its beginning, *Network* was launched on four fascinating levels. The first was the level of Beale: what was eating on him? What was he trying to do? Was he a wild but fair reflection of a popular news analyst? The second level was that of the infighting in the executive suites of what seemed a fairly accurate mock-up of a big corporate television group. Was Diane going to be able, with her absolutely ruth-less ideas of television programing and her viciously aggressive style, to oust Max and grab the news department for herself? The third level was that of the philosophy and policy of programing for TV, as revealed in the ways these frantic people manifested their responsibilities. Were they, especially those in charge of handling what was labeled news, dedicated to serving the public with information that was close to the truth (as clearly, that is, as they could see it) or were they mainly interested in whipping up pseudo-news sensations that would grab the public and promote savings banks and automobiles? And the fourth level, the most fascinating, was that of the audience itself. What are the tastes and interests of that huge amorphous mass that sits out there in front of its TV sets and makes itself known only by the mystical "ratings" and how it buys goods? Does that audience have its own herd instincts? Is it manipulatable? Does it control television or does television control it?

On all these levels, *Network* was vividly expansive and sharp—so fast and so sharp with its transitions and its dazzling satiric jabs that it kept its audiences reeling between amazement and incredulity. Was it truly within the realm of reason that the allegedly obsolete Beale, seemingly abandoned by his sponsors and in a manic-depressive state, should suddenly become the vocalizer of resentment and rage against the "bull-shit" and confusions of "the system" for millions of Americans? And could he, a TV-born Messiah, accomplish such an effect upon his fascinated listeners that they would respond *en masse* to his howling exhortation on the night of a violent thunderstorm, "Stick your head out of the window and yell, 'I'm mad as hell and I'm not going to take this any more'?" Maybe so, maybe not, but as the character was played with demagogic sweep by Peter Finch and the whole scene of TV rabble-rousing was staged so vigorously and colorfully by Mr. Lumet, it revealed a slightly terrifying aspect of this firebrand and the potential of TV. After all, we *had* heard Father Coughlin and *seen* Joe McCarthy do their acts!

As for the drama of the power fight among the top brass of UBS, it was colorful and fluent but not particularly surprising or new. We were all fairly well acquainted with the kind of jockeying and back-stabbing that goes on among some of the corporate executives of most of our large companies. So it followed expectations that Diane should supersede Max and that Hackett should be there with the hatchet to swiftly chop off the head of anybody whose area of operations didn't make money for UBS. Where the screenplay on this level stretched credulity was when it had Max, dethroned and embittered, become sexually involved with Diane and do a September-song with her until he finally saw how cold and cruel she was—and how limited in her thinking. She was "born of the TV generation" and "learned about life from Bugs Bunny," he said. But what made it engrossing and amusing was the splendid way in which it was played by William Holden as Max, Robert Duvall as Hackett, and Faye Dunaway as Diane. The three of them, brilliantly facile, hard, and without sentiment, yet morally flawed and vulnerable in their separate ways, held *Network* together as a drama with the glue of their plausibility, monstrous and dehumanizing though Hackett and Diane were.

But what I liked best was the audacity with which Mr. Chayefsky cut loose in imagining and

In a dramatically lighted and impressive board room, Arthur Jenson (Ned Beatty), the chairman of the board of the conglomerate controlling the UBS network, forcefully persuades Beale to abandon his demagogic espousal of the "independent" man.

satirizing the ultimate news spectacular that Diane produced—the one in which she brought together the freaked-out terrorists of the Ecumenical Liberation Army (to show "where the world is today"), a lady mystic who would forecast *tomorrow's* news, and the ever more anarchistic Beale. Here was the craziest aggregation one could throw into the American public's eyes, and the way Diane went about obtaining permission and putting on the show was just plain wild. Especially so were her negotiations with the members of the ELA who, although they were supposedly communistic, fought ferociously among themselves over contractual details and billings. That was madcap satire at its best.

Equally memorable and searing was the scene in which the lunatic Beale was mesmerized into abandoning his espousal of the "independent" man by the head of the multinational conglomerate that had taken over UBS and induced into preaching a doctrine of man's submission to a world hegemony. "We no longer live in a world of ideologies and nations," this mighty tycoon said. "The world is now one vast ecumenical holding company!" Overwhelmed by such eloquence, Beale agreed. But why, he wanted to know, was he chosen to be the Moses for this crusade. "Because you're on television, dummy!" was the irrefutable reply.

Having reached that peak of lampoon, *Network* had no place to go but into an even crazier windup, and Mr. Chayefsky took it there—fast. Beale, on the tube with his new doctrine, was repudiated by the mass audience. It didn't want to hear enslavement. It wanted to hear anger and escape. His ratings plunged and his employers agreed they'd have to get him off the air. But how? Their solemn conclusion was that they'd have to assassinate him. And that is precisely what happened. Beale was shot and killed in the middle of the great big show, but at the end it wasn't clear who pulled the trigger, UBS or the rebelious ELA. One thing, however, *was* certain. He was "the first man ever killed because he had lousy ratings," as one of his cynical associates said.

Not surprisingly, this disrespectful *Network* caused hackles to rise on the backs of some television people, just as Mr. Chayefsky's *Hospital* had irked some ill-humored medical practitioners with its satire of hospitals a few years previously.

Things just weren't like that in the networks, these irreconcilable critics said; such irrational behavior was preposterous in such a vast and important industry. But, as usual, those partisans of the medium completely missed the point. They failed to see that the picture was imagining preposterous *possibilities*, that it was only presuming what might happen if the lunatics *should* take over the asylum, to borrow an old film-business gag. The way they should have taken *Network*, as I think most intelligent people did, was as a ribald but reassuring warning that there, but for the grace of God and Walter Cronkite, goes TV.

So there was, at last, the movies' riposte, all in a spirit of good mean fun, to the rival that was threatening their continuance. There was, so far, the final word. I feel it is appropriate and ironic that it should be the last film considered in this book.

Beale, thundering his new doctrine of economic "ecumenism" to a studio audience, just before he is shot down by a mysterious assassin.

* Contents of *The Great Films: Fifty Golden Years of Motion Pictures*

** Contents of *Vintage Films: Fifty Enduring Motion Pictures*

ACKNOWLEDGMENTS

In the preparation of a volume of this sort, so many sources must be called upon for help and cooperation in arranging screenings, providing still photographs, extending permission to use copyrighted material and generally obliging with favors of various sorts that the author finds it difficult to express fully his specific thanks or note with suitable mention the generosity of each and everyone. Their readiness to be of assistance was a benefaction without which this book could not have been done.

My particular thanks must go, first, to the Museum of Modern Art/Film Stills Archives and its always cheerful and helpful curators, Mary Corliss and Carol Carey, and to Ted Perry, the obliging director of the Museum's Department of Films; then to all the distributing companies and individuals who have helped in providing and arranging release of stills as acknowledged on the following page of Photograph Credits; to the William Kenly Collection and its gracious organizer and namesake who has been able to provide or turn up several elusive and much-wanted stills; to Donald Rugoff of Cinema Five, Sheldon Gunsburg of the Walter Reade Organization, Bernard Glaser of Avco Embassy Pictures, Richard Brandt of the Trans-Lux Theaters, Joanna Koch of the Lincoln Center Film Society, Al Newman and Dore Freeman of Metro-Goldwyn-Mayer, Eric Naumann of Universal Pictures, to McGraw Hill Films and to the distinguished directors Jan Kadar, Jiri Menzl and Carlos Saura, who provided stills for their films out of their own collections.

I am grateful also to Myron Bresnick of Macmillan Audio-Brandon for arranging screenings of films now handled by his distributing company, and to Paramount, Columbia and other major distributors for providing similar courtesies. And I must note that no one who seeks to see again certain of the great films of the past can fail to be deeply thankful for the fine and intellignetly programmed revival theaters in New York City such as the Bleeker Street Cinema, the Carnegie Hall Cinema, the Regency, and so on. Their performance and success should be models for similar enterprises across the nation.

Lastly, I cannot find words sufficient to express my gratitude to Harriet Dryden, who was indispensable in finding and obtaining stills; to my dear wife Florence, who did the onerous job of typing the manuscript and giving her valued opinions and suggestions on the improvement of same, and to William Targ, my splendid editor at Putnam's, who, after many years in that exasperating role, remains my cherished mentor and friend.

PHOTOGRAPH CREDITS

The Love Parade—*Courtesy of Universal Pictures.*

City Lights—*Courtesy of the Roy Export Company Establishment.*

Grand Hotel—*From the MGM release, "Grand Hotel," © 1932 Metro-Goldwyn-Mayer Distribution Corporation. Copyright renewed 1959 Loew's Incorporated.*

Million Dollar Legs—*Courtesy of Universal Pictures.*

Lost Horizon—*Courtesy of Columbia Pictures Industries.*

The Awful Truth—*Courtesy of Columbia Pictures Industries.*

Destry Rides Again—*Courtesy of Universal Pictures.*

Woman of the Year—*From the MGM release, "Woman of the Year," © 1942 Loew's Incorporated. Copyright renewed 1969 Metro-Goldwyn-Mayer, Inc.*

Hail the Conquering Hero—*Courtesy of Universal Distributing Corporation.*

The Asphalt Jungle—*From the MGM release "The Asphalt Jungle" © 1950 Loew's Incorporated.*

A Streetcar Named Desire—*Courtesy of Warner Brothers.*

The African Queen—*Courtesy of United Artists Corporation.*

From Here to Eternity—*Courtesy of Columbia Pictures Industries.*

Seven Brides for Seven Brothers—*From the MGM release "Seven Brides for Seven Brothers" © 1954 Loew's Incorporated.*

Giant—*Courtesy of Warner Brothers.*

Wild Strawberries—*Courtesy of Janus Films and the Swedish Information Services.*

The Goddess—*Courtesy of Columbia Pictures Industries.*

The Apartment—*Courtesy of United Artists Corporation.*

Psycho—*Courtesy of Universal Distributing Corporation.*

West Side Story—*Courtesy of United Artists Corporation.*

Hiroshima, Mon Amour—*Courtesy of McGraw-Hill Films.*

Breathless—*Courtesy of McGraw-Hill Films.*

General Della Rovere—*Courtesy of the Walter Reade Organization and McGraw-Hill Films.*

Saturday Night and Sunday Morning—*Courtesy of the Walter Reade Organization.*

Two Women—*Courtesy of Avco Embassy Pictures Corporation.*

Divorce, Italian Style—*Courtesy of Avco Embassy Pictures Corporation.*

Hud—*Courtesy of Paramount Pictures.*

8 1/2—*Courtesy of Avco Embassy Pictures Corporation.*

From Russia With Love—*Courtesy of United Artists Corporation.*

A Hard Day's Night—*Courtesy of United Artists Corporation.*

Morgan—*Courtesy of Cinema Five.*

Bonnie and Clyde—*Courtesy of Warner Brothers.*

Elvira Madigan—*Courtesy of Cinema Five.*

The Graduate—*Courtesy of Avco Embassy Pictures Corporation.*

Easy Rider—*Courtesy of Columbia Pictures Industries.*

2001: a Space Odyssey—*From the MGM release "2001: a Space Odyssey" © 1968 Metro-Goldwyn-Mayer, Inc.*

The Wild Bunch—*Courtesy of Warner Brothers.*

The Sorrow and the Pity—*Courtesy of Cinema Five.*

Cries and Whispers—*Courtesy of New World Films, Inc., and the Swedish Information Services.*

Nashville—*Courtesy of Paramount Pictures.*

Network—*From the MGM release "Network" © 1976 by Metro-Goldwyn-Mayer Inc. and United Artists Corporation.*

Index of Films

Index of Names